PALESTINE

A FESTIVAL AT TEL AVIV

PALESTINE

THE REBIRTH OF AN ANCIENT PEOPLE

BY

ALBERT M. HYAMSON

AUTHOR OF "A HISTORY OF THE JEWS IN ENGLAND," ETC.

אם אשכחך ירושלים תשכח ימיני

SIDGWICK & JACKSON, LTD.
3, ADAM STREET, ADELPHI, LONDON

First published in 1917

TO

PHILIPP AND DAVID

PREFACE

OF all the numberless names to be found in the gazetteers there is none that excites so widespread and so intense an interest as that of Palestine. There is no one in whom the name of his own country, especially when found amid alien surroundings, fails to arouse a thrill. Some there are who have personal interests or relationships in foreign lands, which endow the names of those regions with a special personality and life, lacking in the description of regions which, so far as the reader is concerned, belong to the book and to the book alone. To many the names of Greece and of Italy have a special call; to yet others Egypt or Assyria have an attraction of which those for whom archæology has no charm can have no consciousness. Yet all these votaries of their own and of other lands, taken in the aggregate, do not exceed in number those in whom the name of that small and geographically unimportant region whose shore is lapped by the eastern waters of the Mediterranean arouses a vivid interest. Britain, France, Germany, and Russia hold the first place in the minds and affections of most of the inhabitants of those countries. Few of them, if any, have the second place unoccupied, and among the overwhelming number that place is filled by Palestine, a land sacred to Christian, Jew, and Moslem alike.

The number of books on Palestine is legion, yet it is

remarkable how very little is known of the land. It would
almost seem that, at any rate so far as the Western lands
are concerned, every visitor on his return from the Holy
Land considers it his duty to narrate for the benefit of the
public his impressions and experiences.   Thus the literature of modern Palestine seems without end. Yet, despite
its extent, there is a sameness about its content that
renders it depressingly monotonous.   All travellers seem
to have followed the same paths, to have visited the same
shrines and the same sites, to have followed religiously
in the footsteps of their predecessors, to have undergone much the same experiences, and to have recounted
the same story, even though in different words.   Seldom
is it that a traveller or writer steps off the well-worn high
road. He goes to Palestine, not as a man of the world,
but either as a pilgrim, sometimes a cynic, or an archæologist. While there he has the eyes only of a pilgrim or
of an archæologist, and after he has returned to Europe
or America, probably until his dying day, he assumes this
attitude whenever the Holy Land recurs to his mind.
To him Palestine is either the cradle of his faith or a land
of archæological interest.   In either event it belongs
entirely to the past.   It may have a future, but it certainly
has no present.

This book is of a different description.   It has no concern with Palestine either as a religious or an archæological
centre.   The past is of no consequence except in so far as
it serves as an introduction to the present.   These pages
deal with the present and the future, but not the spiritual
future.   The future to which the writer looks forward is
one of material prosperity, which must not be considered
in any degree opposed to spiritual development; of a
land once again flowing with milk and honey, inhabited

by a happy people—a people who, seated in the same
land millennia ago, made mankind its eternal debtor by
the blessings it conferred upon it, and who, once again
restored to those surroundings from which it has been
divorced for two thousand years and more, will resume
its interrupted history and make Zion again the spiritual
centre of the world, and themselves a nation of priests
devoted to the service of humanity. The writer looks
forward to the regeneration of the land of Palestine, which
has been so neglected for centuries that a country which
once was among the most fertile of known lands, proverbial for the exuberance of its productions, now appears
to the superficial observer as a desert incapable of
cultivation and unable to keep its small and scattered
population above the level of beggary. The revival of
Palestine has been in motion for the space of but one
generation. The story of that generation is narrated in
the following pages. In the lifetime of a nation forty
years are but as a day in the lifetime of an individual. In
the most favourable circumstances, relatively little could
be expected after the lapse of so brief a period; but the
circumstances around the colonization of Palestine have
not been too favourable. The Jewish settlers in Palestine have, however, had one advantage over pioneers
in all other climes. These latter, no matter how determined to succeed, how devoted to their enterprise, know,
consciously and unconsciously, that they are going into
exile. But the Jews, who breathe a new life into the
dead bones of the Holy Land, do not go into exile. They
return home, and the home from which by force and by
violence they have been excluded for centuries. The
hunted victims who are taking refuge in Palestine leave
the land of exile behind them. They come out of the

darkness into the light, and the inspiration of their labours lies not only in the hope of creating a home for their weary bodies, a refuge for themselves and also for their children, where they will be secured against the agonies which they and their fathers have suffered in the lands of exile. That alone is a sufficient incentive to ceaseless toil and determination to overcome the insuperable. But in Palestine, which is still the Promised Land to the Jew of the Pale of Settlement, lies another hope, equal to, nay, greater in intensity than, that of the release of the individual from bondage. In Palestine the Jew of Eastern Europe dreams that freedom will be found not only for Jewry, but also for Judaism—freedom to develop on its own lines, unshadowed by the mighty systems that surround it in Europe; at liberty to follow its own course. Given that liberty, the Jew never doubts that Judaism will be well able to justify itself, and that once again, as of yore, "out of Zion shall go forth the Law and the Word of the Lord from Jerusalem."

I am indebted to several friends for assistance in the preparation of this volume. In particular I wish to thank Mr. Leon Simon and Mr. S. Tolkowsky, himself a settler in Palestine, for having read the complete volume in proof, and for having given me the benefit of their much appreciated criticisms and suggestions. Miss Annie Landau, the Head Mistress of the Evelina School of Jerusalem, and Mr. Herbert Bentwich, prominent in the councils, first of the *Chovevé Zion* and afterwards of the Zionist movement in England, have read the chapters which relate more especially to the organizations with which they have been connected and to the phases of the subject which come closest to them, and by their advice I have been enabled to escape many pitfalls into which I should otherwise have fallen. The question of illustration was a difficult one. Palestinian photographs are obtainable by the thousand, but those illustrative of the new life in Palestine exist only in units. Even of the few that have been taken, the War has rendered many temporarily unavailable. The same cause has made it impossible at present to supplement the existing meagre supply. But in this matter also friends have come to my assistance. The majority of the illustrations, none of which have been published previously, are from photographs taken by Mr. Murray Rosenberg, to whom I desire to express my thanks. The few remaining photographs were taken by myself. The map of Palestine is reproduced from " Zionism and the Jewish Future," by permission of the editor, Mr. H. Sacher, and the publisher, Mr. John Murray, C.V.O., of that work, to whom also I desire to admit my indebtedness.

A. M. H.

January 1, 1917.

CONTENTS

xiii

CONTENTS

LIST OF ILLUSTRATIONS

PALESTINE

CHAPTER I

PALESTINE UNDER THE ROMANS

THE year 70 of the present era marks the end of the Jewish
State and the opening of the last and most widespread
of the exiles. The day on which the victorious legions of
Titus spread fire and sword through the city of Jerusalem,
and after having plundered and massacred the wretched
remnant of the inhabitants, razed to the ground almost
every stone of the city, was the death-day of Jewish self-
government. The 9th of Ab, already a fatal day in
Jewish annals, was not the death-day of the Jewish people;
but it marked the end of the Jewish nation. Henceforth
the history of the Jews—a story of inconceivable misery
and suffering, yet one of almost marvellous triumph over
circumstances—lies in the Diaspora, in every part of the
world except in Palestine. The Holy Land alone of all
the lands of the Old World, except on very rare occasions,
lies outside the orbit of Jewish history. The sack of Jerusalem and the massacre of its inhabitants did not, however, utterly destroy the Palestinian Jews. The losses
the Jewish people suffered in the course of the war, in
battle, by massacre, and from starvation, are computed
at more than a million. Almost an equal number taken
captive were sold into slavery or suffered frightful deaths
for the amusement of the populace on some Roman

festival. Nevertheless, Palestine was not denuded of its Jewish inhabitants, and despite vicissitudes and agonies which make the history of the Jews of Palestine a miniature of the history of the Jews in the Diaspora, the country during the succeeding eighteen centuries has never been entirely devoid of Jews or of Jewish communities.

The terrible consequences of the unsuccessful revolt against the Romans rendered impossible any political action on the part of the few survivors who were tolerated in the land, and who for the most part clung to the coast. Those of them who had formerly had means, had been reduced by confiscations to poverty. The others who had never possessed wealth were sunk in even direr distress. The recent terrible events had utterly crushed out of them all national feeling. Broken in spirit, their only thought was to find sufficient food to keep themselves and their families in existence until the end of their appointed time. With one exception the events of the world were no longer of interest or consequence to them. But this exception was the one that had inspired the most heroic defence that history either before or since their day has ever seen. It was the preservation of their spiritual ideal, of the pure creed of Judaism, of the morality on which the whole of the moral system of modern civilization takes its stand. Henceforth the mission of Israel was to keep alive and transmit from generation to generation the religious teachings which directly or indirectly have, from that day to this, been the light of the world.

Judaism is, and always has been, much more than a system of religion or a theology. It is in the fullest sense a civilization, with a literature, a point of view, and an intellect of its own, which need fear no comparison, especially when the oppressive restrictions from which it has at most times and in most countries suffered are considered, with the civilizations of other peoples, European or Asiatic. In its narrowest sense, as a religion, Judaism is dependent entirely on scholarship and learning. This is illustrated by the aphorism that an ignorant man cannot be a Jew. Consequently, if the fall of Jerusalem had carried with it the destruction of the Jewish schools, Judaism would have disappeared with its capital. As a matter of fact, another Jewish centre of learning arose in Palestine even before the last hour of the city had struck. The College at Jamnia, near the coast at Jaffa (or Joppa), was founded by Jochanan ben Zakkai, who is traditionally believed to have escaped from Jerusalem during the Siege concealed in a coffin. Jochanan had been a member of the Synhedrin in Jerusalem, and by him that body, which became the legislative body of the Jewish Church, was reconstituted in his new home, but henceforth it had no political powers. Farther north in Galilee, Agrippa and his sister Berenice, the last of the family of Herod, used the considerable influence which they had with Titus for the benefit of their people. Consequently the recovery from the disastrous war was more rapid in that part of the country, and Tiberias and Sepphoris, which had escaped the destruction prevalent farther south, gained greater importance as Jewish centres.

In the meanwhile the attitude of the Romans towards the Jewish remnant, quite incapable, apparently, of any harm, had become less harsh. Jewish communities began to come again into existence in the depopulated centres; the seats of learning flourished more and more; and there is even evidence that there were individual Jews owning land and slaves. Nevertheless, the Jews of Palestine were little more than helots or outlaws.

In the year 116 Palestine was convulsed by the echoes of
the great Jewish revolt throughout the Roman world.
The victorious rebels marched from Cyrene across Egypt
into Palestine, where they were met by the newly appointed governor, Lucius Quietus, who had recently
destroyed the Jews of Babylon. In the course of the
succeeding operations the Jews of Palestine suffered
terribly. The College and Synhedrin at Jamnia were
suppressed. Quietus was, however, recalled by the
Emperor Hadrian, and the remnant of Jews in Palestine breathed again. Hadrian seemed at first not unsym-
pathetic towards his Palestinian Jewish subjects, and it
is even said that he gave them permission to rebuild
the Temple. Such encouragement restored the spirit of
the people, which showed itself when Hadrian's acts fell
short of his promises, and there were some threats of rebellion, which were quieted by Joshua the Prince and
the Synhedrin, now removed to Usha, of which he was
the head. The subsidence of the movement was, however,
but temporary. Hadrian visited Judæa in 130 and, satisfied of the subservience of the Jews in all things, determined to rebuild Jerusalem—but as a heathen city; and
in furtherance of his plan of Romanization proscribed
certain of the essential observances of Judaism. Thus
once again was Judaism in danger of forcible extinction,
and once again the whole of the Jewish people rose to de-
fend their most treasured possession.

So long as Hadrian remained in Syria the preparations
for the coming revolt were kept secret, but on his with-
drawal the whole of the country burst into flame. The
inspiration came from the world-renowned Rabbi Akibah,
who on the death of Joshua had become the spiritual head
of the people. The leader of the army that sprang into

existence spontaneously was Bar Cochba, who in consequence of his phenomenal success had Messianic powers
attributed to him by his admirers and followers. Immediately on the outbreak of the rebellion the provinces
of Judæa, Samaria, and Galilee were evacuated by the
Romans. Their attempts after the receipt of reinforce-
ments to recapture the country availed nothing against
the rebels, whose army is said to have numbered over half
a million. Julius Severus, the greatest soldier of his age,
was summoned from Britain to restore prestige to the
Roman arms, but even he could not prevail against Bar
Cochba. The latter's army attracted recruits from the
Jewries of all countries. Those who could not serve in
person sent of their treasure. Even non-Jews joined the
rebel forces. The Judæo-Christians alone kept apart,
and from this time may be dated the final breach between
the Jews who kept to the old paths and their kinsmen
who adopted the teachings of the disciples of Jesus.
Jerusalem was made the capital of the rebel State. Bar
Cochba was proclaimed King, and ruled the kingdom
which he had won by his arms. It was, however, impossible permanently to withstand the pressure of the armies
of Severus. From defeat they gradually proceeded to
victory and to yet further victory. Jerusalem was taken
by the Romans, and other strongholds shared its fate.
At length Bither remained the only fortress in the possession of Bar Cochba. On the 9th of Ab—a thrice fatal
anniversary—134, Bither was betrayed by some of its
inhabitants. The Romans entered the fortress, and after
a stubborn battle in which both sides suffered very heavily,
defeated their adversaries and put the survivors to death.
Bar Cochba was either slain in battle or murdered by a
renegade. Akibah was taken prisoner and died under

torture. Of the Jews—men, women, and children—who were caught in all parts of the land, most were massacred: the remainder were sold into slavery. In the fall of Bither alone half a million Jews—including fugitives from the other cities—are said to have lost their lives. Those who surrendered were put to death equally with those who were taken in the open. Most of the survivors fled into Arabia, where they gave rise to the Jewish tribes which in a later century contested with Mohammed the hegemony of the country, and whose descendants still form one of the most valuable elements in the population of the Yemen and of the Aden Hinterland.

With the suppression of the revolt Hadrian was more determined than ever to suppress nonconformity to the official Roman religion. The new pagan city Ælia Capitolina therefore arose on the site of Jerusalem, and not only was a heathen temple erected where the Temple of the Jews once stood, but the Holy Places of the Christians at Bethlehem, and of the Samaritans on Mount Gerizim, were similarly defiled. Jews were entirely excluded from the precincts of the new city, and almost two centuries had to pass before they were again allowed to live on the soil of what had once been Jerusalem. The oppression by Turnus Rufus, the new governor of the province, was so severe that the few Jews who remained in the land were not even permitted to bury their dead. The corpses had to remain above ground as warnings to the survivors. Fortunately Hadrian died in 137, and his successor, Antoninus Pius, proved more humane towards his Palestinian Jewish subjects. As a consequence the religious leaders began to return from exile. A religious capital was again established at Usha, and afterwards transferred to Galilee, which district, and especially the city of Tiberias, remained for long the principal Jewish centre. The considerable ruins of synagogues, dating from this period, which are still to be found in this region, attest the importance of the Jewish population of Galilee during the second and later centuries of the present era. More enduring monuments of the Jewish activity of these times in Galilee are the Mishnah, or code of oral tradition, and the Palestinian or " Jerusalem " Talmud.

The most favourable of the conditions under which the Jews of Palestine lived in the first centuries of the present era was one of oppression, and it is therefore not surprising that their sympathies were with the Parthians in the revolt against Rome in 161. In the resultant campaign Lucius Verus, one of the joint Emperors, came to Syria, where he withdrew the few rights which the Jews still enjoyed and suppressed the Synhedrin of Usha. It was at this time that the spiritual centre was removed to Galilee. Verus' colleague, Marcus Aurelius, dealt more gently with the Jews, and among other concessions permitted them to visit Jerusalem for prayer. During the following century and a half there is little to record of Palestinian history. Jews and Christians were almost equally oppressed. Only the Samaritans obtained relative favour with the Romans. Rabbi Judah the Holy, who was for a long period Patriarch of the Jews, ruled them wisely and well, but he was unable to contend against the extreme poverty into which they were for the most part sunk, poverty due to a large extent to the heavy taxation which the Romans laid upon them.

Henceforward Palestinian history may be said to have been dormant until the era of Constantine and the consequent powerful Christian revival.

Constantine adopted Christianity about the year 324.

He had previously, in pursuance of his policy of religious toleration, placed Judaism formally on a level with the other religions of the Empire, and its Patriarchs and other officers were recognized as ranking equally with the officers of other faiths. The Patriarch of Judæa was, in fact, officially regarded as the spiritual head of all the Jews of the Empire. This was, however, previous to the Emperor's conversion to Christianity. With his new religion he imbibed all the intense hatred which his new co-religionists felt towards the people from whom their own faith had been derived. An era of state persecution of the Jews throughout the Empire commenced, and a regular campaign was initiated for the compulsion of Jews to adopt Christianity. Finally, at the Council of Nice, the last thread that connected Christianity with Judaism— the dependence of the Christian on the Jewish calendar— was broken. Whatever chance the numerically insignificant Jewish population of Palestine had of escaping from the rigour of the new persecution from which their brethren elsewhere were suffering, was destroyed by the interest aroused in the Holy Land by Helena, the mother of the Emperor, who visited Palestine in 326 in order to discover the Holy Places, and thus inaugurated the long line of Christian pilgrims. The Law of Hadrian which forbade Jews to live in Jerusalem, but had been falling into desuetude, was thereupon re-enacted. The Jews, however, were formally permitted to mourn there, on payment, on the anniversary of the destruction of the Temple. At the same time other oppressive laws were introduced, while the Christians were given facilities for the erection of churches throughout Galilee, which was at the time then practically a Jewish land. The persecution reached its height under Constantine's successor, Constantius, by whom a deliberate and long-sustained attempt was made to crush out the teaching of Judaism, and by this and other means to cause the ultimate disappearance of the faith. The oppression by Constantius led to a considerable emigration from Palestine towards the East, and the spiritual hegemony of Jewry permanently left the country. For many years those who remained suffered the direst persecution at the hands of the predominant power. The system of taxation, for instance, seemed deliberately intended for the destruction of the Jewish people. It is not surprising, therefore, that the Jews of Galilee were ultimately goaded to revolt, but the rebellion was suppressed without much trouble, the rebels with their families being put to the sword, and their towns razed. As on the occasion of previous insurrections, many of those who escaped were able to do so only by living for long periods in the catacombs. At this period a change of Emperors meant nothing for the Jews: the intensity of the persecution was in no degree relaxed. This state of things continued until the advent of Julian.

The new Emperor had been an involuntary convert to Christianity, for which religion he had no liking. On his accession to the purple, therefore, he had no hesitation in throwing off his Christian cloak, and henceforth he devoted himself to the furtherance of his ideal of religious toleration. His accession in 361 was a welcome respite for the Jews of Palestine, who were almost at their last gasp. Not only did he remove the immense burden of anti-Jewish legislation, but having through his Christian education and his study of the Bible learnt somewhat of Jewish history and of Judaism, his sympathies were aroused in favour of the Jewish people and the Jewish character. He was probably also influenced by his dislike of the Christians and his desire to mortify them by the favour shown to their former victims. Julian took many means of showing his favour to the Jews: the most important of them all was his letter to the Jewish communities of the Empire announcing his intention of rebuilding the Temple. This was not an empty promise. The Emperor placed funds aside for the work, collected building material, and set an army of workmen to clearing the site of the débris with which it had been encumbered for centuries. The Jews of Palestine had, however, been so thoroughly crushed by their successive misfortunes, that they had not the heart to participate in the undertaking, and could only occupy the rôle of spectators. All hope of the restoration of the Jewish State had by now been driven out of their hearts: they could no longer take any step towards freedom except at the bidding of the Messiah, whose coming they eagerly awaited. Julian, no matter how friendly he might be to the Jews, was obviously not the Messiah. The abstention of the Jews from participation in the work, coupled with several mysterious fires, probably due to the ignition of forgotten stores of oil formerly kept in the vaults under the Temple, discouraged the workers, whose ardour slackened. All possibility of the restoration was, however, destroyed by the fatal arrow which struck Julian down in battle against the Persians within two years of his accession to the Imperial throne. His successors were Christians, but more tolerant than his predecessors had been, and Palestine may again be said to have been without a history, apart from ecclesiastical disputes, until in the division of the Empire in 395 it fell to the Eastern half. But in the interval monasteries, nunneries, and hermitages had been planted by the hundred throughout the land.

CHAPTER II

So far as Palestine was concerned, the division of the Empire had little if any immediate effect. It had since the time of Constantine been under the government of Constantinople, and the change made no alteration in the seat of government nor in the system of government. The succeeding two hundred years formed a period of relative quietude, during which the country had no external history. It was nominally Christian, but the people showed little if any variation from the type of those who lived there when the government of the country rested with the heathens. The only noticeable change was the increasing number of Christian pilgrims who visited the Holy Land in order to worship at the Holy Places, which themselves at the same time increased in number, and the ever-growing army of priests who ministered to them there. Throughout these centuries the Jews led an uneventful life, varied by an occasional outbreak of persecution, but subject always to the extremely oppressive laws which one Emperor after the other enforced against them. Jerusalem had ceased to exist as a Jewish centre. Tiberias was still the religious capital. The bulk of the Jews of the Holy Land were to be found in Galilee, where they followed agriculture as had their fathers before them. Nazareth was probably the only city, the majority of whose inhabitants were

Jews. Until the time of Justinian the oppression of the Jews of Palestine was entirely political and economic. That Emperor, however, who left his mark on Jerusalem in several stately Christian buildings, brought the Jewish religion within the orbit of his oppressive legislation. But pitiful as was the position of the Jews, that of the Samaritans was even worse. In the courts their evidence was not accepted even in cases in which Samaritans alone were the litigants, and they had not the right to dispose of their property at death. So far as the Jews were concerned, Justinian even forbade them to read Isaiah, lest in their abject misery they might derive comfort from the exhortations and promises of the prophet. The Samaritans, less patient than the Jews in their sufferings, repeatedly revolted, but the rebellions were easily suppressed. On one occasion in 556 the Samaritans, assisted by Jews, succeeded in seizing Cæsarea and the neighbouring country, but their success was short-lived, and the punishment of the rebels was ferocious.

In the year 611 a ray of hope shone on the persecuted inhabitants of Palestine. The usurpation of the Emperor Phocas had induced the Persian King, Chosroes II., to invade the Asiatic dominions of the Empire. A Persian army entered Syria from the north, and to the Jews they came as deliverers. All the Jews of Galilee who were capable of bearing arms joined the invading forces, eager to give vent to their enmity against Rome and Christendom, which had been pent up in them for centuries. The Christians of Galilee suffered severely both in person and property. The Persians, reinforced by the Jews, and aided by a band of Saracens, swept through Palestine. Jerusalem was taken by storm in July, 614, its Christian inhabitants put to the sword, and its churches and sanctuaries destroyed. It seemed as if Rome and Christendom had been finally driven out of Palestine. For fourteen years Palestine remained in the hands of Persia. The Jews dreamt that they would be allowed to establish a republic in their ancient home, but their hopes were not realized. Religiously they prospered, and made many voluntary converts from Christianity, but their Persian allies retained control of the country. On the other hand, they inflicted heavy taxation on the Jews, and when differences arose between the latter and the Persians many of the influential leaders of the Jews were banished to Persia. Thus a coolness arose between the allies, and when, about 627, the Emperor Heraclius approached the Jews with promises of tolerance, the latter were not unwilling to favour their ancient oppressor. Chosroes' blindness and age, coupled with dissensions among the Persians, gave Heraclius the opportunity which he seized. Palestine was once again the object of contest among the nations, and when peace was concluded in 628 the country reverted to Byzantium. The Emperor visited Jerusalem the following year, and was pressed by the monks who received him there to exterminate all the Jews. He based his refusal to do so on the treaty into which he had entered with them, but he was assured by the monks that no treaty could hold with the infidel, and that it was his Christian duty to destroy the Jews young and old. As a further incentive they offered to take on their shoulders the responsibility for any sin which their policy might involve. The Emperor yielded, and the only survivors of the Jews of Judæa were those who hid underground or fled into Egypt.

The triumph of Heraclius was short-lived. Within five

years Palestine was again invaded, this time from the south-east. While Persian and Greek had been struggling for the Syrian prize, a new religion and a new power had arisen in Arabia. Mohammed had died in 632, but his successor Abu Bekr, the first of the Caliphs, with the united warriors of Arabia marching behind him, determined to wrest the holy and fertile province of Syria from the hands of the Christian. Abu Bekr died in 634, and was succeeded by Omar. Towards the end of the year 635 Damascus fell to the arms of the new Caliph, and less than a year later Heraclius was finally defeated on the Yarmuk, and compelled to abandon Syria. The Christians of the country defended themselves for some time longer in isolated strongholds, but the dominion of the Emperors in Palestine had come to an end. When Jerusalem had been occupied, peace was arranged, the conditions including certain perpetual restrictions on the Christians. They were, however, guaranteed security of both person and property, and although the erection of further churches or religious institutions was prohibited, the existing ones were declared inviolable, and Mohammedans were forbidden under penalties to interfere with them. Under the guidance of the Christian Patriarch, Omar visited the site of the Temple, which he found defiled by the filth which the Christians had heaped upon it in derision of the Jews. With his own hands Omar helped to clean the site, which subsequently became the second most sacred in the Moslem land. He was urged to visit the church erected over the Holy Sepulchre, but refused to do so, declaring that if he set foot therein, it would probably as a consequence one day be claimed and seized by the Moslems. He wished the church and the site to remain the property of the Christians for ever. The Ordinances of Omar which regulated the attitude of the Caliphate towards the Jews were extremely severe, and if they had been carried out without modification the lot of the Jews in Moslem lands would have been very hard. The application of the Code was, however, far more generous than its letter, and in practice, so far as the Jews of Palestine were concerned, the Moslems came as deliverers and not as oppressors. In 661, as a consequence of dissensions and rivalries, the seat of the caliphate was transferred from Mecca to Damascus. Twenty-three years later, in furtherance of the same policy, the Caliph Abd el-Melek erected on the Temple site one of the world's most beautiful buildings, the Dome of the Rock, which has come to be known as the Mosque of Omar.

Already before the rise of the Moslems there had been an Arab immigration into Palestine, and when the land passed under the control of an Arab dynasty the number of settlers of that race considerably increased. Thus yet another people was added to the mosaic which formed, and still forms, the population of Palestine. Under Omar and his immediate successors the land on the whole enjoyed a peace, and its inhabitants, without distinction of religion, a comfort to which both had for centuries been strangers. Under Moawiya, who ruled the land from 639 until 680, during the last years of that period as Caliph, Palestine was one of the best governed States of the world, and it retained its peaceful character for another two centuries. Towards the end of the eighth century there was a considerable immigration of Karaites,* and many of them settled in Jerusalem as

* The Protestants of Judaism. The Karaites, who reject the Oral Law, the Talmudic developments of the Bible, seceded from the body of Jewry in the eighth century.

Abelim, or Mourners for Jerusalem.   In 831 the Church of
the Holy Sepulchre was restored, to be destroyed again
a century later when the revolt of the Carmathians sent
a large number of fanatical Moslems to Jerusalem.
Previously many churches and other Christian buildings
had been restored by the munificence of Charlemagne.
A few years later the secession of Egypt under the
Fatimites carried Syria with it, and thus again after
many centuries Palestine became an appanage of
Egypt.   The Jewish and Christian inhabitants of Jerusalem had by now become considerable in numbers and
in influence.   In other parts of Palestine also the removal
of the hand of ruthless persecution had enabled the Jews
to stretch themselves in the sun and to prosper and
multiply.   They were to be found in all occupations, but
they were especially prominent on account of their numbers among the minters, dyers, tanners, and money-
changers.

At the end of the tenth century Egypt, and also
Syria, suffered from the rule of an insane Caliph,
Hakim Bi-amrillah, and among the exploits of this mad-
man, who became the prophet of the Druses of the Lebanon,
was the destruction of the Church.   The Jews of Palestine
suffered as severely as their Christian fellow-countrymen
from the persecution of Hakim.   Nevertheless, their co-
religionists in France were accused of having instigated
the destruction of the Church and in consequence were
the object of murderous attacks.   Hakim was assassinated
in 1020, and Palestine passed out of history for the next
half-century.   In the meanwhile the Jewish population
of Jerusalem had been considerably diminished.   However, the city throughout these years of disturbance continued a place of pilgrimage and of settlement to both

Jew and Christian, and there is reason for believing that the Jewish settlers in the eleventh century came in some instances from as distant a region as Germany. Many years previous to this, Jerusalem had again become a centre of Jewish learning, and in the former half of the eleventh century an attempt was even made to revive the Gaonate, the University of Hebrew learning, in Palestine. This was the position of affairs in 1072, when the Seljuk Turkomans from Central Asia, on their march to Egypt, passed through the country and took possession of its strongholds. The Turkomans were defeated by the Egyptians, and Palestine and Syria were recovered, but one of the consequences of the invasion was the removal of the Jewish College from Jerusalem to Tyre.

CHAPTER III

THE CRUSADES AND THE KINGDOM OF THE FRANKS

THE sufferings of the Christians in the Holy Land, and the desecration to which the Holy Places had to submit as a consequence of the period of turmoil through which Syria was passing, echoed and reverberated throughout Christendom. From the time of Constantine the stream of pilgrims from Europe to the Holy Land had run without cessation. Even in the most perilous times there was no lack of Christians willing to brave unknown, the most terrible of, dangers in order to pray at the places which their associations rendered almost divine. Those who returned to Europe reported the miseries by which their fellow-Christians were being tortured at the very birthplace of Christianity, and the narrators did not fail to elicit sympathy and indignation wherever they went or their narratives penetrated. In 1093 Peter, a priest of Amiens, visited Jerusalem. On his return to Europe, so moved was he by the feeling of shame that the holiest places of Christendom should be in pagan hands, that he traversed France, preaching a Holy War for the rescue of Jerusalem. The people of the Continent had been well prepared for such a movement. The active support of the Pope, Urban II., helped it a long way towards success, and soon an army of knights and common soldiers arose spontaneously in France and made their way towards the Holy Land. It is computed that 600,000 men left France in the course of 1096. Only 40,000 of them reached Jerusalem, but this remnant succeeded in capturing the city in July, 1099, and in making their leader, Godfrey of Bouillon, King. Thus began the Latin kingdom of Jerusalem, which endured for eighty-eight years, and whose history has been described as " one of the most painful ever penned." In Syria itself many causes combined to favour the invaders. On the death of Malik Shah, the Seljukian Emperor, in 1092, Syria had become independent of that Empire. The conquest had not been so much a conquest as a military occupation, and the only one of the numerous elements in the country on which the government rested was the Turkish soldiery and officialdom. Of the other elements the most favourable were those that were neutral. Even the Turks themselves were split into hostile sections, and above all, the stability of the state was threatened by the Caliph of Egypt in the south. These factors, far more than the prowess of Godfrey, his fellow-leaders and their followers—among whom were Robert of Normandy, the eldest son of William the Conqueror, Edgar Atheling, the last of the Saxon Princes of England, and Stephen of Blois, son-in-law of William and father of King Stephen of England—contributed to the success of the Crusade. In their march across Europe the Crusaders had prepared for their sacred task by massacring the Jews in every city through which they passed, and in plundering and burning their dwellings. Their course was marked by a river of blood on which shone the lurid flames of burning homes. So appalling were the atrocities they committed that Princes and Bishops were shocked to horrified protest. In the Holy Land they continued this procedure. All non-Christians were to them the enemies of God, and to be utterly rooted out. When

Jerusalem opened her gates every Moslem—man, woman and child—who could be found was put to the sword, so that the Crusaders had to wade knee-deep in blood in order to reach the Church of the Holy Sepulchre. The Jews for their part were driven into their synagogue, where they were burnt.

Godfrey became the first King of Jerusalem, or, more correctly, Advocate of the Holy Sepulchre. Of his companions Tancred became Prince of Galilee and afterwards of Antioch, in which principality he succeeded his uncle, Bohemund. Baldwin, the brother of Godfrey and his successor as King of Jerusalem, became Count of Edessa, and Raymund of Toulouse, Count of Tripoli. Hardly had the Crusaders settled in Jerusalem when they had to repel an attack from Egypt, and in this they succeeded at the Battle of Ascalon. The bulk of the Crusaders thereupon left Judæa, and Godfrey remained with 2,000 followers. Godfrey died in 1100, leaving the kingdom to his brother Baldwin. Before the latter could arrive from Edessa, the Patriarch Dagobert seized the opportunity to attempt to obtain the kingdom for himself. The support he obtained was, however, slight, and Baldwin was in due course crowned and became the first formal King. In the course of the following thirty years the kingdom, which had at first consisted only of the districts of Jerusalem, Jaffa, Ramleh, and Haifa, spread northwards as far as Beirout, and in the south to El-Arish on the Mediterranean, and to the head of the Red Sea. Throughout the period large numbers of Europeans of all classes and of all lands came to Palestine as pilgrims, and many of them settled there. Commercially the country prospered by means of intercourse with the Italian seamen and merchants, who aided materially in the extension of the limits of the kingdom.

The three Frankish principalities in the north, one after the other, came under the suzerainty of the southern kingdom, which, at the death of Baldwin II. in 1131, was at the height of its power. There were a few Jews settled in the trading centres, but the feudal system of government, modelled on that of France, had no room for Jews except as pariahs. One great blessing that the Frankish kingdom brought to the land was that of peace, and the peace was soon followed by prosperity. A stable, energetic government, as was that of the Latins during the first half of the life of the Kingdom, gave security to commerce and to industry. The land which had become a desert through neglect, oppression and warfare, became again as fertile and as fruitful as in the happiest days of the Hebrew State. A wide system of irrigation and adequate protection against marauders from the desert made of the land one huge garden. Sugar-canes, date-palms, banana and pomegranate trees, grew in profusion. Wheat, barley, hay, millet, lentils, sesame, cotton, saffron, and indigo gladdened the heart of the agriculturist. The flax and dates of Palestine rivalled those for which Egypt was famous. Rare fruits flourished like wild-flowers. The melons of Safed made that city famous. On both sides of the Jordan, from the northernmost limits almost to the Egyptian border, the land was once again, as in Bible times, flowing with milk and honey. The products of Palestine were not only exported to, but also acclimatized in, Europe. It was at this period that maize was introduced into Italy, and that the Damascus plum— the damson—and the shalot first appeared in Europe. Later the orange also was introduced from Palestine. From the sugar-cane sugar was manufactured. The industrial and also the commercial activity led to the settlement of a number of small towns throughout the land. Palestine became once again the mart between Europe and the East. The natural routes from Asia to Africa had always run through Palestine. Under a settled government they were more and more frequented. At the same time the ports of Palestine became for Asia the gates of Europe. Through these ports passed the wares of Damascus and of Mecca, of Persia, of India, and even of further China. The products of Palestine also, raw and manufactured, followed the same route. Sugar, silk, soap, camelots, tartans—derived from the city of Tyre—china, and metal-work were all manufactured in the cities of Palestine and Syria, and were exported to Europe. And withal Frank and Moslem co-operated and lived in amity together.

Among the other consequences of the settled state of the country was the arrival of Jewish pilgrims, men of learning and of piety, who came to Palestine to ascertain for the benefit of their co-religionists in Europe the state of the land which loomed so large in Jewish prayers and hopes, and also for the more pious reasons of praying at the Western Wall, the only remnant of the Temple, and at the other Jewish Holy Places, and of visiting the graves of the many illustrious Jews who lie buried in holy soil. Among the most distinguished of these pilgrims was Jehuda Halevi, the Spanish poet and philosopher—perhaps the sweetest singer the Jews of the Diaspora have yet produced—who visited Palestine in 1140 and ended his life while on his pilgrimage there. The resident Christian population had long since lost its crusading zeal, and the Jew was now more free to live in Palestine than in some of the states of Europe. The former Jewish population had been practically annihilated by the massacres and warfare through which they had passed, and as a consequence the Jewish agriculturist who had once been the backbone of the people was now extinct. The new Jewish population consisted to a far greater extent of merchants and traders, and also included many of the most trusted physicians of the country; for the rulers and Bishops of the Frankish States in the Near East, like their brothers in Europe, preferred to entrust their health to the keeping of Jewish and Moslem physicians rather than to those of their own religious community.

During the earlier half of the history of the kingdom of Jerusalem the relations between the King and his Moslem neighbours were often sufficiently cordial to lead to alliances between them. The relations with Damascus in particular were for a long time most friendly. But the conquest of Edessa by the Turks under Nureddin in 1144 may be said to mark the turning-point in the history of the kingdom of Jerusalem. The previous year Baldwin III., the first of the native-born Kings, had come to the throne. The loss of Edessa aroused the remaining Christian Princes to attempt its recovery. As a first measure the friendship between Jerusalem and Damascus was severed, and a considerable step was thus taken towards the ultimate dissolution of the Jerusalem kingdom. When the news of the Christian loss in the East reached Europe, the Pope issued an appeal to France for a new Crusade, and Louis of France immediately took up the Cross. The eloquence of Bernard of Clairvaux was placed at the disposal of the movement, and by him Conrad III. of Germany was induced to take his place at the side of Louis VII. But whatever chance of success the Crusade had was wrecked by dissensions among its members, and the only definite result was the capture of Lisbon. The North German members of the expedition did not even leave their own region, but devoted their energies to attacking the Wends on the other side of the Elbe. Those who reached Asia laid siege to Damascus, and were repulsed without difficulty. By this exploit they not only depreciated the reputation of the Franks in Syria and Asia Minor: they also rendered the relations between the former allies, Damascus and Jerusalem, still more strained. Of the Crusaders but a handful reached the Holy Land itself. So far as Edessa was concerned, the remainder of the principality fell under the Mohammedan rule, and with it went a portion of the county of Antioch. In Europe, as had been the case half a century earlier, the swords of the soldiers of the Cross were baptized in Jewish blood. The Pope, Eugenius III., himself was the first to incite his warriors against the Jews whom they met on their way. The road indicated by him was followed with eagerness. Anti-Jewish outbreaks occurred simultaneously in France, North Germany, Austria, and Spain. In fact, wherever Jew and Crusader were to be found at the same time, the Jew was considered fair game. In Jewish history the Second Crusade opened a long period of murder, rapine, and plunder, which lasted for centuries after the last of Eugenius' warriors had passed to their rest.

In the years that followed immediately after the Second Crusade, Jerusalem under Baldwin and Amalric I. was in effect a dependency of the Eastern Empire. In the meanwhile Damascus passed into the power of Nureddin, who was thus appreciably nearer to Jerusalem. The previous year, 1153, Baldwin of Jerusalem, with the support of the Emperor, had captured Ascalon, a town which had withstood the Franks for half a century, and had thereby opened the road to Egypt, after Jerusalem the principal goal of the Franks. Egypt was, however, also the goal of Nureddin. The two forces met there and fought in 1164. The Turk won. His lieutenant, Shirguh, became Vizier of Egypt, an office in which he was succeeded on his death by his nephew, Saladin, who on the death of the Caliph in 1171 became the sole ruler of Egypt. Jerusalem, caught by the Turkish powers settled in Damascus in the north and in Cairo in the south, was in great jeopardy. Jealousies between Nureddin and his lieutenant in Egypt, however, kept off the threatening blow for some years. The Turkish ruler died in 1174, leaving a child to succeed him. Amalric died the same year, leaving his throne also to a child. Saladin survived in the fulness of his power. The kingdom of Jerusalem gained some respite at the hands of Raymund, Count of Tripoli, who carried his conquests beyond Damascus and supported the heir of Nureddin against Saladin. Ultimately, however, in 1183, the ruler of Egypt brought the northern Turks under his sway.

During this period of disorder, which was leading up to the final catastrophe, the Jewish practice of journeying to the Holy Land was continued. In 1165 the family of Maimonides—the philosopher, physician, and philanthropist, who a few years later reappeared in Palestinian history as the medical attendant of King Richard of England, lent to him by Saladin—in their flight from persecution in Spain and Morocco, paid visits of piety to Jerusalem and Hebron before settling in Egypt. About the same time Benjamin of Tudela, the best known of all medieval Jewish travellers, reached Palestine in the course of his journeyings. He traversed the land

from north to south and back again, and in the narrative
of his travels gives much information regarding the
numbers of the Jews settled in the towns of Palestine
and their condition. He found Jewish communities
of some size in all the coast towns from Gubail to Ascalon.
Although none lived permanently among the Druses in
the Lebanon, Jewish handicraftsmen and dyers were
accustomed to go among them unmolested in pursuit of
their trades. At Tyre, where was a large Jewish community, several scholars had settled. Many of the Jews
of Tyre were men of wealth and owned sea-going vessels.
There were also glassmakers who manufactured the
world-renowned Tyrian glass ware, while the sugar which
grew in the neighbourhood was manufactured and
exported by Jews. Inland, Sebastiya, formerly Samaria,
is described as lying in " a land of brooks of water,
gardens, orchards, vineyards, and olive groves," but no
Jews lived there. Farther south, at Nablous or Shechem,
there were a thousand Samaritans. Jerusalem he described as a city of many tongues—Jacobites, Syrians,
Greeks, Georgians, and Franks, not to mention Mohammedans. He found only four Jews living there. They
had by payment to the King obtained the monopoly of
dyeing. At Bethlehem there were two Jewish dyers.
Hebron was in ruins. The synagogue which had existed
under the Moslems had been transformed into a church.
Nearer to the coast, at Ramleh, a relatively large Jewish
community was found. At Jaffa, however, and at
Jabneh there were no Jews, with the exception of one
dyer at the former port. In Galilee Sepphoris had no
Jewish inhabitants; Tiberias, fifty. Damascus held three
thousand Jews, many of them learned and rich men.
At Tadmor in the Wilderness there were about two thou-

sand, " valiant in war," battling with the Christians and with the Arabs.

A few years later another famous Jewish traveller, Petachiah of Ratisbon, visited Palestine, and wrote the narrative of his journey. His itinerary was shorter than that of Benjamin. Damascus he described as lying " in the midst of gardens and pleasure grounds. There are also high fountains from which the water pours, and many large pools. The Ishmaelites say: ' If Paradise be on earth, then Damascus is the Paradise; and if it be in heaven, then Damascus is opposite on the earth.' " The four Jews of Jerusalem had dwindled to one, who paid a heavy tax to the King in order to be permitted to dwell there.

Petachiah was in Palestine on the eve of the last day of the Frankish kingdom. In these last years the shadow of the approaching Saracen lengthened almost month by month over the doomed kingdom, which in the end fell an easy prey. Its ruler, Baldwin IV., was a child afflicted with leprosy. On his death he was succeeded by the boy, Baldwin V., who was soon poisoned. After him in 1186 came Guy de Lusignan, a French adventurer, whose claim to the throne came through his wife, a daughter of Amalric I. The approaching fate was not unforeseen. For more than twenty years, since all hope of gaining Egypt had been given up, endeavours had been made to turn it aside. In 1184 a great mission, which included the Patriarch of Jerusalem and the Masters of the Orders of the Temple and of St. John, had been sent to Europe to offer the crown, first to Philip Augustus of France and afterwards to Henry II. of England, so as to secure the support of one of those powers in repelling the impending attack. Henry II., as an Angevin, had some claim to the throne on the extinction of the elder line of

Anjou, represented by Fulk, who had reigned at Jerusalem from 1131 to 1143.   But beyond the raising of a special tax in France and England, the mission had no results.   The penultimate stroke came from another French adventurer, Raynald of Chatillon, who, settling to the south-east of Palestine, fitted out a fleet with which to attack the Arabian coast.   Driven from the sea by Saladin, he turned brigand on land.   The capture in 1186 of a caravan in which a sister of Saladin was travelling precipitated the crisis.   Saladin determined once for all to free the Holy Places of Mohammedanism from the Frank, and incident-ally to bring Syria and Palestine once again under Moslem rule.   A new Holy War for the recovery of Jerusalem was preached, this time by the Moslem instead of the Christian.   The war was of short duration.   The whole of the armed forces of the kingdom were destroyed at the Battle of Hattin in May, and in the following October Jerusalem capitulated after a fortnight's siege. By the end of 1189 all that remained to the Franks from Asia Minor to Egypt was the isolated cities of Margat and Tyre and the districts of Antioch and Tripoli. The fall of Jerusalem led to a considerable Jewish im-migration into Palestine, for wherever Saladin's rule ran there was freedom for the Jews as for all other races and creeds.   Jerusalem thereupon again became a Jewish centre.

The picture of the Latin kingdom in its last days has been drawn by Sir Walter Besant in the following passage: " The country was dotted over with castles and strong-holds, the owners of which had learned, since the death of Amaury (Amalric), to despise the authority of the King. Moreover, the pride and power of the Templars set up a sort of rival authority.   Every baron fought for his own land and for his own aggrandizement. There was no more thought of conquest and glory; they fought now for plunder only. When pilgrims arrived from the West, they were made use of by the Syrian barons for their own purposes; and when they were strong enough to fight the Saracens, no treaty was sacred, no convention was kept. The cities, especially those of the sea-shore, were divided into nations, such as the Pisans, the Genoese, and the Venetians, all of whom contended with each other over their privileges, and often fought out their quarrels in the streets. The Templars and the Hospitallers bargained for their arms by demanding the cession of half a town, or a fort, in return for their services. They quarrelled with each other, with the Church, and with the King. And with the depravation of morals had come a total neglect and contempt of religion, with— of which there are not a few traces—the birth of an active spirit of infidelity. Men had begun to question and to compare. There were not wanting renegades to be found among the Mohammedan armies. Islam received its converts from the Christians, but it gave back none in return."

CHAPTER IV

FROM THE FALL OF JERUSALEM TO THE FINAL
EXPULSION OF THE FRANKS

THE fall of Jerusalem reverberated throughout Europe and immediately preparations were begun for the recovery of the Holy City. A new Crusade, the third, was preached. Foremost among those who took up arms were the Emperor Frederick, Philip Augustus of France, and Richard of England, who considered that, as heir to the House of Anjou, Jerusalem had a special claim upon him. The new Crusade, like its predecessors, opened with massacres of Jews, but on this occasion only in England; those of France being merely plundered by Philip Augustus. The town of Acre was the immediate objective of the several armies which set out to recover the Holy Land. The siege of this town had been begun in the summer of 1189 by Guy de Lusignan, who had previously been taken prisoner at the Battle of Hattin and had been released on parole. Difficulties dogged the footsteps of the European armies before they set foot in Palestine. The Emperor found himself on the verge of war with his brother of the Eastern Empire, who was not only unfriendly in disposition to the Westerns, but was almost in alliance with Saladin. Frederick ultimately crossed into Asia, but died by accident while yet a long distance from Palestine. At the same time dissensions and disputes arose between Philip and Richard, who ultimately parted in order to reach Acre by different routes. When Richard arrived at the city the siege had already lasted for more than two years, but within a little more than a month it succumbed to his arms. Philip soon returned to France. Richard made some further conquests on the coast, but devoted most of his energies to negotiations with the object of arranging a marriage between his own sister and Saladin's brother with a view to their accession to the kingdom. Ultimately a portion of the coast, of which Richard's nephew, Henry of Champagne, became King, with the title King of Jerusalem, was ceded to the Crusaders. Richard finally left Palestine in October, 1192. Saladin died the following year.

The Fourth Crusade, which lasted from 1202 until 1204, was directed in effect against the Eastern Empire. Some of the Teutonic knights, however, reached Palestine and recovered Beyrout and other coast towns. Meanwhile Malik-al-Adil, the brother and successor of Saladin, continued his beneficent sway in Syria as well as in Palestine and Egypt. Moslem Palestine had by now become a haven of refuge for the persecuted Jews of Europe. The era of bloodshed and oppression was in full vigour in the West of Europe when, in 1211, 300 of the Rabbis of England and France visited Palestine in order to investigate the prospects of a Jewish immigration on a large scale. The Sultan gave them a friendly welcome. The following year was the occasion of that ghastly tragedy which is known to history as the Crusade of the Children. Dreamers, despairing of the reconquest of Jerusalem by men, in consequence of their apparently innate wickedness and vice, gathered an army of 50,000 children, girls as well as boys, who by their innocence should prevail where their fathers had failed.   But few of these child-pilgrims reached the coast of Palestine.   Even less wandered back to their homes.   The most fortunate were those who were shipwrecked and drowned in the Mediterranean.   The memorial of this army of children is the legend of the Pied Piper of Hamelin.   The Fifth Crusade was proclaimed by Pope Innocent at the Lateran Council of 1215.   It devoted itself to attacking Egypt, where the port of Damietta was taken.   The Sultan Malik-al-Kamil was willing to surrender the greater part of the kingdom of Jerusalem, as well as to agree to other terms, in order to obtain a lasting peace, but the Papal Legate demanded an indemnity in addition.   This was refused, and the Crusaders were attacked, driven back, and forced to evacuate Damietta.   With this disaster the Crusade ended.

The next Crusade, that of 1228, was waged under an interdict, and strange to say, despite its excommunication by the Pope, it proved successful, though not by force of arms.   It was led by the Emperor Frederick II., who had married Isabella, the heiress to the kingdom of Jerusalem, and had assumed the title by the right of his wife. Delays in fulfilling the vow he had taken so enraged the Pope, Gregory IX., that the latter placed him under the ban.   The Emperor nevertheless sailed for Palestine, while the Pope preached and instigated a Crusade against Frederick's European dominions.   Arrived in Palestine, the Emperor was shunned by the Christians already there.   Still, by dint of diplomacy and by playing one Mohammedan party against another, he succeeded in inducing the Sultan to agree to a treaty by which Jerusalem, Nazareth, and Bethlehem, together with a strip of land connecting with the coast, were ceded to him for ten years, and the coast towns already in the hands of the

Christians were retained by them. Frederick then entered Jerusalem, where, as no Churchman would have any dealings with him, he was compelled to crown himself. The following fifteen years were the last in which Christians held rule in Jerusalem. They formed a period of continual struggle between Frederick and his barons, which ended in the advantage of the latter. The barons had hardly, however, secured the victory when the cataclysm overwhelmed them. Towards the end of this period expeditions had come out under the lead of Theobald of Champagne and of Richard of Cornwall respectively, but the excommunication of the Pope, with whom Frederick had again quarrelled after having made peace, prevented their assistance from being of much value. In 1244 Palestine was overrun by a new enemy, and Jerusalem plundered and destroyed by the Kharezmian Tartars. The Franks, not satisfied with having to face these marauders, made an alliance with Damascus and went to war with Egypt. But at the Battle of Gaza they were deserted by their allies, and beaten by Bibars, who afterwards became the Mameluke Sultan of Egypt. Jerusalem was the prize. Ascalon, which had been strongly fortified by the Franks, fell three years later.

The answer of Europe to this calamity was the immediate preaching of a new Crusade, directed against both the infidels in Palestine and the heretic Emperor in Europe, and of the two campaigns the Pope showed a decided preference for the latter. St. Louis of France, however, preferred the Holy Land, but when his army reached Cyprus he deflected it to Egypt. The invasion led to a disaster which included the capture of the King himself. He was released after payment of a ransom and then went to Acre, but the whole of his power in the

CHAPTER V

THE TURKISH DOMINION

PALESTINE was once again joined to Egypt under one ruler, and under the tolerant rule of the Moslem it became to some extent a land of refuge for the Jews of Europe. Jews were quite free to come to the land, and if they wished to settle there, they ran no risk in doing so. Palestine thus became a centre of Jewish pilgrimage, and the Jews of Egypt and Syria, as in the days of the Temple, began to flock to Jerusalem to celebrate the Jewish festivals. Many of the new-comers settled in the country and engaged in agriculture, in industry, and in commerce. A few employed themselves in secular studies and in the practice of medicine; a large number devoted the remainder of their lives to Jewish scholarship. In fact, during this period Palestine became again a centre of Jewish learning where European scholars of repute studied and taught. In Jerusalem to an especial extent Jewish students and scholars settled, but artisans, merchants, and physicians were also to be found there. The new Jewish population of Hebron devoted themselves more to weaving, dyeing, and the manufacture of glass ware. In the South of Palestine the new-comers adopted a pastoral life. Their Rabbi was also a shepherd, and used to teach his people while he and they were tending their flocks. The Jewish settlers in Palestine during the fourteenth century came from homes as distant as Western

36

Europe. A large number of them had come from France, where the fourteenth century was a period of almost ceaseless persecution. At the same time Christians gradually resettled in the land and rebuilt the churches at Jerusalem, Bethlehem, and Nazareth.

The year 1402 saw the country overrun and ravaged by the Tartar conqueror Timur (Tamerlane), but his death three years later restored Egyptian authority. With the return of peace the favourable conditions antecedent to the inroad of the Tartars were restored. So comfortable, in fact, were the Jews of Palestine, compared with those of other lands, during the earlier half of the fourteenth century, that the rumour spread in Europe that the Jews had bought Mount Zion and the Holy Sepulchre, and had demolished the buildings upon them. Without attempting to confirm the rumour, the Christian powers of Europe accepted it as an excuse for giving a few further turns to the screw of persecution. Although the material power of the Jews of Jerusalem did not approach so great a height, their spiritual power waxed to such an extent that for a time the rule of the Chief Rabbi of Jerusalem was accepted by Jews throughout Egypt and Syria. The prosperity of the Jews of Jerusalem was, however, not of long duration. Plague, famine, and economic depression, followed by an unfavourable change in the political conditions, dealt repeated blows at the community after the middle of the fifteenth century had been passed. Emigration commenced, and a traveller who visited the city in 1481 reported that there were then only 250 Jewish families there. Within a few years the number had fallen to seventy families, all in a state of poverty.

Jerusalem Jewry remained in this condition for a very

short time. The year 1492 saw the expulsion from Spain of the whole of its large and in many respects illustrious Jewish population. The refugees scattered along both shores of the Mediterranean, but the Moslem lands were almost the only ones in which they were able to find undisturbed shelter. Palestine profited greatly from the migration. The number of Jews in Jerusalem increased so largely that the place of the one congregation previously existing was taken by four. The community also rose appreciably in self-respect and in status, and under the guidance of the saintly scholar, Obadiah of Bertinoro, who had settled in Jerusalem some years earlier, secured again a considerable influence over the Jews of the East. The same cause made Safed almost as important a Jewish centre as Jerusalem. Spanish immigrants raised its Jewish population to 10,000, over whom Joseph Saragossi held a position similar to that of Obadiah at Jerusalem. So widely recognized was the value of the influence of these two men that Mohammedans vied with Jews in showing them honour; and when there was a fear that Saragossi was about to leave Safed, the governor of the town made every effort to persuade him to remain. In Damascus also the Jewish population became sufficiently considerable to justify the formation of several congregations.

The year 1516 witnessed the beginning of the last period of the history of this country which had undergone so many vicissitudes and had obeyed so many masters. The final struggle between Asia as represented by the Ottoman Turks, and Egypt, which was still under the Mameluke dynasty, had been long impending. The Sultan of Egypt was defeated and killed in battle by the Turks in August, 1515, and the following year Syria became a portion of the Turkish dominions. On the 20th of January, 1517, Cairo was taken, and within a short time the Ottoman Sultan Selim became Sultan of Egypt, and the African empire was incorporated in the dominions of the Turks. So far as the people of Palestine were concerned, the change of rulers made little difference. The system of government remained as before, and almost the only change was that the product of the taxes went to Constantinople instead of to Cairo. After some years, however, Suleiman the Magnificent erected a series of important buildings in Jerusalem. In 1537 the walls which still stand were raised. At the same time the Tower of David was restored and a system of water-supply for the city completed. Suleiman accorded his Jewish subjects full liberty, and they were free to engage in any occupation they wished. The tolerant attitude of Suleiman was duly appreciated in contemporary Jewish writings. The numbers of the Jews in the city increased, and many merchants of relative wealth, from Italy in particular, as well as scholars of distinction, settled there. Among the trades followed by the Jews of Jerusalem at this time, those of goldsmith, silversmith, weaver, and shoemaker predominated. A considerable number of the inhabitants traded among the neighbouring villages, making the city their headquarters. The settlement of Joseph Caro, the renowned Jewish jurist, at Safed about the same time made that city the intellectual centre of Jewry. He died there in 1575. In 1538 an attempt was even made to re-establish the Synhedrin at Safed, but Jewry was not then ripe, nor is it yet, for so great a step towards national rehabilitation. Safed had for very many years been a centre of cabbalistic learning, the Jewish mystical philosophy. It was but natural, therefore, that a mystic like Solomon Molcho, who afterwards loomed so large in European Jewish history, should visit the city in order to reinvigorate himself. Isaac Luria, the founder of the modern Cabbala, also made that city his headquarters, and created a school at the head of which he was succeeded by his disciple Hayyim Vital Calabrese. Earlier than that period, in 1567, there was a considerable migration of Jews from Jerusalem to Safed on account of the heavy taxation inflicted on them by the Turks.

Suleiman the Magnificent, the greatest of the Sultans, stands out in Jewish history as the protector of the Jews of Europe against their persecutors. It was he who was able to compel the Pope, the Republic of Venice, and the other rulers of Italy, to withdraw the hand which had already been stretched forth to light the faggot of the Inquisition fires. During his reign Turkey became the land of refuge for the hunted fugitives from European cruelty. The number of Jews who settled in Salonica made that port almost a Jewish city, and incidentally raised it to the pinnacle of commercial prosperity, a position which it retained so long as the Crescent waved above it. Other benefits, also, Suleiman and his empire derived from the humane attitude he adopted towards the Jews. Above all was the wise and statesmanlike advice offered to him and accepted from the Spanish refugee Joseph Nasi, a prince among philanthropists and merchants, who with his relatives had taken refuge in Constantinople to avoid the oppression and greed of half of the Sovereigns of Europe. Nasi's services to the State were rewarded by Suleiman, and by his successor Selim, with many great dignities. By the former he was presented with the town and district of Tiberias in order that he might settle Jews there. To increase the security of the grant Suleiman obtained the agreement of his heir and of his heir's heir to it. Nasi, assisted by his aunt, Donna Gracia Mendes, the modern Esther, and aided by a State subvention, devoted a fortune to the enterprise. He had the walls of Tiberias rebuilt despite great difficulties with the Arab workmen, who were taught by a sheikh that the raising of the walls of the city would mean the universal dominion of Judaism. He invited the persecuted Jews of Italy to settle in his domain, and large numbers left Italy for that purpose, especially on the expulsion of the Jews from the Papal States. In the spirit of true statesmanship Nasi encouraged agriculturists and artisans to settle. He planted mulberry-trees for the breeding of silkworms, and introduced the manufacture of wool and silk. Nasi's energies were, however, after a time directed to other channels—to Naxos and other islands of which he was made Duke, and to Cyprus, of which he had some expectation of becoming King—and the promising experiment of Tiberias sank into oblivion.

Of the history of Palestine during the succeeding two centuries there is very little to record. The local government sank gradually into a condition of neglect and corruption, and the people of all races and religions suffered accordingly. During the first decades of the seventeenth century the Druse Prince Fakhr ud-Din, who had in Italy acquired a veneer of European culture, seized the coast as far south as Acre, and held it despite the efforts of the Turks to dislodge him.

Oppression and poverty had by then reduced the Jews to a level from which it took centuries to raise them. The principal means of existence was the alms which the pious Jews of Europe were accustomed to send to their co-religionists in the Holy City, who were expected in return to devote themselves to prayer and to study. Thus grew up a dependent population whose spiritual descendants even to-day form a large proportion of the Jewish inhabitants of the city.

The seventeenth century was unfortunately a period of massacre and spoliation for the Jews of Poland, in which kingdom the greater part of the Jews of Europe had taken refuge from similar treatment in the south and the west of Europe. The sufferings of the Jews of Poland reacted in Jerusalem in the cessation of the customary revenues. In this manner the atrocities committed by Chmielnicki and his Cossacks led directly to the starvation of the Jews of Jerusalem. In the midst of all these troubles came one of the periods of fiscal oppression by the uncontrolled Pasha of Jerusalem. In their dire distress the wretched victims looked to their co-religionists abroad for assistance; and Sabbathai Zevi, the most famous of the pseudo-Messiahs who in the course of nineteen hundred years brought misfortune on Jewry, being then a resident of Jerusalem, was sent to Egypt to obtain it. For a few months after his return from Egypt, Jerusalem was the scene of the exploits of this most romantic figure, and in consequence the city gained a fame or notoriety to which it had long been a stranger. On the departure of Sabbathai, however, Jerusalem sank again into oblivion. By the year 1690 the Sabbathaian movement had been quite forgotten so far as Palestine was concerned. In that year there was a considerable settlement of ultra-pious Polish Jews, Chassidim, from Galicia in Jerusalem. They brought no wealth with them, and increased the material poverty of the community, but

one benefit that was due to the immigration was the
sympathetic interest in the condition of the Jews of the
city shown henceforth by the Austrian Government.   By
the end of the eighteenth century the population of the
city amounted to more than ten thousand, one-tenth of
whom were Jews.   The latter had at least twelve colleges,
the majority of which were supported or had been
endowed by pious Israelites in Europe.   In the meanwhile Safed, which had hitherto been the principal Jewish
centre in Palestine, had declined greatly in importance.
It suffered much from the plague in 1742, and from the
earthquake of twenty-seven years later. The latter
misfortune led to the emigration of practically all the
survivors to Damascus and other cities, so that of the ten
thousand Jews who were to be found in Safed two and a
half centuries earlier, only seven families remained
Within a very few years, however, there was a new immigration of Russian Jews, who lived under the protection
of the Russian and Austrian Governments, and henceforth Safed remained one of the few important Jewish
centres in Palestine.

CHAPTER VI

THE NINETEENTH CENTURY

The eighteenth century, although far advanced, was still
to witness several more invasions of Palestine from Egypt.
The first of these commenced in 1771, when Ali Bey,
having made himself independent, sent a force into Syria
in order to incorporate that province in his dominions.
His General, Abu'l Dhabab, was joined by Zahir, the
Governor of Acre, and with his assistance succeeded
easily in taking the chief cities, including Damascus.
At this point he transferred his allegiance from Ali to
the Sultan, and proceeded to invade Egypt in the interest
of the latter potentate. His example was followed by
others of Ali's Generals, and it was not long before the
latter was a fugitive at Acre dependent on the protection
of his friend, Zahir. At Acre he received assistance
in men and stores from Russia, always anxious to harm
the Turks, and was able to recover several of the coast
towns which had been temporarily conquered for him the
previous year. Of these he gave Jaffa to Zahir. Ali
was, however, soon defeated in battle after he had again
been deserted by those on whom he depended, and
Syria with Egypt resumed its former position in the
Turkish Empire. The punishment of Zahir, however,
remained to be inflicted, and a force, by which Palestine
was again overrun, was sent from Egypt for that purpose.
Still later in the century Acre was under the beneficent

44

government of Dhaher el Amir, a local sheikh. Among
the refugees whom he protected was an Albanian slave,
Ahmed el Jazzar, who had fled from Egypt. After a
few years El Jazzar returned to Egypt, and when shortly
afterwards Dhaher revolted against Turkey, his knowledge of local conditions was utilized, and he was sent to
Acre to suppress the revolt. In this he was entirely
successful, and as a reward was appointed governor in
the room of his opponent and former host. El Jazzar's
rule at Acre was noteworthy for considerable building
activity, but he also justified his surname of El Jazzar,
or the Butcher. Among his other exploits was the expulsion in 1791 of the colony of French merchants which
had been settled at the port for more than a century.

In 1798 Egypt was invaded by Napoleon, ostensibly
in the interests of Turkey, and was conquered within
six months. Turkey, however, did not agree that her
interests required a French invasion, and she sent expeditions by sea and by land to recover the country. The
latter was to have followed the customary route through
Palestine, but Napoleon, determining to forestall it,
himself crossed the Desert of El Arish and invaded
Palestine. He easily took El Arish, Gaza, and Jaffa, at
which latter town he massacred his prisoners. Continuing his march along the coast, he took one town after
another, until he arrived at Acre, where he halted. Sending
forces inland, he defeated the Arabs, and took Nazareth
and Tiberias. In the meanwhile the news of Napoleon's
advance and his cruelties drove the population, Jewish
and non-Jewish, before him. The inhabitants of Jerusalem were filled with consternation. That city was
thought to be the invader's objective. Measures were
immediately taken to fortify the city, and Jew and

non-Jew, Rabbi and layman, vied with one another in assisting in the raising of ramparts. Napoleon on his part issued a proclamation promising to present the Holy Land to the Jews and to restore the glories of Jerusalem, and calling on the Jews of Asia and Africa to join his forces. But the Jews distrusted the conqueror, and there was no response to the invitation. In the meanwhile Napoleon was laying siege to Acre, which was still in the hands of El Jazzar, whose Jewish Minister Farchi was the soul of the defence. Its body was, however, the British forces under Sir W. Sidney Smith, which were hastily thrown into the town and succeeded in compelling Napoleon after an ineffectual siege of two months to withdraw from this originally half-ruined fortress. The failure at Acre was the end of the Syrian campaign and the beginning of the end of the French occupation of Egypt.

Meanwhile the misfortunes of Safed, which had already been of long duration, continued. At the beginning of the nineteenth century, the plague that was prevalent there caused a further emigration and led indirectly to an increase of the Jewish population of Jerusalem. In 1812 four-fifths of the remaining Jewish population are said to have died of the same disease. Seven years later the survivors received the unwelcome attentions of the governor of Acre, a grandson of El Jazzar, who was noted for his rapacity and cruelty. The Jews were all imprisoned and held to ransom. The following year he murdered the Jewish Minister of his grandfather, who had inspired the defence of Acre against Napoleon. This crime led indirectly to the occupation of the whole country by Mehemet Ali, in 1831. The six preceding years were a period of great civil and political disturbance, harmful

to the interest of all the inhabitants without distinction
of race or creed. Great distress prevailed, and messengers
begging for assistance were sent as far as the United
States. Nevertheless, throughout this period the immigration of pious Jews, mostly settlers desirous of spending their few remaining years on holy soil, continued.
They came for the most part from Austria and Russia,
which two empires had now, in conjunction with Prussia,
absorbed the remainder of the Polish dominions. These
settlers were, however, not deserted by their Governments. Austria sent a representative to Jerusalem to
look after their interests, and both the Austrian and the
Russian Governments repeatedly brought pressure to
bear in Jerusalem on behalf of their nationals. The year
1827 was marked by the first of the several visits paid by
the great Anglo-Jewish philanthropist, Sir Moses Montefiore.

While these events were happening among the Jewish
communities of Palestine, the relations between Mehemet
Ali, the Pasha of Egypt, and his master the Sultan, were
becoming strained to breaking-point. The former had
been promised Palestine and Syria as the price of his
assistance against the Greek rebels, if the rebellion were
suppressed. The intervention of the Powers had, however, taken the decision in the matter of the rebellion
out of the hands of both Mehemet and the Sultan. It
is doubtful whether Mehemet really considered that he
had any claim to these provinces, but the growing cer-
tainty that the Sultan would sooner or later make war upon
him made the necessity for a previous *casus belli* against
Constantinople urgent. It was found in the claim for
Syria and Palestine, fortified by some minor matters of
less consequence. These were the circumstances that

led in 1831 to yet another invasion of Palestine from Egypt. Mehemet's progress was at first unopposed. He was met at Jaffa by his fleet and without difficulty occupied not only the coast towns, but also the remainder of the country. Acre hindered the army for a moment, but was stormed and sacked. The further progress of the army was then uninterrupted, and within a few days over six months from the crossing of the Palestine-Egyptian frontier, Damascus was reached and taken. The explanation of Mehemet's rapid progress was the welcome given him by the population. His army met with no further opposition until it reached Homs. There, and again at Hamah and at Beilan, the Turkish forces were defeated; and the Egyptian incursion did not come to a standstill until the banner of Mehemet Ali had been carried well into Asia Minor. Then the Powers intervened. The threat of Russian interference, nominally in the interests of Turkey, brought Britain and France into the negotiations, and they practically compelled the Sultan to cede Syria, Aleppo, Damascus, and also Adana in Asia Minor, to Mehemet and his son.

The rule of Mehemet in Syria was not successful. The reforms in the government which he introduced proved so unpopular as to lead to a revolt in 1834, which Mehemet suppressed only with difficulty. The outbreak of the rebellion was the signal for the turbulent Druses of the Lebanon to swoop down upon Safed and to sack the Jewish quarter. Whatever property escaped from the first attack succumbed to a second one which followed shortly afterwards. The bandits did not, however, remain unpunished, for when Ibrahim, Mehemet's son, arrived he imposed an indemnity on the surrounding villages, and devoted it to making good in part the losses of the Jews. The suppression of the revolt of 1834 did not settle the difficulties of Mehemet in Syria, for the Powers, with the exception of France, were opposed to his retention of the Asiatic provinces. But a premature attempt by Turkey to oust him failed, and when the Sultan subsequently offered him a portion of Syria for life, relying on French support he declined to compromise. Ultimately the Powers grew tired of the protracted negotiations. In September, 1840, the fleets of Britain, Austria, and Russia, under Sir Charles Napier, bombarded Beyrout, and an accompanying Turkish force took the town. Simultaneously the population of Syria rose again in rebellion. Exactly a month after the fall of Beyrout a similar fate overtook Acre, and Mehemet Ali's empire in Syria was at an end. The previous year Great Britain had appointed a Consul to Jerusalem, thus being the first Power to do so. The other Powers soon appointed Consuls also, and contemporaneously the Turkish Government strengthened its hold on the country at the expense of the hitherto semi-independent sheikhs.

It was fortunate for the Jews that the European Powers had their representatives in Syria at this time, for the year 1840 was stained by one of those terrible anti-Jewish campaigns which have sprinkled the history of civilization with blood. Mehemet Ali was still in control of Syria when the disappearance of a Capuchin friar at Damascus, which then had a large Jewish population, was used by his fellow-monks to revive the terrible charge of ritual murder against the Jews of the city. In this campaign they were ably assisted by Ratti Menton, an Italian adventurer and renegade to Mohammedanism who was the representative of France in the city. France was at this time the only friend that

4

Mehemet possessed. The influence of her representative with the local government was therefore supreme. The governor of Damascus found it politic to support the charge, all the more because the murderer was known to be a Moslem, and an anti-Jewish campaign was soon in full course among the local Christians and Moslems. The leading Jews of the city were arrested and put to the torture. Even children of three and four were taken from their parents and subjected to starvation so that their agonies might induce their mothers to denounce their kinsmen as guilty of a crime which had not been committed. The other Consuls allowed these proceedings to continue without heeding them until the representative of Austria was forced to intervene by the arrest and threatened torture of an Austrian subject. The Christians of Damascus in their attacks on the Jews were joined by their co-religionists throughout the Turkish Empire. At Rhodes also the charge of ritual murder was brought against the local Jewish community, members of which were put to the torture. In many cities the Jews were attacked: in all they and their faith were slandered.

Reports of the proceedings in the East soon spread to Europe, at first under the false colours given to them by Ratti Menton, but the truth in time became known through other sources, and sympathy began to be roused for the unfortunate Jews of Damascus. The Jews of England and France appealed to their Governments. The latter, although it offered fair words, took no steps to repress the criminal zeal of its representative. Palmerston, on the other hand, took a far more active line. He sent out instructions to the British representatives at Constantinople and Alexandria to use every effort to bring the cruelties to an end. Metternich at Vienna, on his own initiative, took a similar line. The light of publicity was being turned on the atrocities of Damascus. So far as the Rhodes accusation was concerned a formal trial was held, as a consequence of which the tables were turned on the Greek accusers, who were found guilty of bringing forward baseless charges against their Jewish fellow-citizens.

The Damascus affair was more difficult of treatment, for Mehemet was in control there. Any steps towards justice which he might have taken spontaneously were stopped by the influence of the French Consul-General, who was determined to support through thick and thin his subordinate at Damascus. The Austrian Consul, acting on instructions from Vienna, was, however, importunate, and he ultimately succeeded in getting the charge against the Jews remitted to a court composed of the British, Austrian, Russian, and Prussian Consuls at Alexandria. But France was still zealous on behalf of her Consul, and succeeded in getting Mehemet to withdraw his commission. Europe thus became divided into two camps, and in particular all the forces of clericalism were mobilized in the Latin countries in order to fasten the hateful Blood Accusation around the neck of Jewry. The Jews of France, hopeless of obtaining justice from their own Government, then determined to send their own representative to Alexandria to plead with Mehemet Ali. Their choice fell upon the orator and statesman Adolphe Crémieux, and with him went Sir Moses Montefiore as the representative of the Jews of England. In the House of Commons, Sir Robert Peel, the leader of the Opposition, pleaded the cause of the persecuted Jews, and Palmerston, the Foreign Secretary, warmly supported him. At the same time the Lord Mayor of

London convened a meeting in order to protest against
the charge that had been brought against the Jews of
Damascus, and through them against the entire Jewish
people. In Egypt the deputation obtained the hearty
support of the British Consul-General and the undisguised
opposition of his French colleague. Mehemet himself
temporized. His fate, not only in Syria but in Egypt
also, was in the balance, and he was naturally very
anxious not to offend either party. Ultimately he gave
way to the combined pressure of all the Powers excepting
France, and those of the imprisoned Jews of Damascus
who had not died of the cruelties perpetrated upon them
were released.

One of the immediate consequences of the Damascus
affair was the issue by Palmerston of instructions to all the
British representatives in the Levant and Syria, placing
the Jews under their special protection and informing
them that so far as non-British subjects were concerned
the Turkish Government desired their attention to be
directed to any case of oppression, and had promised the
British Ambassador that " it will attend to any repre-
sentation which may be made to it by the Embassy, of any
act of oppression practised against the Jews." The
services of the British Consul at Jerusalem were required
in this connection on several occasions, notably on one
in 1847, when he was instrumental in suppressing in its
first stage a revival by the Greek priests and pilgrims of
the terrible Blood Accusation. On another occasion a
Russian Jew, recently arrived from Europe, and unacquainted with the local customs, was almost murdered
by Christian pilgrims for having passed too close to
the Church. Although he was not a British subject,
the Consul intervened on his behalf; but the Greek

ecclesiastics claimed in their defence that if they had killed the man the penalty for which they would have been liable would have been a fine of ten paras (a halfpenny). As a consequence of this and similar incidents the British Government issued specific instructions to the British Consul to undertake the protection of foreign Jews whose own Consuls refused to act for them. There had by this time been a considerable influx of Russian Jews into Palestine, and their own Government, not caring to be troubled with their affairs, declined all responsibility for them, but told them when in need of advice and of assistance to apply to the British Consul. The Jews themselves were overcome with joy at the change of protector.

It was during the consulate of James Finn, who had shown himself especially sympathetic to the Jews, that the Anglican bishopric was founded. It was established by the Queen of England and the King of Prussia jointly, and the original arrangement was that the nomination of the Bishop should fall to each alternately. The first Anglican Bishop, who entered on his office in 1841, was Michael Solomon Alexander, a convert from Judaism. The Protestants were looked at askance by both the Greeks and the Latins, and were occasionally the object of attack by them. The hostility shown towards the Protestants was, however, insignificant compared with the hatred which the Latins and the Greeks had and still have for one another. The jealousy between the two communions in Palestine is as old as the Secession. It showed itself repeatedly during the period of the Crusades and the Latin kingdom, although the Latins had then definitely the upper hand. The quarrels ranged especially around the Holy Places, and much of the violence that one party did to the other took place within the sacred precincts themselves. The Christian Holy Places, which were definitely given over to the Christians, always needed the safeguard of a neutral Power in order that outrage and violence might be prevented there. Thus the Turkish Government, undesirous of interfering between Christian and Christian, was yet compelled by circumstances not only to adjudicate between them, but often to station an armed guard even within the Church of the Holy Sepulchre. In 1620 the Sultan had formally granted to the King of France the protection of all Christians, French or stranger, in Palestine, and Roman Catholic ecclesiastics were guaranteed certain rights in the Holy Places. These rights were confirmed by a later Sultan in 1740. During the succeeding half-century the numbers and influence of the Orthodox Greeks in Palestine, supported by Russia, grew year by year, and while France was, so far as this question was concerned, in a state of lethargy, the Greeks staked out claims, both material and moral, for themselves. No serious movement was made by France until the time of Napoleon III., but his Government made a formal demand for the restoration of all the rights and privileges of which the Latins had gradually been deprived. The negotiations which proceeded out of this demand culminated in the Crimean War.

The negotiations at Constantinople had been accompanied and preceded in Palestine by a tireless struggle between the supporters of the two parties. In 1847 the Latin world had been scandalized by the theft by the Greeks of the Holy Star from the Church at Bethlehem, which, since it bore a Latin inscription, was anathema to them. Previous to the theft the church had been the scene of a fight between the two parties. During the night the Greek monks had built a wall inside the church which deprived the Latins of access to the sanctuary. The Latins, when they found the obstruction in the morning, proceeded to demolish it, whereupon the Greeks attacked them. At Jerusalem, on another occasion, each party had proceeded piecemeal to strip the dome of the Church of its lead, so that the right to repair it, and thus to obtain a claim to the sacred edifice, might be secured. While these rival claims were being pressed the edifice itself suffered severely from the penetration of the rain, but it was not the welfare of the building that was the consideration of the litigants. Ultimately, in order to preserve the uneasy *status quo*, the Sultan had the damage repaired at his own expense, and thus neither party gained the prize. At one time, in 1848, when the Pope was an exile from Rome, there was a project to make Jerusalem the Papal capital. Fortunately or unfortunately, the proposal was not adopted. The French protectorate over all the Roman Catholics in the East continued until 1901, when one of the numerous affrays between the rival communities in the Church led to investigations, one consequence of which was that henceforth the Consuls took charge of the interests of their own nationals, and French subjects only were left to France.

After the close of the Crimean War there was a considerable influx of Christian visitors to Jerusalem, and as a consequence a number of churches were erected and the permanent Christian population increased. The first Christian missionaries to settle in the city were the American, who came in 1821, followed five years later by English fellow-workers. In 1845 the seat of the

Greek Orthodox Patriarch was removed from Greece to Jerusalem, and in 1847, as a counter-stroke, the Latin patriarchate was reorganized. The year 1849 saw the foundation of the Jerusalem Literary and Scientific Society, out of which developed the English Palestine Exploration Fund.

CHAPTER VII

THE GROWTH OF THE TOWNS

By no means can the change which has come over Palestine —the country and the people—during the course of barely more than the span of one generation, a change which justifies the use of the title " The Rebirth of Palestine," be better illustrated than by a comparison between the numbers of the Jewish inhabitants and their relative importance at intervals during the past century. The figures on which such comparisons can be based are, of course, not absolutely correct. They are estimates whose reliability varies with the source from which they come. It has never been possible accurately to ascertain the numbers of any section of the population of Palestine. Even to-day there is a wide diversity between current estimates of the Jewish population even of Jerusalem. However, for the present purpose the estimates of men of some reliability only have been taken into consideration, and one is justified in accepting the figures if not as literally, certainly as generally, correct. To facilitate comparison, the present* Jewish population of Palestine may be considered to amount to about 125,000, exclusive of the twelve thousand Jews of Damascus.

About the year 1770, when Palestine had been free

* By " present " here and henceforth is intended " prevailing immediately previous to the outbreak of war."

for centuries from outside disturbance, according to the statement of a Rabbi—Isaac Karigal, of Hebron— as recorded by Ezra Stiles in his diary, there were about a thousand Jewish families in Palestine. These were to be found not only in the four Holy Cities, Jerusalem, Tiberias, Safed, and Hebron—always the centres of Jewish piety—and in Damascus—a city which since the dawn of history has always been a great Jewish centre —but also in Gaza, Shechem (Nablous), Acco (Acre), Sidon, and Jaffa. Of these the largest Jewish centres were Jerusalem, Safed, Hebron, and Damascus. The unrest and almost ceaseless warfare which prevailed during the succeeding half a century were not conducive to a growth of population either from immigration or from an excess of births over deaths. Nevertheless, there was a small increase in the number of Jews in the country, and when Sir Moses Montefiore paid his first visit to Jerusalem in 1827, he found about five hundred and sixty Jews there. Of these two hundred were elderly widows. The condition of the community was one of great poverty. Not much less than half of the Jews of Jerusalem were Ashkenazim—that is to say, immigrants or the children of immigrants from Europe; whereas not many years before it could be said that there were no Ashkenazim in Jerusalem. The few who were in Palestine had settled at Safed and Tiberias in Galilee. This appearance in Jerusalem was the beginning of a movement which has made of Jerusalem an Ashkenazi Jewish city.

In the year 1839 the Committee of the General Assembly of the Church of Scotland for the Conversion of the Jews sent two of its members—Andrew Bonar and Robert Murray M'Cheyne—to Palestine to report on the

condition of the Jews in the country. They traversed
the land from El Arish on the Egyptian frontier, to
Beyrout in the north, and visited every Jewish centre.
They reported that there was very little natural increase
of the population, and that the gain from immigration just about covered the loss by death. The condition of the Jews was one of deep depression. By the
Mohammedans they were regularly oppressed, but by
the Christians of all denominations they were actively
persecuted. The only friend whom the Jews of Palestine
possessed was the British Consul. They estimated the
number of the Jews of Palestine at from 11,000 to 13,000.
Of these about half—five to seven thousand—lived at
Jerusalem, two thousand were at Safed, fifteen hundred
at Tiberias, from seven to eight hundred at Hebron, and
about two hundred at Nablous. On the coast there were
about two hundred Jews at Beyrout, sixty at Jaffa, one
hundred and fifty to two hundred at Haifa, two hundred at Acre, one hundred and fifty at Tyre, and three
hundred at Sidon. About five hundred Jews lived in
the villages of Galilee. In addition there were about
five thousand Jews in Damascus. Of the Jews of
Jerusalem, about two thousand were Ashkenazim from
Russia, Poland, and Hungary. A couple of years previous
to the visit of the Scottish missionaries there had been
a slight redistribution of the Jews of Palestine in consequence of earthquakes at Safed and Tiberias, which led
to a large emigration from those cities. By this means
most of the communities in the coast towns had been
established, although some of the settlers there were
Algerian Jews who had been driven from their homes by
the warfare which followed the invasion of the French.
The earthquake of 1837 also led to a large migration to

Jerusalem. This emigration of Jews from Algeria was not favoured by the French Government, who warned the emigrants that if they did not return they would forfeit all claim to French protection, and would, so far as France was concerned, be considered Ottoman subjects.

The condition of affairs in Palestine about the year 1840 is described in an account given by a European resident there. " Commercial intercourse with the country people is utterly impossible, on account of their extremely un-civilized and savage state, even where they are not addicted to stealing and rapine. Their idle habits prevent their cultivating their fields beyond what absolute necessity requires; the ground remains fallow, while the price of corn rises higher and higher. A demand for merchandise is very seldom found among the country people, because the climate in a great measure exempts them from the necessity of dress. On this account, retail traffic with the country people is rendered impossible.

" The inhabitants of Jerusalem can also derive no maintenance from the pursuit of husbandry, because the wild Arabs, if they do not destroy and pillage the planta-tions when first laid out, are sure to appropriate the ripe fruit to their own use.

" The Jews in Jerusalem must therefore seek for a liveli-hood in the town itself, which cannot, however, possibly suffice for its inhabitants, in the present low state of industry and the want of mercantile interests and con-nexions. There are shoemakers and tailors enough, and they find a livelihood; but all cannot follow those trades, just as all cannot earn their daily bread by studying or teaching the Talmud."

Another European, writing from Safed in 1845, said: " The Jews here are still sorely oppressed by the Turks;

they are robbed, injured, and insulted, and have no
appeal. Every man doeth that which is right in his
own eyes. A Turk will enter a shop and demand so
much money; if the poor man threatens to go to a judge,
he is told, ' My sword is the judge—give or take the
consequences !' This has really happened since our
return to a poor Jew, and was told us by another Jew.
If they begin to have anything to do with Christianity,
they would be liable to suffer perhaps little less from
their own unbelieving brethren."

A third witness, Joseph Israel, known as Benjamin II.
(the first of that name was Benjamin of Tudela), a famous
traveller in his generation, visited Palestine in 1847
His account confirms the two previously quoted:

" Deep misery and continual oppression are the right
words to describe the condition of the Children of Israel
in the land of their fathers. I comprise a short and
faithful picture of their actual state under the following
heads:

" 1. They are entirely destitute of every legal protection and every means of safety. Instead of security
afforded by law, which is unknown in these countries,
they are completely under the orders of the Scheiks and
Pachas, men whose character and feelings inspire but
little confidence from the beginning. It is only the
European Consuls who frequently take care of the oppressed, and afford them some protection.

" 2. With unheard-of rapacity tax upon tax is levied
on them, and with the exception of Jerusalem, the taxes
demanded are arbitrary. Whole communities have been
impoverished by the exorbitant claims of the Sheiks, who,
under the most trifling pretences and without being
subject to any control, oppress the Jews with fresh

burthens. It is impossible to enumerate all their oppressions.

" 3. In the strict sense of the word, the Jews are not even masters of their own property. They do not even venture to complain when they are robbed and plundered; for the vengeance of the Arabs would be sure to follow each complaint. . . .

" 4. Their lives are taken into as little consideration as their property; they are exposed to the caprice of anyone; even the smallest pretext, even a harmless discussion, a word dropped in conversation, is enough to cause bloody reprisals. Violence of every kind is of daily occurrence."

The Jews of the four Holy Cities—that is to say, practically the whole of the Jewish population of Palestine —were supported to a very large extent by the system of *Chalukah*, the organized collection of funds in the Diaspora, the lands of the Dispersion, for the support of the pious scholars of Palestine. The system is practically coeval with the Christian era. In theory it was a voluntary tax levied on the Jews outside of Palestine, who were themselves unwilling or unable to return to the land and to devote themselves there to the pursuit of Jewish learning, for the support of those who were living in Palestine and spending the whole of their lives in study. The *Chalukah* in its essence may well be compared with the medieval Christian system of supporting students at the Universities. The Holy Cities of Palestine were the Universities of Jewry. But not only the students themselves, but also their families, and in time their remote descendants, were eligible for support from the *Chalukah*. So long as the fund was devoted strictly to the encouragement of learning and to the support of the aged and infirm—for

gradually the Holy Land became the almshouse of Jewry
—criticism of the details of administration alone was
justified. When, however, as in due course occurred,
it became a huge machine for the pauperization and the
consequent degradation of the Jews of the Holy Land,
the system as a whole laid itself open to well-justified
attack. The *Chalukah* system is largely responsible for
the only Jewish problem existing in Palestine to-day—
the huge mass of helpless poverty in Jerusalem and the
other Holy Cities.

This tribute from the Diaspora was collected by means
of *meshullachim*, or duly accredited messengers sent out
periodically from the Holy Land, not only to all parts
of Europe where Jews were settled, but also to America,
Egypt, Persia, Asia Minor, and even to Australia and
South Africa. These messengers received very liberal commission, and seldom failed to find their mission very profit-
able. Gradually local societies arose in Europe for the
support of the Jewish inhabitants of the Holy Land.
The Jews of Palestine at the same time split into congregations, each representing a district in Europe from which
its members originated. A definite relationship came into
being between the Palestinian congregation and the
European society or committee. In the meanwhile the
European societies were affiliated to a central organization
formed at Amsterdam. And in Palestine the fissiparous
tendency displayed in the creation of local congregations
led also to the formation of a central committee, in whose
care were those applicants for relief who, coming from
relatively unimportant centres in Europe, had no local
congregations in Palestine to join. To this central committee was entrusted the payment of the general expenses,
including the salaries of the Rabbis, the communal taxes,

and the customary and necessary baksheesh to the Turkish functionaries. The total income of the *Chalukah* is as a rule very considerable; nevertheless, in most cases the amount of relief given per head is quite insufficient for the support of the recipient.

The Russo-Turkish War of 1878, by draining Palestine, in common with other parts of the Turkish Empire, of a large part of its young Moslem manhood—at that time non-Moslems were not permitted to serve in the Turkish Army—led to a widespread decay of prosperity. Colonel Conder, visiting the country in 1881, found villages which had been prosperous when visited a few years previously, fallen or falling into decay. Those of the proud and relatively wealthy chiefs who had survived had become paupers. Their lands were sold or were for sale to any comer. The peasants had lost their freedom and had become serfs to the usurers. Their lands had passed permanently out of their possession. A new landowner was appearing in the person of German and Jewish colonists who began to settle in the land. The Jewish population did not suffer from the same causes, but the war caused a considerable diminution in the volume of immigration, and as this was the larger source from which the Jews of Palestine drew their numbers, the numerical advance consequently suffered a set-back.

In the history of the Jews of Palestine the close of the Russo-Turkish War marks a definite epoch. Previously the Holy Land had been to but an insignificant extent a land of colonization or settlement for the Jews of the Diaspora: it had been merely a land of pilgrimage for the pious, in which many remained to the end of their days. The Jewry of the Holy Land was not only not self-supporting: it was, in the absence of new elements, incapable of ever becoming self-supporting. Its function was to study, to pray, and to die on holy soil: that of the Jews of the remainder of the world was to keep them and their dependants alive until the time came for their burial in sacred ground. In such circumstances the Jews of Palestine not only had no future, but despite their numbers, may be said to have had no present.

The Russo-Turkish War, as is usual with successful wars, was followed by a period of reaction. In all such periods the class in the population that suffers most bitterly is the Jewish. The Jews of Russia had for many years previously enjoyed relative liberty. They were being gradually admitted as equals into the life of the Russian nation and the Russian people. Assimilation was spreading among them. Among the intellectual classes their Judaism was regarded not only by themselves, but also by their non-Jewish neighbours, as only a matter of religious belief. The liberal policy of Alexander II. was succeeding in all directions, and the Jews felt themselves Russians, equally with the other races of the Empire children of the Tsar. But the orgy of massacre which opened the period of reaction shattered all these beliefs and hopes. The Jew of the professional classes, equally with his brother of the proletariat, found himself in effect an outlaw. Many lost hope so far as their own country was concerned. The great exodus to Western Europe and America commenced. The more spiritual, perhaps the more statesman-like—a very small minority—turned their eyes towards the Holy Land. A new class of settler began to arrive there. The story of the regeneration of Palestine at the hands of these refugees will be told in a later chapter. It should be stated at once, however, that the arrival of the first of them marked a turning-point in the history of the country.

In the year 1880, immediately before the beginning of the new immigration, the Jewish population amounted to about 25,000 souls. In the course of the subsequent thirty-five years it has multiplied fivefold.

The story of the Jews in Palestine must henceforth be dealt with under the headings of the different settlements, new as well as old. On only a few points can they be treated as a whole. The rapid increase in the number of Jewish settlers, especially from Russia—a country of which Turkey has always been suspicious—caused the authorities some uneasiness, especially when the Russian Consul at Jerusalem openly boasted that he had more " subjects " than those of all the other Consuls combined. The year 1887 consequently saw a tightening of the administration of the immigration laws. In order to prevent further Jewish settlement the period of stay of Jewish visitors was limited to one month, almost immediately extended to three months. The reasons for this step given to the American Ambassador were "that the spirit of religious fanaticism rose to such a high pitch at Jerusalem that at certain seasons of the year, during Easter, the Jews were compelled to remain within their houses to avoid coming in contact with the Christians, who would attack them and perhaps murder them"; and also " the report that had spread abroad that the Jews throughout the world intended to strengthen themselves in and around Jerusalem with a view, at some future time, of re-establishing their ancient kingdom there." The United States were not satisfied with these explanations, and protested against the restrictions so far as their subjects were concerned. The protest was supported by the British and French Governments also in defence of the interests of their subjects and protégés. Russia and Germany, however, supported Turkey in her proposed restrictions. But the protests of the liberal states were in effect successful. The projected expulsions were abandoned and the Turkish Government explained that the regulations were intended to apply only to immigration on a considerable scale. The restrictions still remained in existence, on paper, as a dead-letter; but for a time Jews were prohibited from purchasing land in Palestine.

CHAPTER VIII

JERUSALEM

THE Jews of Jerusalem may be said to have been discovered by their wealthier co-religionists in Western Europe in the year 1840, when the city was visited by Crémieux and Montefiore in the course of their mission to Damascus. Montefiore had been in the city thirteen years previously, but this visit was merely a preliminary reconnaissance with no apparent result so far as the discovery of Jerusalem by the emancipated Jews of the Diaspora was concerned. From the second visit of Montefiore, however, an ever-increasing interest in Palestine and the Jewish inhabitants of that country began to permeate the Jewries of the world, until to-day Palestine is probably the region that looms largest in the hopes and fears of the Jews. The exodus from Safed and Tiberias two or three years before this visit had considerably increased the Jewish population of the ancient capital of the Jews, whose numbers had thereby been raised to about three thousand souls. The newcomers were, however, not a gain to the community. If the poverty of those who were already living in the city could have been rendered more intense, this influx would have done it. Like those whom they were joining, they were all steeped in the direst poverty, living in conditions inconceivable to their more fortunate brethren whose necessities, if known, would have been considered un-

68

attainable luxuries by their brethren in the holy cities of Palestine. The poverty was not due to disinclination from toil on the part of those who were capable of undertaking it. The chief cause of the poverty was the absence of demand for anything that the Jews could produce. The native population—the Arabs—had no needs which they themselves could not supply. No customers or employers could be found by Jewish artisans among them. An export trade did not yet exist, even in embryo, so far as Jerusalem was concerned. Commerce and manufacture were thus out of the question. Agriculture, the only other possible resource, was equally impossible on account of the insecurity of the country. Thus the only support of the Jews of the city was the charity of their more fortunate brethren in other lands.

In the course of the following ten or fifteen years the number of Jews in Jerusalem almost trebled, until they came to form almost a third of the total population. Their condition showed little improvement, but whatever industry was to be found in the city was almost entirely in their hands. Tailors, bakers, blacksmiths, shoemakers, watchmakers, glaziers, etc., were almost without exception Jews. Also without exception, they failed to obtain employment during the greater part of the year. A few attempts began to be made to deal with this huge mass of unemployment and consequent poverty and misery, but they were on so small a scale as not even to touch the fringe of the problem. Of two houses of industry one, that for men, was conducted by the London Society for Promoting Christianity among the Jews. It was doomed to inefficacy from its initiation. The conversionist movement has never had the slightest success among the Jews of the Holy Land, despite their extreme poverty.

The institution aroused suspicion on account of its sponsors, and the Jews of Palestine preferred death from starvation to living by bread which to them was tainted. The other house of industry was for women and children. It was founded by a Miss Cooper without any proselytizing tendency.   As a consequence, instead of being boycotted, it met with a success that strained its resources.   These resources were of very small dimensions, and although the work the institution performed was of great value, it had no appreciable effect on the problem.   A third institution, whose usefulness has continued until the present day, was founded about the same time by the British Consul, James Finn, and his wife.   They recognized the urgent need of industrial occupation if the spirits as well as the bodies of the wretched Jews of Jerusalem were to be preserved alive, and with no missionary *arrière-pensée* they set to work to succour them. " Abraham's Vineyard," as Mrs. Finn's work of charity came to be called, commenced in the most modest manner. The wife of the British Consul hired a very small piece of ground just within the city walls, and set two Jews to cultivate it.   To her is due the honour of being the first in modern times to place rakes and spades in the hands of Jerusalem Jews.   The work prospered so greatly, and the applications for employment were so numerous, that within a few years—in 1852—Mrs. Finn found it necessary and possible to buy a larger piece of land.   Ten acres were purchased for £250.   The Jews flocked to it for employment.   All who could be taken were admitted, and by their industry and devotion to work these hereditary paupers, and those who came after them, so improved the land entrusted to them, that when valued twelve or fifteen years ago it was considered to be worth £20,000.

The experiment of Abraham's Vineyard, apart from the benefits it conferred on those whom it employed and their dependants, showed that the Jew of Jerusalem was not unemployable: he needed only the opportunity for work. The work performed unaided by Mrs. Finn and her husband for many years was afterwards taken over by an English society known as the Syrian Colonization Fund, or the Society for the Relief of Persecuted Jews. The workers were at first employed in agriculture. They were soon also employed in building and blasting the rock in order to form huge cisterns for the storage of water. But the industry carried on at Abraham's Vineyard that is most widely known is the manufacture of soap from the products of the olive-tree and from alkali, which also is to be found in Palestine. This soap is exported from the country as well as sold for home consumption.

The visit of Montefiore to Jerusalem in 1840 led directly to the establishment three years later of a dispensary which was afterwards merged in a local hospital. A few years later he founded a school for Jewish girls, in which, among other subjects, dressmaking, embroidery, and domestic economy were taught. The school had to be discontinued in 1857 for want of funds. About the same time he gave his adhesion to the first project for the building of a railway from Jaffa to Jerusalem, a project which ultimately came to fruition thirty-five years later, after Montefiore's death. It was in the fifties also that the first of the Jewish " colonies " outside the walls of Jerusalem was founded. The means that rendered the erection of the houses possible were forthcoming under the will of Judah Touro, an American Jewish philanthropist, who appointed Montefiore his executor. The latter, to whom a considerable discretion was left, wanted at first to erect a hospital, but a hospital was one of the several institutions for the benefit of the Jews of Jerusalem founded at that very time by the French Rothschilds, acting on the advice of their almoner whom they had sent to the East, Albert Cohn. The Touro Bequest, supplemented by a large sum from the pocket of Montefiore himself, was thereupon devoted to the erection of almshouses for Jewish men of learning. The overcrowded state of the city rendered an expansion beyond the walls inevitable: the *Mishkenoth Shaanannim* (Dwellings of those who live at ease), as they were named, so that the feelings of the inmates should not be hurt, were the pioneers in this expansion.

The hospital founded by the Rothschild family of Paris on the occasion of the visit of Albert Cohn in 1854 was not the only beneficent institution that the Jews of Jerusalem at that time owed to the same family of philanthropists. Albert Cohn visited Jerusalem on five occasions during the period 1854 to 1869. On the first he went as the representative of the *Consistoire Central des Israélites de France*, which had been requested by the Jews of Western Europe to investigate the condition of their co-religionists in the Turkish Empire, and to endeavour to alleviate it if desirable. On Cohn's advice a society of manual workers, a girls' school—the original of the present Evelina School—and a loan society were founded in addition to the hospital. A couple of years later the Austrian poet, Ludwig August Frankl, visited Jerusalem at the request of Elise von Herz-Lämel in order to take the necessary steps for the establishment by her of the Lämel School, whose activities still continue. In the meanwhile the proportion that the Jews of Jeru-

salem bore to the general population was continually
rising, until in 1863 it was estimated that of the three
classes into which the population might be divided—
Jews, Mohammedans, and Christians of eleven or more
sects—that of the Jews was the most numerous.

The extension of Jerusalem beyond the walls was very
noticeable to Montefiore, who remarked upon it in his
diary when he visited the city in 1875, and practically
the whole of the extension was Jewish. He also noticed
a considerable increase in the traffic on the road from Jaffa
to Jerusalem, and a welcome appearance of self-reliance
and independence on the part of a section of the Jewish
population of the city. In fact, a new population—quite
different from the aged and pious, who had in the past
composed the greater part of the Jewish inhabitants—
was settling in the city. In 1870 had arrived the first
of the Georgian settlers from the Caucasus, who already
numbered two hundred at the time of Montefiore's visit.
Physically they were very different from the older type
of settler—the Sephardim, the Ashkenazim, and the
Maghrabim or Moroccans. They came with the full
approval of the Russian Government, in whose military
service several of them had gained medals, which they
wore with pride. Apart from these Georgians, however,
the Jews of Jerusalem were no longer almost entirely
dependent on the bounty and charity of their co-religionists in Europe. A fair proportion were engaged in industry and commerce. Tailoring, shoemaking, carpentry,
weaving, working in metals, as well as the unskilled work
of labourer and porter were all pursued. The Jews of
Jerusalem had even created a foreign trade. Some had
raised themselves to positions of relative affluence; one
even to that of British Vice-Consul at Jaffa. Another

sign of the great advance that had been made in recent
years was the formation of co-operative societies for the
erection of houses in the new quarter outside the walls.
There were three such building societies in existence in
1875, and by means of them their members were building
for themselves comfortable houses in healthy surroundings.   To commemorate this, the last visit of Montefiore
to the Holy Land, the Montefiore Testimonial Fund was
raised in London.   It was to a small extent employed
in the encouragement of new industries, but the bulk of
the Fund was devoted to loans for the erection of houses
in the new quarter.   The loans are repayable over a
term of years, and the money as it comes in is again lent
for a similar purpose.   Thus the important work which
the Fund performs never ceases, and with its assistance
a large colony of substantial stone houses has come into
existence.

The progress continued, although it was much diminished by the outbreak of the Russo-Turkish War, so that
in 1880, on the eve of the great Jewish migration from
Russia, which opened a new era in Palestine, the Jewish
population of the city amounted to about 15,000 souls.
Of these the Sephardim—practically all natives of the
Holy Land or of some other portion of the Turkish
Empire—and the Ashkenazim—immigrants or the near
descendants of immigrants from Eastern Europe—about
equalled one another in numbers.   There were in addition
twelve or thirteen hundred Moroccan Jews, who also
formed a community by themselves.   The artisans—
one-fifth among the Sephardim and Moroccans, and nearly
a third among the Ashkenazim—had spread into a variety
of occupations; watchmakers, goldsmiths, lacemakers,
bronze-founders, and even umbrella-makers, being found

IN THE "BOX" COLONY

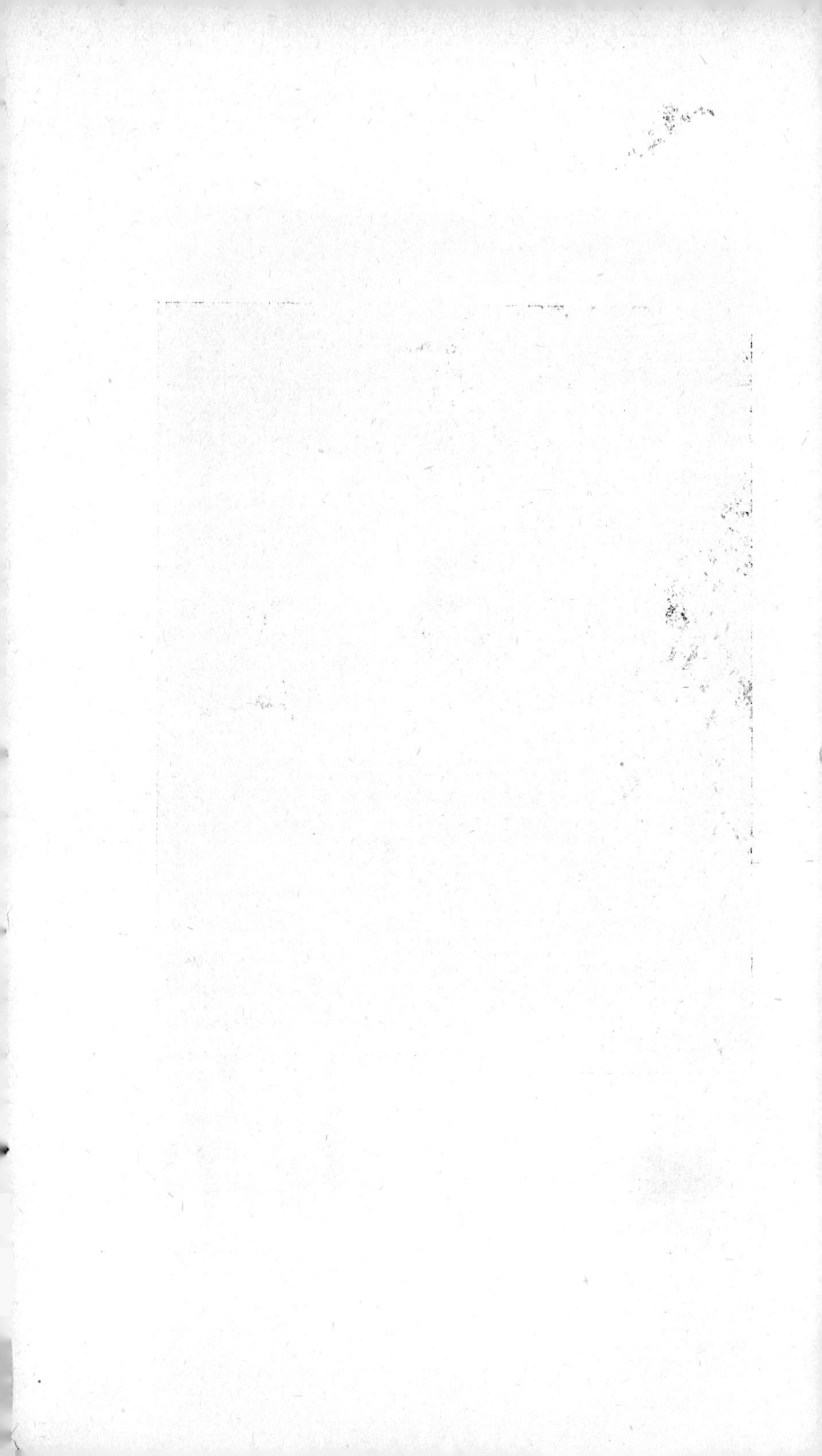

the conditions of the Persian and Yemenite Jews in common with that of their co-religionists. The inhabitants of the Box Colony are for the most part porters and masons, but as the opportunity has been forthcoming, they have entered largely into agricultural pursuits, while Yemenites, trained at the Bezalel School of Arts and Crafts, have shown themselves adepts at filigree-work. As a consequence of this spread of employment the Box Colony is gradually being evacuated for human habitations.

Near the Persian-Yemenite Quarter is the small colony of the Jews of Orfa, from the head waters of the Euphrates. They differ little either in customs or in prosperity, or lack of it, from their Persian brethren. Apart from the Bokharans and a few Georgians, the Jews from Aleppo in Syria are the only immigrant Sephardim in Jerusalem whose condition shows any approach to prosperity. These used to be for the most part engaged in commerce. In Jerusalem they considered themselves the aristocratic section among the Jews, and for the most part keep to themselves. Of late years, however, their condition has been much reduced. But the condition of the Moroccan Jews, who number about 1,200, is the most terrible. So abject is their misery that it would seem that no circumstances could redeem them from it. The remainder of the 20,000 or so Sephardim of Jerusalem are native-born or immigrants from Turkey in Europe. They include many Rabbis and students of Jewish learning, but also a large number of artisans and labourers, as well as shopkeepers, and one banker. The forty thousand Ashkenazi Jews of Jerusalem also are to a very large extent dependent on foreign charity, and on this account are organized in communities bound together by a common geographical origin. Many of the recipients of charity spend their lives in study and prayer, while others are engaged in the service of the community. A minority is employed in useful labour, but the size of this minority is dependent on the scarcity of the demand for such labour. Experiments such as Abraham's Vineyard have shown that the Jews of Jerusalem, Ashkenazi as well as Sephardi, are eager for work, and that the cause of their unemployment is a lack of opportunity. It must also be remembered that there is an excessive proportion of old men and other unemployables among them. If these were eliminated from the calculation the proportion of genuine unemployed would not be excessive.

The most favourable picture of the Jews of Jerusalem is, however, not a pleasant one, and if they were typical of the Jews of the Holy Land there would be no hope for them during the lifetime of the present generation, and the development of a Jewish future in Palestine would be hardly yet in embryo. But among the Jews of the Holy Land there is a clear division into two classes, the old and the new. The Jews of the four Holy Cities, of which Jerusalem is the chief, belong to the former of these two classes. In the other three cities the Jewish population is entirely of the old class; in Jerusalem, however, there is a considerable ingredient of the new. For this reason, although Jerusalem Jewry cannot be said to be dead, the life in it is but an embryo, which, cut off from outside influences, would be little likely to develop into a living being. The hope of Jerusalem does not lie in the old city or in its inhabitants, but in the new Jerusalem outside the walls which has come into existence in the course of the past two generations. In this new city two-thirds of the 80,000 inhabitants now dwell. Here are to be found most of the best-

managed and the best-organized of the numerous charitable and educational institutions which are supported
and endowed by the Jews of the remainder of the world.
Here in the open air, free from the walled-in alleys and
courts and cellars of the medieval town, are now to be
found some two hundred Jewish settlements of varying
size. The number of houses is increasing month by
month, almost day by day, for the growth of the Jewish
population, which is continuous, means the growth of
suburban Jerusalem. The lesson of the Jews of Jaffa
with their garden city has been learnt by their brethren
in the capital. Land has been acquired for the formation of a Jewish garden suburb outside of Jerusalem,
and when peace is at length restored and normal life
returns to the land, this great work for the regeneration
of Jerusalem will proceed.

CHAPTER IX

THE OTHER TOWNS

TIBERIAS, the second in importance of the Holy Cities of Palestine, owes its inclusion in that category to the tombs of Jewish saints that are to be found there. It is situated in Lower Galilee, in the most beautiful district of Palestine, on Lake Gennesareth (Kinnereth). Tiberias was for long the most important Jewish centre in Palestine. But the earthquake of 1837, and the cholera epidemic of 1865 and 1866, affected its fortunes considerably and scattered many of its Jewish inhabitants. The great migration from Russia which commenced in 1881 sent ripples even to Tiberias and the other little-known centres of the Holy Land. The total population of the town is now from 9,000 to 10,000, about 7,000 of whom are Jews. They, however, practically all belong to the " old " class, and as a consequence the life and economic condition of the town are still stagnant.

Safed, the third of the Holy Cities, is in Upper Galilee, and has for long been a centre of Jewish learning in Palestine. It suffered severely in the earthquake of 1837, when four thousand of its Jewish inhabitants are said to have been killed and a host of the survivors migrated to other towns. Of the 18,000 inhabitants of Safed one-half are Jews. Their condition is somewhat more advanced than is that of their brethren in Tiberias, as is evidenced by the existence of a Zionist Society and a

lodge of the American Jewish Order of the B'nai B'rith,
as well as of two well-organized schools among them.
Yet Safed must be classed with Tiberias as a city of the
" old " type of Palestinian Jew, as distinguished from
the " new."

Near Safed is the village of Pekiin, which contains a
score of families of Arabized Jews who are engaged in
agriculture, and are hardly to be distinguished from the
Arabs. Their settlement is of considerable age, and it
may well be that their claim to be directly descended
from the Jews who lived in the land at the opening of
the Christian era is well founded.

Hebron, the fourth of the Holy Cities, is the only one
in which Jews are in a minority. They number only
a thousand to fifteen hundred out of a total population
of 20,000. As the burial-place of the Patriarchs Hebron
is also a Mohammedan Holy City, and as such is a
centre of fanaticism from which the Jews suffer greatly.
Here also the great majority of the Jews are dependent on
charity, although a few artisans are to be found among
them.

Outside of these four towns there were until forty years
ago very few Jews in Palestine. James Finn, who was
British Consul at Jerusalem in 1852, mentions in his
" Stirring Times " that Jews used sometimes to come
from Haifa and Nablous (the ancient Shechem) to obtain
his advice and assistance. The latter city was then, as
now, the centre of the Samaritan sect, whose ancient
hostility to the Jews burnt undiminished. As a consequence Jewish residents at Nablous have always been
few in number. In 1888 there were a hundred and
twenty there out of a total population of 18,000. In the
past twenty years this latter number has increased, but

the Jewish population remains stationary.   The Samaritans, who are about equal in number to the Jews in Nablous, are diminishing.

The Jews of Beyrout numbered about a thousand in the year 1880.   There were very few paupers among them, and those were supported by their Jewish fellow-townsmen, most of whom, by means of trade, had attained to comfortable positions.   Their number increased rapidly. New-comers came at first from other parts of Turkey, and later also from Russia.   The community has throughout been self-supporting and prosperous, and possesses many valuable educational and other institutions.   By 1897 the Jewish population had grown to 2,500, and it is probable that now it numbers not many less than four thousand.

Sidon, the port twenty miles to the south of Beyrout, has about eight hundred Jews, the most comfortable of whom are not far removed from a state of poverty. Acre has now about fifty Jews out of a total population of 10,000.   This number shows a considerable reduction on previous years, due to emigration to Haifa.   Gaza, farther south also, despite its long Jewish history, has now less than a hundred Jewish inhabitants.   El Arish, which is in Egyptian territory, has even less.

The two towns in Palestine which hold out the greatest hope for the Jews of Palestine are the coast towns of Jaffa and Haifa.   The one, the ancient Joppa, is the port of Jerusalem and of the fertile plain of Sharon, and the starting-point of the railway to the capital; the other, beautifully situated on the Bay of Acre at the foot of Mount Carmel, is the port of Galilee and of the fertile plains of Trans-Jordania—already connected by railway with Damascus and the Hedjaz railway run-

ning north and south, and within the last few months
with Jerusalem also, and destined by nature in the future
to be one of the great ports of the Eastern Mediterranean.
The Jewish community of Jaffa, now in many respects the
most important in Palestine and Syria, is less than a
century old. It was founded by a handful of Algerian
Jews, who were shipwrecked off Haifa, and wandering
to Jaffa, remained there, and were reinforced a few years
later by a small immigration of Ashkenazim from Europe.
So poor was the community then and for many years
afterwards that it could not afford to purchase a cemetery,
and had to send its dead to Jerusalem for burial. In
1880 the Jews of Jaffa numbered about a thousand, one-
fifteenth of the total population. They were for the
most part very poor, and although they had several
places of worship, none deserved to be dignified by the
title of synagogue. By 1888 the Jewish population
had doubled. Seven years later the Jewish position had
been so strengthened as to earn from a visitor the description of having " become almost a Hebrew port.
The shop-fronts are crowned by Hebrew names and
sign-posts. The market is a Jewish forum, and the very
infants speak Bible Hebrew."* By 1900 the population
had again doubled. The most remarkable development,
however, is that which has taken place within the last
few years. With the assistance mainly of the Anglo-
Palestine Company, one of the financial instruments of
the Zionist Movement, a garden suburb, Tel Aviv,† or
the Hill of Spring, has grown up in the neighbourhood;
and if its recent rate of extension is continued, it will
soon reach to the seashore. Of the ten thousand Jews

* E. N. Adler, " Jews in Many Lands," p. 139.
† *Vide* Ezekiel iii. 15.

of Jaffa more than a quarter have settled in this new suburb. They comprise people of all classes—artisans, shopkeepers, teachers, engineers, and members of the learned professions. Hundreds of houses, all surrounded by gardens, have been erected in wide and shaded avenues. The building society principle has been adopted in advancing the money for the erection of these dwellings, so that the occupiers will in due course become the owners of their homes. The public lighting and water-supply are on the best European lines. The centre of the suburb is the excellent Hebrew grammar school, whose education attracts pupils from Europe and Egypt, as well as from the Turkish dominions. Its leaving certificate is accepted as the equivalent of matriculation by several European Universities. Other educational institutions in Jaffa and Tel Aviv comprise kindergartens, primary and secondary schools, a training college for teachers, and a school of music. In all these Hebrew is the language of instruction. There are also literary, musical, dramatic, and scientific societies, a public library, a gymnastic club—in fact, all the concomitants of intellectual communal life in Europe.

The following are among the conditions imposed on settlers in this garden suburb: (1) Every house must occupy at least 700 square yards, two-thirds of which are to be devoted to garden. (2) The minimum width of a street is 39 feet, and all houses must stand apart from their neighbours. (3) Provision is made for public gardens, which must in no circumstances be built upon. (4) Certain districts only are reserved for shops. (5) Every male inhabitant has to take his turn, in company with paid watchmen, in police duty.

The administration of Tel Aviv is autonomous, and is

similar to that of the numerous Jewish agricultural colonies which have sprung up throughout the country during the past thirty years.

Tel Aviv is the finest illustration of the benefits the recent Jewish colonization of Palestine has brought to the land. The traveller on his first arrival has at hand both this splendid Jewish settlement and also the squalid Arab streets and houses which were characteristic of the country before the Jews arrived. If he wishes to compare the new Jewish settlements with the older ones he can judge of the difference between Tel Aviv and Safed or Tiberias. Such a comparison will assure him that if the Jewish settlers are only allowed freedom to develop along their own lines, free from all external interference, there need be no fear regarding their future in a land whose present prosperity, limited as it is, may be said to be due entirely to the exertions of the Jewish immigrants, the only progressive element of any size in the country. Ideally situated, with the blue sea and sunny sky of the Mediterranean stretching out far beyond the horizon; with golden sands extending north and south, farther than eye can reach; nestling on the edge of the fertile Plain of Sharon, embedded in orange groves and vineyards; with a growing population of sturdy Jews and beautiful Jewesses, possessing all the advantages of town and country life, enjoying healthy minds as well as healthy bodies—the future of Jaffa, whose very name signifies " beautiful," is indeed full of promise.

Haifa, the port at the foot of Mount Carmel, is less important at present from the Jewish point of view, although its situation as the sea gate of Damascus, the Hauran and Trans-Jordania generally, points to the probability that it will one day become commercially the most important town of Palestine. The modern Jewish community of Haifa is about sixty years old. In the middle of last century there were only seven Jewish families in the town, but shortly afterwards others came from Constantinople, Smyrna, Syria, and Morocco. Henceforward the Moroccan element has always been relatively considerable. By 1875 the local community had grown sufficiently to support four synagogues and several charitable institutions. The community was in fact, although not rich, self-supporting, and was able to maintain its own poor without any assistance from outside. The immigration which set in at the beginning of the eighties had perhaps an earlier and more marked effect at Haifa than in any other of the towns. Within a few years the town had grown tenfold in size. From an Arab village similar, except in situation, to other villages, it became a clean, tidy little European town, endowed with natural beauties of which many a larger and more prosperous town may well be envious. Haifa was in fact admitted to be the most spacious and tidiest town in all Palestine, and the prosperous and cheerful little colony of Germans from Wurtemburg who had settled at a distance of about a mile many years earlier, added to the attractiveness of the town, which soon spread over the intervening ground. The new Jewish colonists came for the most part from Roumania. They brought with them a standard of living higher than that of the native Jews, but it was not long before the latter rose to it. The new standard created new wants. Shops were soon opened to satisfy these, and thus the prosperity of Haifa and of its population of all creeds rose. In the course of the last fifteen years the population of the port has doubled; that of the Jewish population has increased threefold. The number of inhabitants now amounts to about 20,000, about one-fourth of whom are Jews. The projected establishment of a garden suburb, Herzliah, on lines similar to those of Tel Aviv, and the completion of a Jewish University college, rendered possible by the munificence of a few wealthy European and American Jews, will increase vastly the importance of Haifa as a Jewish centre and at the same time its importance among the ports of the Levant.

CHAPTER X

THE EARLIER COLONIZATION PROJECTS

ALTHOUGH the systematic colonization of Palestine by Jews is a movement of less than forty years' duration and in fact only contemporary with the latest cycle of Jewish suffering in Russia, the Jews of Palestine were not, like their co-religionists in Europe, divorced from the land during the preceding centuries. There is no evidence that the Jews of Palestine were ever legally prohibited from engaging in agriculture. Insecurity of life outside the towns, poverty and ignorance of agriculture, natural in an immigrant population coming from lands in which settlement outside of the slums of the cities was forbidden, were the principal factors in keeping the Jews from the land in Palestine during the greater part of the Christian era. If, however, there was no systematic colonization of the land by Jews throughout this period, it must not be taken for granted that the Jews without exception left the cultivation of the land entirely to their neighbours. There is plenty of evidence of the pursuit of agriculture by Jews throughout the centuries between the Roman occupation and to-day. There are even one or two Jewish villages whose inhabitants to-day claim a continuous history extending far back into the past, perhaps to the time when Jews took their full share in all the industries of the land. There is Pekiin, near Safed, whose inhabitants, Mista'arbim or Arabized Jews, are indistinguishable from the surrounding native population except in their religious practices. They are now few in number, and many have emigrated of recent years. Those who remain are still agriculturists as their ancestors have been for innumerable generations. The land at their disposal is barely sufficient, their methods are primitive, and their material condition consequently not very satisfactory. Of recent years a Rabbi and teacher has been sent to them from Safed by the generosity of Baron Edmund de Rothschild, but the boys have little time for study, for their labour is required in the fields. The Jews of Pekiin are therefore as little learned as prosperous, but in physique they show that health, vigour, and sturdiness are, given encouraging conditions, as possible to the Jew as to the Gentile. As is the rule in most village communities, agriculture is supplemented by a subsidiary industry—among the Jews of Pekiin, shoemaking. This Jewish village was mentioned by the late Lord Kitchener when, as Lieutenant Kitchener, he was engaged on the Palestine Survey.

The settlement has survived until the present day. Its survival is, however, an accident, an exception from the rule of annihilation which overwhelmed the more widespread Jewish agricultural activities that went under in the course of one or other of the vicissitudes which would have destroyed the land a score of times if it were possible utterly to destroy a country. When Benjamin of Tudela and Petachiah of Ratisbon visited the country during the last decades of the twelfth century, they found a portion of the small Jewish population engaged in agriculture. Three centuries later grapes and cereals were being cultivated by Jews in the neighbourhood of Gaza. The settlement at Tiberias formed by

Joseph Nasi at the end of the sixteenth century was mainly an agricultural one, and there is evidence that at the time Jews were engaged in other parts of the land in the cultivation of cotton, mulberries, and vegetables, and in the breeding of silkworms and bees.

Europe first became interested in the agricultural employment of Jews in Palestine about the time of the second visit of Sir Moses Montefiore early in 1839. The Scottish divines who visited the country in 1838 heard of the village of Bukeah (otherwise Pekiin), near Safed, where a few families of Jews were living like Fellah agriculturists. Montefiore, who displayed much statesmanship in his treatment of Palestinian Jewish problems, strongly favoured the employment of the Jews in agriculture. When in Safed on this same visit he found the local Jewish population anxious to find employment on the land. Some of them had, unaided, attempted to obtain such employment, but they were sorely hampered by lack of means even more than by inexperience. Whatever chance of success these handicaps might have left to their efforts was destroyed by the jealousy and even hostility of the neighbouring Moslems. Montefiore had, however, considerable hopes of success, and planned a somewhat ambitious scheme. Writing in his diary at the time, he said: " From all information I have been able to gather, the land in this neighbourhood appears to be particularly favourable for agricultural speculation. There are groves of olive-trees, I should think, more than five hundred years old, vineyards, much pasture, plenty of wells and abundance of excellent water; also fig-trees, walnuts, almonds, mulberries, etc., and rich fields of wheat, barley, and lentils; in fact, it is a land that would produce almost everything in abundance, with very little skill and labour. I am sure if the plan I have in contemplation should succeed, it will be the means of introducing happiness and plenty into the Holy Land. In the first instance, I shall apply to Mohammed (Mehemet) Ali for a grant of land for fifty years; some one or two hundred villages; giving him an increased rent of from ten to twenty per cent., and paying the whole in money annually at Alexandria, but the land and villages to be free, during the whole term, from every tax or rate either of Pasha or governor of the several districts; and liberty being accorded to dispose of the produce in any quarter of the globe. This grant obtained, I shall, please Heaven, on my return to England, form a company for the cultivation of the land and the encouragement of our brethren in Europe to return to Palestine. Many Jews now emigrate to New South Wales, Canada, etc.; but in the Holy Land they would find wells already dug, olives and vines already planted, and a land so rich as to require little manure. By degrees I hope to induce the return of thousands of our brethren to the Land of Israel. I am sure they would be happy in the enjoyment of the observance of our holy religion, in a manner which is impossible in Europe."

The plan was favoured by the governor of Tiberias, who invited Montefiore to settle there and become the head of the proposed colony. The representative Jews of Jerusalem also expressed themselves in favour of the employment of their people in agriculture, a proposal which obtained the support of the British Consul at Jerusalem. Montefiore left Palestine on that occasion full of schemes for the welfare of his people in the Holy Land. On his return journey he stayed in Egypt in order to obtain Mehemet Ali's approval of his proposals.

Among other concessions for which he asked were permission for land and villages to be rented on a lease of fifty years, free from all taxes or claims of governors, the rent to be paid at Alexandria; permission to send people to assist and instruct the Jews in agriculture in general, and in the cultivation of the olive, the vine, cotton and mulberries, and the breeding of sheep, in particular; and a firman to establish banks at Beyrout, Jaffa, Jerusalem, and Cairo. Mehemet expressed himself sympathetically. Every effort to obtain his sanction in writing, however, failed. He was probably most interested in the proposal to establish banks with a capital of a million pounds, but this was the last of the concessions for which Montefiore asked. The whole promising scheme lapsed finally with the fall of Mehemet as the Lord of Syria.

About the middle of last century some Moroccan Jews settled at Shefa'Amr near Nazareth, and cultivated corn and olives there. The settlement was encouraged and assisted by a few English Jews and Christians, but the settlers removed before long to Haifa, where they engaged in trade. At the same time, the first American Consul appointed to Jerusalem, Warder Cresson, who on adopting Judaism later took the name of Michael Boaz Israel, was becoming ever more interested in the welfare of the Jews of the Holy Land. To him agriculture appeared the only method of removing the intense poverty which he saw around him in Palestine. He devoted his private fortune, as well as sums placed at his disposal by public-spirited Jews in America and in Europe, in founding an agricultural colony in the Valley of Raphaim, not far from Jerusalem. Even if the human material available had been satisfactory sufficient means were not forthcoming to assure success. Nevertheless, it was long before Cresson abandoned hope, if he ever did so.   He may have had the satisfaction of knowing that although his colony was an apparent failure, that and other similar failures were the seeds out of which success was to spring in the not distant future.

Still earlier Colonel Gawler, of the British Army, had formed in London a colonization society for a similar purpose, but the disturbed conditions which followed the expulsion of Mehemet Ali from Syria were an insuperable bar to success at that time.

In the meanwhile Montefiore had by no means abandoned hope of obtaining concessions which would enable Jews to settle on the land in Palestine.   On the occasion of his fourth visit to the East in 1855 he obtained interviews with both the Sultan and the British Ambassador at Constantinople, Lord Stratford de Redcliffe, for the furtherance of his schemes.   Montefiore also approached Lord Clarendon, the Foreign Secretary, in London, and a few months later Lord Palmerston, who had by then become Prime Minister.   Both were sympathetic, but the times—the period of the Crimean War—were unpropitious, and Montefiore received no support from the British Government.   Nothing daunted, Montefiore still determined to proceed with his project of an agricultural settlement in the neighbourhood of Safed and Tiberias. Drought, cholera, pestilence, civil war, and other misfortunes, however, overtook the colonists, to ensure whose success in the first instance too small a capital had been set aside.   As a consequence, this experiment also was of but short duration.   Nevertheless, at Bukeah were sown seeds which were to fructify a generation later, while so far as the people themselves were concerned the craving for an agricultural life was unabated, as was evidenced by the petitions Montefiore received on the occasion of subsequent visits to the Holy Land.

In Europe, and in England also, the subject of the settlement of Jews in Palestine as agriculturists remained a living one, and interest in it was much encouraged by the progress of the colonies of Germans who had settled near Jaffa and near Haifa. The Montefiore Testimonial Fund, an institution with activities in Palestine, founded in 1874 by English Jews in recognition of Sir Moses Montefiore's exertions on behalf of his co-religionists in all parts of the world, found itself unable to undertake agricultural work in Palestine, greatly to the regret of the philanthropist whose name the institution bore. Another English institution, the Palestine Society, a non-sectarian one, had no such qualms. The leading spirit in this movement was Colonel Gawler, who had by no means been dispirited by the failure of his efforts of a quarter of a century earlier. Out of the Palestine Society developed a Palestine Colonization Fund, in the activities of which Jew and Christian worked side by side. A deputation from the Society was received by the Turkish Ambassador in London, who informed it that his Government would welcome settlers in all parts of the Turkish dominions, who might either remain under the protection of their Consuls or become Ottoman subjects. In the latter case grants of land would be made to them. Such settlers would be exempt from all taxation for a period of twelve years, and after twenty years would have complete control over their land, with the right to dispose of it if they so wished. Among the privileges granted to the settlers were the power of electing judicial and administrative bodies and collectors of tithes, autonomy for religious communities, and freedom to hold and dispose of their property. These favourable conditions were granted on the authority of the Turkish Government. Yet they did not meet with any appreciable response. The difficulty was the disinclination to trust, not the good-will, but the power of the Turkish Government. The Society, and the references to it and to related matters which frequently appeared in the public press, served to keep alive an interest in the subject of the Jewish colonization of Palestine.

This interest was by no means peculiar to England, although outside of Jewish circles it is in Great Britain mainly that the settlement of Jews in Palestine has been looked on with favour. For instance, when Montefiore was in Venice in 1875, he recorded in his diary the meeting with a Signora Randegger-Friedenberg, who had a proposal for the establishment of an agricultural school for girls in Palestine.

Five years earlier a definite undertaking was commenced in Palestine, whose activities still continue, and have had a direct and beneficent effect on the fortunes of the Jews of Palestine. This is the Agricultural School, Mikveh Israel ("The Gathering of Israel"), founded by the *Alliance Israélite Universelle*, an institution for the protection and improvement of the Jews in general and of those in the East of Europe and in the Moslem lands in particular. The impetus for the foundation of the school came from a group of enlightened Russian Jews, prominent among whom were Hirsch Kalischer and Elijah Gutmacher, who foresaw in the settlement of Jews in Palestine on a considerable scale, the readiest and most promising means of easing the situation of the Jews in the Diaspora. In France the idea was accepted eagerly by Charles Netter, who devoted a large portion of the remaining years of his

7

life to securing the success of the experiment. A grant
of land of over six hundred acres was made by the Turkish
Government for the purposes of the school. The experiment proved a success almost from the day of its opening.
There were difficulties at first in obtaining a satisfactory
staff, and also in a certain prejudice against it on the part
of intensely conservative native Jews. At a later date
the language question led to trouble, the local people
being desirous of replacing French, the language of the
school, by Hebrew. These difficulties were in due course
overcome. The school had at one time over two hundred
pupils. Hebrew is now the language of the school which
has recently undergone a complete re-organization. All
branches of agriculture and horticulture are taught
there, even stockbreeding and silkworm-raising. For
many years past the school, which has by now attracted
around itself a small Jewish colony, has supplied expert
gardeners and teachers of agriculture to all parts of the
Near East, to Moslem as well as to Jewish employers.
In fact, Mikveh Israel is justified in calling itself the
foster-mother of the numerous Jewish agricultural colonies
which have sprung into being in Palestine in the course of
the past thirty years.

A far more ambitious project was that of Laurence
Oliphant, who, after many wanderings and adventures
in all parts of the world, suddenly in 1879 adopted a
scheme for a large Jewish agricultural settlement in
Palestine. He had developed the project considerably
before his first visit to the Holy Land. It was, in his own
words, " To obtain a concession from the Turkish Government in the northern and more fertile half of Palestine,
which the recent survey of the Palestine Exploration Fund
proves to be capable of immense development. Any

amount of money can be raised upon it, owing to the belief which people have that they would be fulfilling prophecy and bringing on the end of the world. I don't know why they are so anxious for this latter event, but it makes the commercial speculation easy, as it is a combination of the financial and sentimental elements which will, I think, ensure success. And it will be a good political move for the Government, as it will enable them to carry out reforms in Asiatic Turkey, provide money for the Porte, and by uniting the French in it, and possibly the Italians, be a powerful religious move against the Russians, who are trying to obtain a hold of the country by their pilgrims. It would also secure the Government a large religious support in this country, as even the Radicals would waive their political in favour of their religious crotchets. I also anticipate a very good subscription in America." The project had the unofficial approval of the Prime Minister, Lord Beaconsfield, and of the Foreign Secretary, Lord Salisbury.

Oliphant's first business on reaching Palestine was to explore the country in order to find a suitable site for his colony. This he chose to the east of the Jordan, near the upper end of the Dead Sea, a region of remarkable fertility, but perhaps somewhat too tropical for immigrants from the more temperate regions of the East of Europe. This difficulty did not, however, occur to Oliphant, whose mind was captured by the luxuriant vegetation, the great industrial possibilities, and the beauty and magnificence of the region which he had discovered. Since leaving England he had been still further encouraged in his project by the success of Jews as agriculturists in Russia, Galicia, and North Africa, and above all in Palestine itself, where he mentioned in particular the success of fifty-five Jewish families which had then but recently settled at Lydda, near Jaffa. A number of Roumanian Jews, who were suffering very severely at the hands of the Roumanian Government, despairing of their native land, had about that time formed a Society for the Colonization of the Holy Land. They had some capital, but no experience, and appealed to the Jewish Board of Deputies in London to assist them to settle in Palestine. The negotiations were somewhat protracted, and led to no result in so far as the London Board was concerned. They, however, encouraged Oliphant in his scheme, which also gained the approval of King Edward, then Prince of Wales, and of the French Government. Unfortunately the year 1880 saw a change of government in England, and the sympathy of the Conservative leaders was not continued by their Liberal successors.

The change of government in London had its reaction in Constantinople. Hitherto the proposals had found some favour with both the Sultan and his Government, and Oliphant's only complaint was of the *vis inertiæ* which had for long rendered patience so valuable at Constantinople. In fact, a charter for a colonizati n company, drawn up by Oliphant, had been submitted to the Porte, and elaborated and amended by the latter's legal advisers so as to safeguard the interests which to them seemed supreme. So far had the negotiations proceeded. The accession of Gladstone to power, however, changed the entire situation. Turkey immediately became suspicious of every English project, and if Oliphant's scheme had previously had a prospect of success, that prospect was utterly destroyed by the polls in the English boroughs. Oliphant's dream of a prosperous and happy Jewish population in Palestine, loyal to the Ottoman Govern-

ment, which on its part would profit both by the prosperity
of the land and the loyalty of its inhabitants, and also
in the protection, so far as that region was concerned,
from external enemies, which it would derive from the
active sympathy of Great Britain, faded away like a
mirage.

Oliphant's scheme did not stand alone.   He was an
idealist and a dreamer.   Edward Cazalet, a contemporary,
who also published in 1879 a scheme for the resettlement
of the Jews in Palestine, was of a different character.   A
man of affairs and an industrialist, he had, while furthering
his projects in Russia, come into contact with the Jews
there.   His intercourse with them assured him of the
necessity of efforts to relieve the endless agony under which
they were living, and also of the magnificent material
they could offer for the industrial development of Palestine.   Satisfied on these two points, he launched a scheme
for the institution of a British protectorate of Palestine,
on lines practically identical with those which were a
few years later applied to Egypt, and the settlement
of large numbers of Jews who, with the assistance of
capital privately subscribed, would assure the industrial
regeneration of the country.   All that was required of
the British nation was the protectorate and the supply of
the nucleus of a government.   To secure the permanence
of the British protectorate, Cazalet pressed for the
building under British auspices of a great work such as a
railway to the Euphrates, which would at the same time
provide employment for a large number of Jewish
artisans, and thus encourage their immigration.   As
another influence to attract a permanent Jewish settlement of the right character, he advocated the establishment in Palestine of a college or University which should

serve as a centre of Jewish philosophy and science. " Nobody," concluded Cazalet, " who has any knowledge of the Jewish character can for a moment doubt that if the Jews were restored to their country under an English protectorate, they would prove true to our nation, and that Syria would become as firmly united to England as if it were peopled by our countrymen."

The projects of Oliphant and of Cazalet to a large extent supplemented one another. They were involved in a common fate.

CHAPTER XI

THE COLONIZATION OF PALESTINE

FROM the foregoing chapter it will be seen that the project of the resettlement of the Jews in Palestine was one that had exercised the minds of statesmen and philanthropists, of practical men and of dreamers, for half a century or more before any practical step was taken. It is probable that this theoretical period would have lasted very much longer if the course of events in Eastern Europe had not made the question of Jewish migration once more a very practical one. An outburst of intense persecution in Russia and Roumania in the late seventies and early eighties of last century raised to torrential force the intermittent stream of Jewish wandering. Jews by the tens of thousands fled from Russia and from Roumania. The flow was almost entirely westwards, to Germany, to England, to France, and to America. A small part, composed to a great extent of students and other young intellectuals, whose gradual assimilation and absorption into the general population had been suddenly interrupted by the outbreak of Anti-Semitism, looked towards Palestine rather than towards Europe or the New World. Influenced by the Zionistic writings of Kalischer and Hess and others of their school, they dreamt not of a land of refuge for the individual, but of a haven for the Jewish nation, of a centre where free Jews living a free life would combine to preserve their joint heritage, to restore health to the Jewish spirit which had been battered and bruised during nearly two thousand years of oppression and persecution. They looked forward to the creation of a centre whence Judaism and the Jewish spirit, reinvigorated by the air of freedom, would breathe fresh life into the weakened and declining Judaism of the Diaspora. In short, they longed for the re-creation of the Jewish nation in a Jewish land. Striving towards this, a band of pioneers left Russia and Roumania to start the Jewish colonization of Palestine, to turn the first sods preparatory to digging the foundations of the new Judæa.

The first of the agricultural colonies was, however, settled by seven Jews from Jerusalem. They acquired land about ten miles inland from Jaffa, and made their homes on sites which are now included in Petach Tikvah (The Gate of Hope), now the largest of the Jewish agricultural colonies in Palestine. The first years of Petach Tikvah were not fortunate. The colonists had plenty of zeal, but little practical experience. The original situation was unhealthy, and malaria made severe ravages among them. As a consequence the settlers were soon compelled to remove their homes to a healthier site a short distance away, at Jehudieh, but they continued to cultivate their lands. Moreover, the available capital of the colonists was insufficient. It is not surprising, therefore, that this first attempt proved a failure. The present Petach Tikvah may be said to be separate and distinct from the colony founded in 1878. About the same time some of the more progressive Jewish families of Safed founded a settlement in the neighbourhood of that town. They had opposed to them the full

BREAKING THE SOIL AFTER 2,000 YEARS

COLONISTS AT WORK

Face p. 104

force of the conservative school in Jewry, which was, and is, exceptionally strong in Safed, and considers all progress heresy. This and other difficulties proved insuperable, and the settlement did not prosper. About the same period one of the wealthier inhabitants of Jerusalem had acquired an estate in the neighbourhood which he proposed to cultivate. These represented the whole of the agricultural activities of the Jews of Palestine in the year 1880, when the great migration from Russia had not yet commenced. Poor as they were, they yet inspired an Anglo-Jewish traveller, Sydney Samuel, who was in Palestine in that year, to a prophecy which cannot be said to have lacked fulfilment: " In these colonies a far-seeing eye may, perhaps, discern the Shadow of the Coming Restoration. At any rate, their encouragement will do much to promote the firm occupation of the land by the Jews."

The Colonization Movement commenced in full force in the year 1882. Among the refugees were seventeen Russian Jews who settled on the site of the Biblical En-Hakkore, the scene of one of Samson's exploits, about an hour and a half's journey south-east of Jaffa, now known as Rishon le Zion (The First in Zion), perhaps the best-known of the colonies. These colonists were members of the *Bilu*, an organization of Russo-Jewish students formed for the colonization of the Holy Land. The first of the *Bilu* unions was formed at Charkow, and Rishon le Zion was the first of their settlements. The immigrants, although members of the learned professions and graduates of Universities, worked on the land as common labourers, so intense was their zeal for the colonization of Palestine, so steadfast their faith in ultimate success. Gradually these *Bilu* settlers became absorbed in other colonies as they came into existence, or built up colonies of their own.

At the same time refugees from Roumania, where a severe social and political persecution had set in, began to arrive in Palestine. They settled further north, at Zammarin, now known as Zichron Jacob (The Memorial of Jacob—*i.e.*, the father of Baron Edmund de Rothschild) in Samaria, and at Rosh Pinah (The Cornerstone) in Galilee. These colonists were assisted out of a fund raised in Roumania for the settlement of Roumanian Jews in Palestine. The story of the foundation of Zichron Jacob is a romantic and chequered history. The arrival of the colonists in Palestine was attended by the severest hardships, privations, and drawbacks. Their agents, who had been sent in advance to purchase the land for the colony, had allowed themselves to be cheated. Bribes and baksheesh had absorbed a large portion of the funds with which they had been entrusted. As a consequence, when the settlers arrived at Haifa, twenty-three miles from their destination, they found themselves homeless, penniless, and destitute. They were, however, not friendless. Laurence Oliphant was at that time at Haifa. He came to the assistance of the immigrants, supported them for a time out of his own purse, aided them in the negotiations which preceded their settlement on their land, interested friends in Europe, and above all Baron Edmund de Rothschild, of Paris, in their welfare. As a consequence Zichron Jacob became in a few years the centre of a happy, self-supporting community, one of the most prosperous and largest in Palestine, the model of what a Jewish colony can be.

Contemporary with these two Jewish movements emanating from Russia and Roumania was the establish-

ment of the Society for the Relief of Persecuted Jews, or
the Syrian Colonization Fund, under the presidency of
Lord Shaftesbury. This was, as has already been
mentioned, a development of the work of Mrs. Finn, who
had many years previously, when her husband was
British Consul at Jerusalem, been the first to give employment to the Jews of Jerusalem. Its purpose was to
use Mrs. Finn's original institution, "Abraham's Vineyard," as a training-school for agricultural colonists, to
fit the workers to become farmers and agriculturists, and
to settle on the land. The task was a considerable one,
and adequate means were not forthcoming. The Syrian
Colonization Fund was therefore a hope rather than an
accomplishment. It occupies a place, however, in the
history of the return of the Jews to Palestine.

The colonies which had in the meanwhile been established by the Russian and Roumanian refugees found
their position very critical. Almost completely lacking
in experience, with moderate means, and also to some
extent objects of suspicion to the Government of the
land and to the surrounding population, it is probable
that if they had remained unaided the experiment which
they were initiating would have been overwhelmed in
failure. The pioneers in Palestine, however, had eager
sympathizers and ardent well-wishers in the lands from
which they came. Societies sprang into existence in
many of the Jewish centres of Russia, for the practical
encouragement and assistance of the colonists. At the
same time other societies for the propagation of the
nationalist idea in Jewry were also formed. Of all these
societies, that of Odessa was the most important and
soon became the leader. Ultimately they all became
organized as the Odessa Committee, an institution whose

valuable work in and for Palestine has left a permanent
mark on the prosperity of the land. Before that time
these societies formed part of a world-wide movement
which became known as the *Chovevé Zion* or Lovers of
Zion.

The first leaders of the *Chovevé Zion* movement in
Russia were Leo Pinsker, the author of the epoch-making
" Auto-Emancipation "; Rabbi Samuel Mohilewer of Bya-
listok ; Moses Lilienblum, the man of letters; Wolf Wissotzky, the millionaire philanthropist; and Saul Phinehas
Rabbinowitch, the historian. By November, 1884, the
movement for the colonization of Palestine was sufficiently strong to justify co-operation between the many
independent societies with a view to the organization
of the movement. A conference of representatives of
these societies was accordingly held at Kattowitz, in
Prussian Silesia, in that month. From this conference
may be dated the organized world-wide movement for
the resettlement of the Jews in Palestine. The conference was weak, but the consciousness of its weakness did
not daunt it. It immediately took steps to assist the
infant colonies that had not yet found their feet in
Palestine. It voted money for the provision of houses,
implements, wells, etc., and for the maintenance of the
colonists until the harvest. At the same time five young
men were sent by the Kattowitz Conference to Zichron
Jacob to study agriculture there. A second conference
was held in 1887, at which it was decided, among other
things, if possible to obtain the permission of the Russian
Government for the establishment of an official Palestine
Association, and for the creation in Palestine of an office
for the purchase and sale of land. This permission was
not forthcoming, and as a consequence the work of the

organization was much hampered. A third conference of the Russian *Chovevé Zion* was held in 1889.

The *Chovevé Zion* Movement soon spread beyond Russia. Besides those already in existence in Roumania, similar societies were formed in Germany, in Austria, in England, and in the United States. In England it first manifested itself in 1885, directly or indirectly through the agency of Russo-Jewish refugees. A meeting was held in London in that year for the purpose of founding a society for the promotion of the Jewish national idea, and for the establishment of Jewish colonies in Palestine. The meeting had no immediate practical consequences. Two years later, the *Kadimah*, a London society of a theoretical rather than a practical character, was founded. The *Chovevé Zion*, as a practical colonization movement, was not established in England until early in 1890. From that year onwards the movement in England continually gained strength, until the greater Zionist Movement created by Theodore Herzl in 1896 absorbed it. At first the wealthier classes in Anglo-Jewry for the most part held aloof, and for some time it drew practically the whole of its strength from the poorer and foreign elements in the population. There were, however, some notable exceptions, and the interest increased as the ideal became better known and the work more effective. Elim d'Avigdor and his kinsman Colonel A. E. W. Goldsmid were successively the heads of the movement; and among their most energetic lieutenants were Mr. Herbert Bentwich and Mr. Joseph Prag. Other well-known English Jews who took a prominent part in the work of the *Chovevé Zion* were the Rev. S. Singer, Sir Joseph Sebag-Montefiore, and the late Lord Swaythling. On the platform of these "Lovers of Zion" were also to be found

at one religious extreme Dr. Hermann Adler, and at the
other Dr. A. Löwy, Sir John Simon and Sir Julian Goldsmid.   Young Israel was represented by branches of
the *Chovevé Zion* formed at the Universities of Oxford
and Cambridge.   The English Movement, like the greater
one in Russia, devoted much of its resources to the assistance of the existing colonies, but in addition it aided in
the establishment of more than one new one.

At length, in February, 1890, the Russian Government
approved the formation of a " Society for the Relief of
Jewish Agriculturists and Artisans."   In this body,
which became known as the Odessa Committee, the
Chovevé Zion societies of Russia were merged.   Under the
presidency of Pinsker, it entered upon a career of great
activity.   An executive was installed at Jaffa.   Renewed
attention was given to the colonies in which the *Chovevé
Zion* had been interested, and additional ones were taken
under the protection of the new organization.   This
work and that which arose immediately out of it monopolized the resources of the Committee.   Houses, water-
supply, drainage, afforestation, capital—all were needed,
and had to be supplied.   Then came the demand for
schools, libraries, hospitals, and other similar institutions.
The function of the Odessa Committee was to satisfy these,
and further extensions had to be left to other bodies and
individuals.   In the meanwhile difficulties arose both in
Russia and in Palestine.   A recrudescence of persecution
in the former country affected the relationship between
the Government and the Odessa Committee, and caused
the latter to be much hampered.   It also set in force
another wave of emigration, some ripples of which found
their way to Palestine.   These latter emigrants were
encouraged by a number of irresponsible societies and

bodies which wanted also to share in the colonization of the Holy Land, but whose capacities fell far short of their ambitions. The evil of land-speculation, with its undesirable accompaniments, also appeared upon the scene. Money was wasted: unsuitable immigrants were sent to Palestine, and hardship to individuals and harm to the general welfare followed. The unfortunate state of affairs which began to arise attracted the attention of the Turkish Government, which, in order to put an end to the evils, determined, in true Turkish fashion, to prohibit the immigration of Russian Jews or the purchase of land by them. The Turkish authorities were, in fact, nervous of the intervention of the Russian Consuls in Palestine on behalf of their Jewish nationals there.

In the meanwhile the *Chovevé Zion* in England had been continuing on its course. It presented a petition to the Porte, which was actively supported by both the outgoing Foreign Secretary (Lord Salisbury) and his successor (Lord Rosebery), and had also the practical sympathy of the United States Minister to Turkey. The restrictions on the purchase of land were soon removed, through the influence of Baron Edmund de Rothschild, of Paris, as well as of the British and American Foreign Offices, and in 1892 the English society joined forces with its co-workers in Ekaterinoslaw and New York to acquire land in the Hauran, east of the Jordan. After the setback of 1891 the organization of the Russian Society had been improved. About the same time, in 1893, the whole of the movement throughout the world was brought into closer co-operation by the formation of a central representative committee at Paris, at the instance of the eminent Russo-Jewish physicist Dr. Waldemar Haffkine, who was then resident in Paris. The reorganization was followed by the adoption of a new policy—the foundation of a model colony, Castinieh, whose inhabitants were drawn not from the inexperienced town-dwellers of Europe, but from colonists who had already served their apprenticeship in other Palestinian colonies. The advent of Theodore Herzl and his new Zionist Movement practically absorbed, though it did not destroy, that of the *Chovevé Zion* outside of Russia, and it largely reduced the number of its adherents within that empire. Its separate activities have, however, by no means ceased. They are engaged now principally in the direction and organization of education in Palestine, and in work, such as the encouragement of artisan settlements, garden cities, etc., for which no other institutions specifically exist. The German branch of the movement, the Ezra Society, has also continued in operation until the present day, but it confines its activities to tasks of detail such as the care of the health of the settlers in Palestine.

The movement for the restoration of the Jews to Palestine, whatever success it may attain in the future, can never repay the debt which it owes to the *Chovevé Zion* and to their leaders. Without the encouragement and assistance of that organization, many of the colonies would never have survived their first years. Like children, they needed protection and guidance. The *Chovevé Zion* came into existence to supply those necessities, to fill the place of guardian and helper. And as each colony progressed sufficiently to be able to assist itself, to stand alone and to supply its own needs, the control and direction were gradually withdrawn. During the first years the organization was always at hand, but the object of the training which it gave—self-dependence— was never forgotten, and even after the necessity for all direct assistance had passed, the organization was always ready to render advice whenever required.

The *Chovevé Zion* was, however, as has been explained, a federation of societies each consisting of hundreds of members. The work performed by it therefore represented the Palestinian efforts of thousands of European and American Jews. The whole of the beneficent work of the *Chovevé Zion* in Palestine has been equalled—nay, in a sense exceeded—by that of one individual, a prince among philanthropists, but one who did not subordinate his head to his heart, as so many philanthropists do who devote their millions to performing the task of Sisyphus. He is also a statesman among philanthropists, one whose good deeds have of themselves multiplied a hundred times in his own lifetime, and scattered the seeds and the fruits of his beneficent actions and labours throughout the length and breadth of Palestine. This builder of the future Jewish State in Palestine is Baron Edmund de Rothschild, of Paris. "The Baron," as he is called throughout Jewry, had his attention first drawn to the possibility of the colonization of Palestine by Laurence Oliphant, when the latter was seeking means for the assistance of the Roumanian immigrants whom he had taken under his protection at Haifa. Rishon le Zion, Zichron Jacob, Petach Tikvah, one embryonic colony after another, the Baron took under his care. He bought land to provide for the growth of existing colonies and for the establishment of new ones. He appointed agents in all parts of the land to assist the colonists, and allowed them to draw upon him almost without limit. He assisted and encouraged the colonists to introduce new cultures; and when, as in the case of wine, he found that their exertions resulted in overproduction, he provided the

8

means himself for the purchase of their produce at a price which would afford them an adequate remuneration. Marsh lands were drained at his expense, and eucalyptus-trees planted.*   Wine-cellars, with all the latest machinery for the manufacture and preservation of wine, have been provided by him.   Even a factory for making glass bottles was established. For seventeen years " the Baron " supported not only the colonies Ekron and Metullah, which he had himself planted, but also, at one time or another, Rishon le Zion, Petach Tikvah, Chederah, Zichron Jacob, Rosh Pinah, and Yesod Hamaaleh. Not only did he assist the colonists whenever they needed him. He bought land continually in order to extend their holdings and to enable the colonies to expand. When, however, Baron Edmund found that the assistance he was rendering to the colonists was making them dependent instead of self-reliant, he altered his procedure. He transferred the administration of the colonies to the Jewish Colonization Association, the institution formed and endowed by Baron Maurice de Hirsch with his millions, and devoted to the assistance of Jewish emigration from the East of Europe, and to the establishment in the first instance of Jewish agricultural colonies in North and South America. The Ica, by which name this institution is known, made drastic reforms, and had to cope with several difficult situations. It encouraged other forms of cultivation besides the vine, and in the course of four years reduced the production of wine by two-thirds. At the same time the Ica assisted in the formation of a society for the manufacture and disposal

* The health-giving and rapidly-growing eucalyptus was introduced into Palestine by the Jews, and is known among the Arabs as the " Jews' Tree."

of this produce through the ordinary market channels. To fit the colonists for the new conditions, their holdings were enlarged where necessary. The administration of the Ica proved successful. The colonies and colonists were placed on their feet, and in many places the tutelage and support of the Ica were gradually withdrawn, until at length there were very few colonies that still needed financial assistance. The experiment initiated by the *Chovevé Zion* and adopted and extended by the Baron had obtained success. A number of self-supporting prosperous Jewish agricultural colonies had been established in the Holy Land. The Jew, once he had been granted the opportunity, had shown himself capable of living as an agriculturist, without sacrificing the intellectual position which is his heritage; culture of the soil, accompanied by culture of the intellect, may well form the basis of a nation.

The example set by the Rothschild colonies was followed by the others. The Ica itself, although at first not very favourably disposed towards Palestinian colonization, became to some extent infected by the success of the colonies which had been entrusted to its care and extended its advice and assistance to other colonies. It even acquired land of its own near Tiberias and settled Jewish labourers upon it with a view to their becoming later small farmers. A proposal was made in the Council of the Ica that a large tract of Crown-lands in the Hauran should be purchased, but the opposition of the anti-Palestinians was too strong for the proposal to be adopted. In other directions, however, the Ica has devoted much attention to Palestine. It has introduced many industries —silk-weaving, wool-weaving, knitting, and dyeing. It supplies knitting-machines to poor families, accepting payment from them in instalments. It acts as a building society in order to enable shopkeepers, artisans, and others of moderate means to acquire their dwellings. It has established a loan bank for the same class of client, and a school where girls are taught lace-making.

The pioneer Jewish colonists in Palestine were at first faced by difficulties that only a determination inspired by an enthusiasm which was both a religion and a patriotism could overcome. Failure and disillusionment were frequent, and many of the weaker—in spirit or in body—of the colonists succumbed to the difficulties which barred their way to success. But the idea was far stronger than the combined strength or weakness of individuals. Individual colonists dropped out of the contest, but the colonies persisted. No matter how bitter the disappointments, how heart-rending the failures, the spirit of the Jewish Revival clung to the land. Ultimately the confidence in the future overcame the despair of the present, and as a consequence the resettlement of the Jews in Palestine—a movement the growth of which events may retard, but which they cannot cause entirely to cease—has commenced. In other lands colonies have been founded by men and women bred to agriculture. With very few exceptions this was not the case in Palestine. The colonists came from a people which had been forcibly excluded from the land for centuries, from which the artificial conditions in which it lived had, it was generally considered, permanently eradicated that love of the land which is among the natural instincts of a people. So deeply had the iron of oppression entered into the soul of Jewry that there were many who denied it any title to nationality and who preferred to regard it merely as a race or a religion. The Jew was considered essentially a townsman, to whom the life of the country was something alien. From such material were the pioneers of Palestine colonization drawn.

The number of mistakes that a pedlar, a shopkeeper, or a student, suddenly planted in an almost virgin country, would make, can easily be conceived. These colonists, however, met with difficulties from which they would have been free if they had settled in some no-man's-land elsewhere. The land they purchased was in many cases unhealthy or otherwise unsuitable for settlement, and the prices they paid excessive. Starvation and disease pounced upon them as easy victims. Of the conditions of the land, and of the language of the natives, the settlers were entirely ignorant. The natives, failing to understand them or the objects of the settlements, grew suspicious and became a source of difficulty and sometimes of danger. When the settlers became acquainted with the conditions amid which they found themselves, they learnt that their task was to introduce Western methods of life and of progress into a land and a people both of which had been dormant for centuries, which the Oriental spirit of indolence and fatalism claimed as its own. The acquisition of land was beset by innumerable difficulties. Ottoman subjects alone were permitted to make purchases, and the new-comers were with few exceptions aliens. Plots of suitable size were seldom available. Even when the preliminary difficulties were overcome, it was often found necessary, in the negotiations for a single estate, to deal with a host of vendors. Among the best equipped of the settlers capital was scarce, and to obtain any in the land itself except on ruinous terms, was practically impossible. Misgovernment, civil and external war, extending over the greater part of two millenia, had even gone far to destroy the natural fertility of the land, and to interfere with the supply of water on which the land depends. Successive armies, of invaders and of defenders, had to a very large extent denuded the land of the forests which were among its natural defenders against drought and sand. The encroachments of the desert and of the seashore continued from year to year, and there was no government to make any attempt to stay them.

One by one these difficulties were overcome, or were in the course of being overcome, when the outbreak of war put the results of a generation's laborious toil, of work for which the labourers had in many instances given their very lives, in jeopardy. Experience in due course had come to the original settlers and to those who followed them. The prognostications of those who thought that the agricultural instinct had been entirely eradicated from the Jew of the Ghetto had been falsified. The undying adaptability of the Jew had displayed itself in Palestine as elsewhere. The child of the walled-in alleys of the Ghetto had become the child of the open air, of the green and golden fields and the orchards and the fruit gardens, of the blue skies. By the establishment of banks and by other means the capital which was so necessary to the development of the colonies had been forthcoming. New-comers with means of their own had also settled in the land. The unpleasant attitude adopted by the native Arabs had soon given way to one more sympathetic. They had found that they had nothing to fear from the new-comers; instead of losing by their advent they would gain. The native landowner had found the value of his land increase; and seeing the success in Jewish hands of new methods of cultivation, he had often adopted them to his own advantage. The peasants had found new and remunerative markets for their labour, and profited also to some extent from the ideas introduced by the new-comers. These latter had also brought with them new needs, some of which the natives, in the towns as well as in the country, were able to satisfy. Other general improvements—for instance in education, in sanitation, in the administration of justice, in the making of roads—had benefited all the inhabitants of the land, Arab as well as Jew. As a consequence of all these advantages, friendliness soon took the place of the suspicion which the first arrivals had engendered, and the native recognized in the advent of the Jewish colonist a benefit and not a disadvantage.

In the earliest days of the colonies much use was made of native labour both in the preparation of the land for settlement and in the cultivation of it. Arabs are still employed in many of the settlements, but side by side with them has grown up a class of Jewish labourers distinct from the colonists who, on their part, occupy the position of farmers. These labourers, however, advance in the social scale, and in due course become colonists themselves. They are recruited, not only from Europe, but also from the cities of Palestine, from among a population whose greatest misfortune is a chronic unemployment. The increase in this labouring class, the facility with which they learn the work entrusted to them, the intelligence and zeal with which they perform their tasks, all tend to augment the value of this class in the population. Intellectually and educationally, they are far superior to similar classes in other countries. In breadth of outlook and in ambition, too,

they soar above their fellows in other lands. They
look forward to the day when they will no longer be
labourers, but farmers, and perhaps proprietors also.
In the meanwhile they conscientiously perform the tasks
allotted to them. The number of Jewish labourers increases year by year. Of late years many have come
from the Yemen in South Arabia, where the Jews who
have been settled there since the beginning of the
Christian era and earlier have suffered so severely at
the hands of the native chiefs as to render their lives
unbearable. There are still some thirty thousand Jews
in the Yemen, all capable, with a little instruction, of
agricultural or any other manual labour. Migration from
the Yemen to Palestine has now become regular, and
in due course the greater part, if not the whole, of the
Jewish population should remove from South Arabia
to Palestine to the advantage of the land as well as of
themselves.

At first, of course, the lack of experience on the part
of the colonists had to be compensated for by the employment of agricultural experts as directors. These experts
were not Jews, and had to be sought outside of Palestine.
As the experience of the colonists grew, the need of these
directors in the older colonies diminished. There always
remained, however, a call for scientifically trained agricultural experts. In much less than a generation the
source of supply of these directors has changed entirely.
The Jewish agricultural training-schools in Palestine
and elsewhere have shown themselves well qualified to
satisfy the need, and the Jewish material on which they
draw includes also children of the colonies, who, after
a course of training at Mikveh Israel or elsewhere, return
to their homes or settle in other colonies to take their part

YEMENITE CHILDREN

Face p. 125

in the Jewish rehabilitation of the Holy Land. Arbori-culture, especially fruit-farming, and agriculture are the staple industries in the colonies. Wine-making has from the beginning been a considerable industry. Many minor industries, some of which may grow to consider-able importance, have also sprung up. Among these are floriculture, the distilling of perfumes, soap-making (from the fruit of the olive-tree), agriculture, cattle-breeding, fruit-preserving, tobacco-growing, silkworm cultivation and silk-spinning, and poultry-farming.

CHAPTER XII

MIKVEH ISRAEL, the oldest of the existing Jewish agricultural settlements in Judæa, is not in its main purpose a colony. In an earlier chapter an account has been given of the establishment by the *Alliance Israélite* of an Agricultural School. This school, together with its dependants, has become the nucleus of a small colony of which it forms the greater part. The curriculum of the school covers a wide range, and a practical knowledge of many branches of agriculture is given there. Among the many advantages which Palestine owes to Mikveh Israel is the acclimatization of the Damascus cow, which gives four times as much milk as the native variety. Cereals, vegetables, oranges, vines, olives, and almonds, are all cultivated there and with commercial success. The extent of the settlement is, however, not very considerable—about 600 acres—and its population does not exceed 200. Mikveh Israel's function is still that of an example; it is still a centre of instruction rather than of production. The establishment in 1914 of a Palestinian Agricultural Society, which includes in its membership trained and practical agriculturists in all parts of Palestine, still further increases the value of Mikveh Israel to Palestine.

The earlier history of Petach Tikvah, the first district to be settled as a colony, has already been narrated.

A part of the land abandoned by the first settlers was purchased by new-comers from Bielistock, in Russia, in 1883. They also, like their predecessors, had to pay dearly for their inexperience, although they profited to some extent by the failures of the earlier colonists. For instance, in order to avoid the malaria which had so sorely stricken the first settlers, they made their homes on the higher ground, the houses being built with the assistance of the Russian *Chovevé Zion*. In the year 1887 Baron Edmund de Rothschild came to the assistance of the struggling colony. He bought about half of the site of the original holding and settled twenty-eight selected families upon it. To check the ravages of malaria he planted eucalyptus-trees around the neighbouring marshes. Hitherto corn-growing had been the principal industry, but the Baron introduced the vine into Petach as well as into the other colonies, in which he began to take an interest at about the same time. Another philanthropist who devoted attention to the colony in these early days was Emil Lachmann, of Berlin, who bought a portion of the land and planted an orange grove and grape vines.

The twenty-eight new families, together with the survivors of the earlier settlers, were soon reinforced by a number of further arrivals, some of whom became colonists, but most of whom entered the employment of the earlier settlers or of the Administration. The colonists were for a time unable to support themselves by their own produce alone, and had to supplement the income thus derived, by wages earned in the employment of others. The great trouble of the colony in those early days was, however, the malaria caused by the unhealthy situation. The removal of this trouble was taken cornfields and the grass-lands of Petach also must not be forgotten.

Once the colony was firmly set upon its feet, it progressed continuously, with hardly a set-back. It grew continually in extent and absorbed small neighbouring settlements which had already been planted. Of these, Ain Ganim, a working-men's settlement, consists of about 700 acres, with a population of a hundred. The land at Kafr Saba, which is about two hours north of Petach, was acquired in 1892, but development did not commence until twelve years later. This settlement is also worked by working men, who cultivate the almond, the olive, and the eucalyptus. Its immediate success gave great promise for the future. In five years the value of its products increased fourfold.

The productive land of Petach Tikvah now extends to about 8,000 acres, and its population approximates to three thousand, having more than doubled during the past ten years. The colony has its waterworks (for both domestic and irrigation purposes), a dispensary, two large schools (one supported out of the revenues of the Lachmann estate, and the other provided by the Ica), a synagogue, club and library (provided by the Jewish National Fund) and other public buildings, public gardens (presented by Baron Edmund), and two hotels. The colony is, in fact, no longer a village, but a garden city. The dwellings all stand in their own gardens. The roads are avenues of mimosa or acacia. In the centre of the colony is a fountain from which streams radiate in all directions. The settlement itself is embedded in orange groves and almond plantations. The price of land in the colony—which when the Jews first came there was practically uninhabitable—has risen from £3 12s.

to £36 per acre in the course of twenty-five years. The wages paid to Arabs employed in the colony amount to almost a million francs per annum. Thirty years ago the Government received in taxation from the district an annual sum of 2,000 francs: now 85,000 francs a year are received, and the taxation is not excessive. In 1880 the value of the land of the colony was estimated at £1,200: now it is worth £600,000. No commentary on these figures is necessary to show the value of the Jewish immigration into Palestine to the Government and to the Arabs. The prosperity of the neighbouring port of Jaffa has been correspondingly affected.

Petach Tikvah, like the other colonies and Tel Aviv, enjoys autonomy. The *Waad*, or local council, has a wide scope. It is elected annually by all adult land-owners and resident tax-payers of three years' standing, independent of sex. To this council the Turkish Government assigns full powers of local administration. The Central Government, in fact, takes no further interest in the colony beyond requiring annually the taxation for which it is liable. The Central Government has reserved to itself the right of interference in a case of murder, but as murders are never committed by the Jewish settlers, this right has by force of circumstances fallen into desuetude. The *Waad* consequently has far greater powers and responsibilities than a town or district council in Europe. The registration of births, marriages, and deaths, and of titles to land, rests with it. It is responsible for the division of both the local and central taxation among its constituents. Schools, syna-gogues, public hygiene, including the services of physician, chemist, and nurse, water-supply, public baths, and many forms of public charity, are under its control   It concerns itself also with the quality of the food offered for sale.

The Council acts through a number of committees, which deal with such matters as finance, education, and public security. An arbitration committee settles any disputes which may arise between settlers. So successful have these arbitration committees been in securing the general confidence that their services are often sought by Arab litigants, not local residents, who are more willing to accept the decisions of these Jewish committees than those of the Government Courts appointed for the purpose of trying their causes.

Rishon le Zion, the best-known of the colonies on account of the attribution of its name to the wine produced by all the Palestinian colonies, also was not founded under the best of conditions. The first settlers were essentially men of the town, devoid of all acquaintance with rural life. The choice of a situation for their settlement at once gave evidence of their inexperience. There was no water at hand, and the supply of the colony was dependent on a source at a distance. The prospects of the success of this colony were very dismal when it came under the notice of the Baron. His first assistance took the form of a loan of 25,000 francs. He also sent the colonists an expert horticulturist to teach them the art of planting. Henceforward his interest in Rishon was untiring, and he is computed to have devoted millions of francs in one way or another to the welfare of the settlement. In 1885 he bought sufficient neighbouring land to double the size of the colony. This was necessary in order to accommodate several new families which had arrived. Two years later a further considerable purchase of land was made. At first the

A COLONIST'S HOUSE

A STREET IN PETACH TIKYAH

Face p. 128

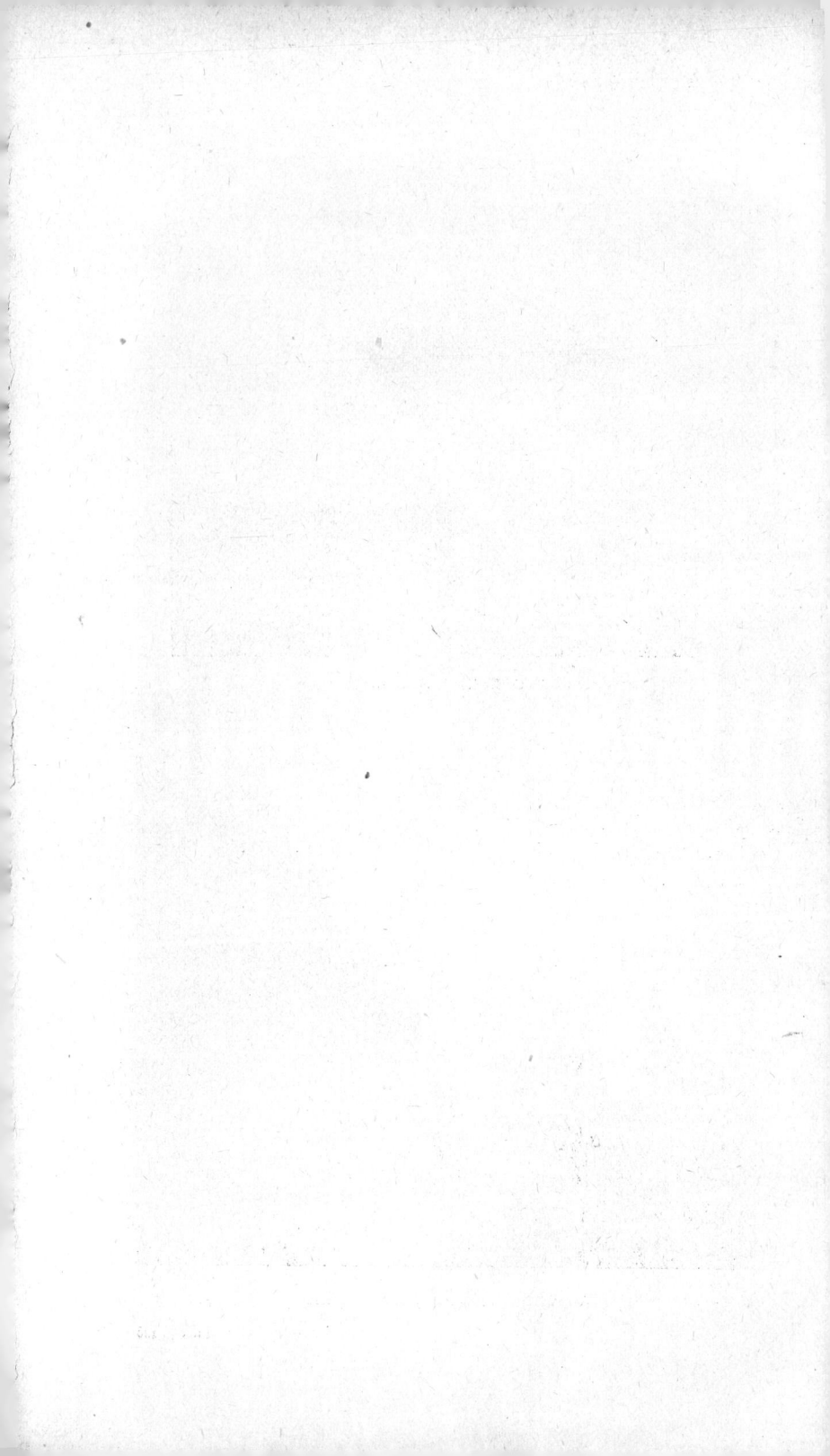

production of corn was undertaken, but the ambition of the Baron was to make Palestine a wine-producing land, and Rishon was chosen as the point of the new departure.   French varieties of vine were introduced and grafted on American stock so as to render them immune from phylloxera.   From first to last a million and a half vines were planted in Rishon le Zion.   The most capacious wine cellar in the world—containing 104 vats, each holding 60,000 pints—was constructed and fitted with two 150 horse-power steam-engines, cooling vats, etc. Rishon was thereby enabled to deal not only with its own produce, but also with the fruit of all the other Palestinian colonies.   Unfortunately the supply of Palestinian wine soon exceeded the demand.   Much of the stock became unsaleable, and it is probable that the colonization experiment in Judæa would have been submerged in an economic crisis, if the Baron had not again stepped in, saved the situation, and purchased at a fixed price all the wine that was offered.   As this price was above the market value, and as no commercial machinery was then available for disposing of the produce, in order to set free the storage accommodation for further purchases, the wine already purchased was sold at a considerable loss.   For fifteen years the Baron continued this expensive policy of, in fact, subventioning the colonists.   At length, after he had handed the administration over to the Ica, the situation was eased by a considerable reduction in the area devoted to viticulture, and by the formation of a syndicate for the disposal of the produce on commercial lines, which by a judicious system of advertisement brought Palestine wine under the notice of a large and widespread public. Compensation was paid to the colonists whose vineyards

were destroyed, and almond, olive, orange, and other
fruit-trees, for the produce of which there was a surer
market, were planted in place of the vines. Moreover,
additional land suitable for the cultivation of cereals
was purchased.

Under the Ica administration the extent of the colony
was much increased by the purchase of corn-land, with
the assistance of loans granted by the Association. The
planting of fruit-trees—fig, pomegranate, apple, mulberry
(for silkworms), and citron, as well as almond, olive, and
orange—was also encouraged, and the cultivation of
barley, sesame, and water-melons introduced. Cattle-
breeding was also undertaken. By means of this variety
of produce the economic position was secured. Rishon
le Zion, having passed out of its period of anxiety, became
prosperous, and is now the third largest Jewish agricultural settlement in Palestine. Although the extent
of viticulture has been reduced almost 50 per cent., it is
still by far the most important industry in the colony.
Next to it in importance comes the orange industry.
The cultivation of the almond does not fall far short.
Corn-growing is also important. The mulberry-trees
exceed 20,000 in number. The quality of the vines
varies, and several kinds of wine are manufactured. It
is exported to Europe and America, and especially to
Egypt, where Rishon le Zion wine is widely consumed.
A good brandy is also manufactured and exported. All
the work relating to the manufacture and export of the
wine is performed by the Jewish settlers, for whom even
a cask factory was established in Rishon, and a bottle
factory, which was afterwards discontinued, at Tantura
in Samaria.

The population of the colony now amounts to between

1,100 and 1,200 souls. It extends over about 3,000 acres. The inhabitants consist of artisans, labourers, professional men, and shopkeepers, as well as of the colonists proper. The houses are of stone, with flower and kitchen gardens, vines, and fruit-trees attached. Every family owns at least a horse and cart, a cow, and some poultry. The colony contains three large wells, a synagogue, schools, a splendid library, a club, public baths, municipal buildings; a hospital with six wards. Periodicals, Palestinian and foreign, are easily obtainable in the colony, the intellectual and social level of which is relatively high. The streets are broad and well paved, lined with the houses surrounded by trees. A palm garden, planted by the Baron and presented by him to the colony as a park, is the finest in Syria. A diligence runs regularly between Rishon and Jaffa, which is two hours distant. The country around Rishon, except where the lands of Rechoboth and Wad-el-Chanin lie, is sandy and uninhabited—a wilderness in the midst of which the Jewish colonies blossom as oases. The land they occupy was once as that which surrounds them. If these Jewish fugitives had not settled there it would have remained so. Rishon le Zion, seated in the wilderness, is one more witness of the value to the land of Jewish colonization.

Wad-el-Chanin, or Nachalat Reuben (The Heritage of Reuben), a settlement with 200 inhabitants, to the south of Rishon and in similar surroundings, was founded in the same year by Reuben Lehrer, of Kherson, who purchased 336 acres, and, settling in the colony, sold some of the land to other Russian settlers. They engaged mainly in viticulture, and suffered very severely in the crisis which overtook that industry. The small amount of land belonging to the colony also depressed the fortunes of the settlers. The Odessa Committee and the Baron had early rendered assistance to the colonists, and the Ica later advanced them a loan of 100,000 francs. Still later, in 1906, the Vintners' (Wine Growers') Syndicate advanced money wherewith to convert much of the land previously planted with vines into almond, orange, and other fruit orchards. Further land was also bought with the assistance of the Ica and the cultivation of corn undertaken. To tide them over the period of transition, the Ica gave employment to the colonists in its own orange plantations which it had established in the colony. In due course the economic situation improved. The loans have for years been repaid with regularity. The colony is now self-supporting: its future is full of promise. Agriculture is pursued in the colony on a relatively large scale. Orange production has become the main industry. Experiments have also been made in cotton-growing.

Jehudieh, a very small colony to the south of Petach Tikvah, was founded in the following year.

Ekron, founded by Baron Edmund in 1884 on the Biblical site of the same name, near Jabneh, was named by him Maskereth Bathia, after his mother. He commenced the colony with eighteen families of Jewish agriculturists from Russia, who engaged in the cultivation of corn, to which they were accustomed. The land was not altogether suitable for cereals, and as a supplementary industry, fruit-tree planting was introduced. This was a form of agriculture with which the colonists had had no previous acquaintance, and for a time the colony did not prosper. Ekron was transferred by the Baron to the Ica, together with his other interests in Palestine, and further ground was thereupon bought and sown with corn. From this time forward the independence of the colonists was assured. Supporting themselves in comfort, they soon repaid the money which had been advanced to them by the Baron. The staple industry of the colony is wheat production, which is now conducted with great success. Sesame, lucerne, and barley are also grown. The number of fruit-trees, comprising oranges, citrons, almonds, olives, pomegranates, apples, mulberries, apricots, bananas, dates, and figs, is also considerable and increasing. Among the subsidiary industries is that of silk production. The colony now owns about 3,200 acres, divided among a population of about 320. Every family has a stone house, one or two horses and cart, and several head of cattle, sheep, goats, and poultry.

Katrah or Ghederah, situated about four miles southwest of Ekron, was founded in the same year, by a number of student members of the *Bilu*, by other Russo-Jewish immigrants from Charkow, and by the *Chovevé Zion*. The original settlers had far more zeal and enthusiasm than capital or experience. Their willingness to labour and to exert themselves had no apparent limit, but through want of knowledge much of their labour was wasted. The deficiencies were to some extent made good by the *Chovevé Zion*, which with great generosity came at once to the assistance of the settlers. This society gave them the means wherewith to build houses, to bring water to the colony, and to plant vines. With this assistance the colonists soon forged ahead until the wine crisis came. To tide them through this the Ica granted them loans, but only seven of the settlers, those who were the most deeply engaged in wine production, needed this assistance. The Ica also improved the water-supply of the colony and erected a mill, worked by motor power, for it. The cost of these improvements was repaid in annual instalments. In 1895 the manufacture of cognac was first undertaken with satisfactory results. Katrah did not suffer so severely as the other colonies from the wine crisis. The cause of its partial immunity was the special suitability of its land for the growth of vines. The crisis, nevertheless, led to a reduction in the area devoted to vineyards, and the land thus set free, as well as other land acquired a little later, was devoted mainly to the production of corn and almonds. Not more than 20 per cent. of the produce of Katrah now consists of wine. The great hardships endured by the original settlers caused many of them to leave the colony at one time or another. Thus but few of the original settlers or their families remain at Katrah. Their places have been taken by new-comers from the neighbouring colonies. The population is still small, not more than 150, who occupy 1,250 acres. Every family is now prosperous. Without exception they own houses, cattle, and poultry. To every house vineyards and gardens—flower and kitchen—are attached.

Castinieh, or Beer-Tobiah, the southernmost but one of the colonies, lies to the south of the Katrah, about fourteen miles north-east of Ascalon. The land was originally acquired by a party of Roumanian or rather Bessarabian Jews, who in 1888 sold it to the Baron. The colony was not a success. In 1895 the *Chovevé Zion* societies of England and Russia, the Central Committee in Paris, and the Ezra Society of Berlin, acquired it on very favourable terms, and set about to make of Castinieh a working men's colony. They settled twenty-one colonists, providing them with land, cattle, agricultural

A LABOURER'S HOUSE

YEMENITE BOYS AT WORK

Face p. 134

implements, and small subventions to assist them until
they could become self-supporting. With three exceptions these colonists were drawn from among the labourers
in other colonies. Of the exceptions, two were graduates
of the Mikveh Israel Agricultural School. The settlers
threw themselves with eagerness into the work of
home-making. In the somewhat quaint English of
a contemporary report to the English *Chovevé Zion*:
" It was a true pleasure to see the feverish activity which
reigned in the colony at the time of building; everyone
contributed to the work—men, women, and children
carried the stones on their backs, the sand, the clay, the
lime, and the water (at the commencement there were
only two carts for hire in the colony). They kneaded
the clay and they built the houses with very small stones.
The women plastered the earth floor with clay, and made it
smooth and straight. They worked with zeal to put
their houses in good order and to make things decent
in these houses deserted since nine years. Workmen
swarmed at all points—large and small, male and female—
and the result has been truly fine. Behind the houses they
have built poultry-houses, kitchens, small stables, and
storage for coal and other things necessary in a country-
house. Each had his little project and arranged the inside
of his house according to his pet ideas."

As was natural, the colonists encountered many unexpected difficulties. Some of the oxen which they had
purchased had been badly trained, " and lay down when
at work, and the colonists were unable to make them
work." The horses also were accustomed to the pack-
saddle rather than the plough, and it was difficult to
get them to adopt their new calling. The ploughs
proved in practice too heavy, and a lighter kind had to

be obtained. These, however, and other difficulties were as nothing when the fire of the colonists' enthusiasm was turned upon them. " Among the colonists there were only a few who knew how to till. The most of them are very good, are careful workmen, but have never handled the plough; some of them even did not know how to put to a horse. I must say, however, to be just, that they very soon learnt how to look after horses and oxen as well as to handle the plough, and it was beautiful to see their radiant faces when they came to tell of their success. In fact, these colonists, who a few months ago did not know how to put to a horse, now till the ground from morn till night, make good straight furrows, and acquit themselves in a satisfactory manner of all the work of the field."

Although Castinieh depends mainly on wheat production, it grows barley and fruit of several varieties also. Its roads are avenues of mulberry-trees: its boundaries consist of eucalyptus woods. The population of Castinieh is between 150 and 200 souls. Its area extends to 1,600 acres.

In 1890 the smallest, with one exception, of the Judæan colonies, Mozah or Kaloniyeh, was founded on the site of an unsuccessful attempt at colonization by some of Kalischer's disciples in 1873, by the international Jewish society, " The Independent Order of the B'nai B'rith " (Sons of the Covenant), by which organization, and also by the Ica, it has been to a large extent assisted. Mozah is situated on the Judæan hills, three-quarters of an hour's journey from Jerusalem on the road to Jaffa. The vine and the olive are cultivated there and wheat is also grown to some extent. One colonist devotes himself entirely to the production of vegetables, and another to dairy-farming. Both find a ready market for their produce in Jerusalem. Mozah has become a holiday resort for the children of Jerusalem.

In the year 1890, also, the colony of Rechoboth, four miles south of Rishon and the same distance from the Jaffa-Jerusalem railway, was founded by a number of Russian Jews, mainly of Warsaw, of whom Rabbi Samuel Mohilever, of Bielistok, was the most prominent. Most of them, however, did not themselves settle in the colony. Over 2,500 acres of land were acquired in the first instance, and devoted for the most part to viticulture. As many of the landowners remained in Russia, Rechoboth was to a large extent at the beginning a workers' colony. At first many difficulties were placed in the way of the colony by the Turkish authorities, but in 1894 a *modus vivendi* was reached. Henceforward Rechoboth flourished. In course of time the cultivation of the vine was supplemented and partly replaced by other forms of agriculture. Almonds came to occupy an important position in the economy of the settlement and promise to do so still more in the future. Olives and oranges are also important, while mulberries (for silk), figs, and cereals are also grown.

The population now numbers about 900, inclusive of 270 who have come from the Yemen and are employed by the colonists. Rechoboth was, in fact, the first colony to make the introduction of Jewish workmen a success. All the houses are comfortable and adequate, but not imposing or luxurious. They have stables, flower and kitchen gardens, horses and carts, cows and poultry. Mulberry-trees form avenues along the streets, and in the centre of the village, in the most prominent situation, stands the school. Other noticeable buildings are the synagogue, the public baths, the library, the dispensary, and the new great "Beth-Am" ("The People's House") where, during the evenings and on Saturday afternoons, literary and scientific lectures are given and other forms of intellectual recreation are pursued. The village has in all three schools.

Close to Rechoboth the *Chovevé Zion* Society and the Ezra Society of Berlin in 1895 founded a small working men's colony, known as Ezra, whose first inhabitants were selected from among the labourers in other colonies. Every family was given five acres of land, a house built of stone, three cows, and a stock of poultry. The income derived from these was supplemented by wages earned in Rechoboth. The settlers were by these means enabled not only to keep themselves and their families in comfort, but even to save money, and in time to obtain larger holdings and take their places in the ranks of the established colonists.

The foregoing exhausts the list of the principal Jewish colonies in Judæa. During the past ten years small settlements have been made at Ben Shamen (600 acres, 100 inhabitants), Bir Jacob (500 acres, 70 inhabitants), and Hulda (455 acres, 40 inhabitants). Ben Shamen is to a large extent an olive-tree plantation. In 1910 workmen of the Bezalel School of Arts and Crafts of Jerusalem were settled there, and made of the colony the first garden-city (in miniature) based on domestic industry. There the filigree craftsmen work in silver, and their wives weave carpets and work lace. A model poultry farm and a model farm of the Jewish National Fund have been established, and the village is also the site chosen for one of the forests of olive-trees which are being planted by the last-mentioned organization.

Earlier in its history Ben Shamen was the site of a Hebrew Agricultural School, and in 1907 the industrial settlement of the " Athid " oil and soap factory was established there.

Still earlier, in 1896, a Bulgarian Jewish Colonization Society acquired 1,125 acres at Artuf, not far from Jerusalem on the railway, where an English mission to the Jews had previously, without success, attempted to found a Jewish colony. Insufficiency of means was a source of much anxiety and hardship at first, but later the Ica came to the assistance of the colonists with loans and the position was greatly eased. The colony is still a small one, about 1,200 acres with a population of ninety-five. Corn, grapes, figs, and olives are grown. The settlement possesses a mill and an oil distillery, and shortly before the outbreak of the War a large dairy farm was established there.

At Hulda, not far from Lydda, on the Jerusalem-Jaffa railway, the Jewish National Fund bought land in 1906. The great olive grove which is being planted in memory of Theodore Herzl is situated at Hulda.

The first steps for the colonization of Djemama, twenty-six miles south of Castinieh, had been taken before the outbreak of war, and the question of settling Jewish colonists still farther south, in the Egyptian territory of El Arish, was being seriously considered.

CHAPTER XIII

THE COLONIES IN DETAIL—II. GALILEE

THE Galilean colonies, of which there are sixteen, lie for the most part near the western shore of the Sea of Galilee and the western bank of the Jordan, previous to its entrance into that sea. They stretch, however, almost half-way to the Mediterranean. The northernmost, Metullah, is on a level with the ancient port of Tyre: the southernmost, Merchavia, lies on the Haifa-Damascus railway. The district in which these colonies are situated is perhaps the most fertile in Palestine, and would, together with that beyond the Jordan which the railway serves, under satisfactory political conditions, become one of the granaries of the world. When the Ica took over the administration of these colonies from Baron Edmund in 1899, almost the first task that met them was the transformation of a wine-producing area into one for the cultivation of cereals and for cattle-raising. For this purpose additional land had to be purchased. The Baron had already acquired considerable tracts in Lower Galilee, but as they had remained uncultivated, they had, in accordance with Turkish law, reverted to the Government. The Ica after much difficulty regained possession of these tracts and founded on them a number of colonies. In fact, the colonization of Southern Galilee, which is more intensive than that of any other part of Palestine, may be said to have been largely due to the exertions of the Ica. About 60 per cent. of the land in these colonies has now passed definitely into the possession of the settlers.

Of the colonies in Galilee, Rosh Pinah (The Cornerstone), north of the Sea of Galilee, three miles from Safed, is the longest established and also the largest. It is most picturesquely situated on the mountain-side, with magnificent views of Mount Hermon, " The King of the mountains of Palestine," in the far distance, and the Sea of Merom in the middle distance, to the north. At its feet runs the Jordan, hastening on its way to the Sea of Galilee, whose blue waters are to be seen to the southeast. Behind the observer to his right and his left stretch the highlands, every ridge still more attractive in appearance than the one below it. The climate is excellent and the spring-water the best in Palestine. According to the statement of the local doctor, only the very young and the very old are buried in its cemetery.

Rosh Pinah was settled in 1882 by Roumanian immigrants, who devoted practically the whole of their industry to viticulture. When Rosh Pinah with the other colonies was taken over by the Ica, it was there that the transformation to agriculture, in the narrow sense, and cattle breeding was first undertaken. Rosh Pinah was less fitted than the Judæan settlements for success in the wine industry, but on the other hand was far more adapted for the alternative industries. To facilitate the change, some of the colonists were transferred to Judæa, but Rosh Pinah soon recovered from the temporary loss of population, and although its increase has not been as great as that of its contemporaries—the nature of the staple industries necessitated sparser settlements—it has attained to a condition of unquestionable prosperity.

Corn—wheat and barley—and cattle-raising are the principal occupations. In addition the almond industry is relatively considerable. There are also some orange and citron orchards and tens of thousands of mulberry-trees. A silk-factory which gave employment not only to some of the inhabitants, but also to some of the younger Jews at Safed, was in existence for a time, and the silk produced in the other Palestinian colonies was sent to Rosh Pinah to be manufactured. This industry commenced under very promising auspices. It had, however, to be abandoned on account of the difficulty, in the absence of satisfactory roads, of keeping in touch with the outside world. Tobacco cultivation was also undertaken and proved successful, but the industry was destroyed by the very heavy taxation levied upon it by the Turkish Government on account of possible competition with the State monopoly.

The population is now about 800, and the land under cultivation about 9,500 acres. The houses are built of stone, every one surrounded by flower and kitchen gardens and orchards. Every household is the owner of horses, asses, cattle, and poultry. Among the public buildings of the village are the synagogue, the school, public baths, and a dispensary. The streets are well paved and lined with avenues of trees. All the fields and plantations are surrounded by hedges of mimosa, whose fragrant blossoms are sent to the perfume factory at Yesod Hamaaleh. The village owns a pretty park.

The following year Yesod Hamaaleh (Excelsior) was founded by a number of Polish immigrants on the western shore of the Sea of Merom. At first they had a very severe struggle on account of their insufficient means, but in due course the Russian *Chovevé Zion* and the Baron came to their assistance, and henceforward their path was easier. The site also proved unhealthy, and steps had to be taken to eradicate the malaria which was rife. On the other hand, the water-supply for irrigation purposes is inexhaustible. The warm climate is especially suitable for the cultivation of flowers. Large tracts are therefore devoted to nursery gardens, roses, mimosa, tuberoses, jessamine, geraniums, wild oranges, apricots, etc., being cultivated. To deal with the produce of these gardens a factory for the manufacture of attar of roses, eau-de-Cologne, and other perfumes, was erected by Baron de Rothschild. The nursery gardens of Yesod Hamaaleh also supply the other colonies of Upper Galilee with their young trees. Moreover wheat, oats, barley, maize, beans, and sesame are cultivated, and to a less extent, mulberries, apricots, and almonds. Cattle-breeding, bee-keeping, and fishing are pursued, and the colonists own a vessel which plies on the Sea of Merom. Tobacco-growing was formerly attempted and proved successful, but the industry, as in Rosh Pinah, was killed by the Turkish authorities on behalf of the " Dette Publique," which possesses the tobacco monopoly.

The prosperity of the colony is now assured. Its population consists of about 300 souls, occupying over 3,000 acres, and employing not only themselves, but also labourers from the neighbouring colony of Mishmar ha Yarden. The colony possesses the usual public institutions.

In 1884 a tract of land was purchased at the Bridge of Jacob, not far from the issue of the Jordan from the Sea of Merom. On one-half of the tract twenty labourers from the then existing colonies settled: the other was acquired by a teacher and twenty-five labourers from

Safed. These settlers possessed nothing but enthusiasm. They had no means whatsoever. The land they obtained on credit without much prospect of ever being able to pay for it. Apart altogether from the conditions of their tenure, the extent of the land was insufficient to allow the prospective colony to become self-supporting. The houses in which the colonists were to live were built by means of loans. Their great asset was that indestructible confidence in the future, that unquenchable optimism which has preserved the Jewish people for twenty centuries. The name which they gave to the settlement was Gesher ha Yarden (The Bridge over the Jordan). These pioneers were, however, not left to die of starvation. The *Chovevé Zion* and the Ezra Society of Berlin, and also the Baron, came to their assistance. Money was advanced to enable them to pay for their land and their houses. They were assisted to build additional houses; irrigation works were provided; furniture, cattle, and money supplied. The insurmountable difficulty was, however, the insufficiency of land, as a consequence of which, in despite of all the assistance, the numbers of the settlers dwindled, and the stability of the settlement seemed unattainable.

An improvement set in in 1898, when the Ica began to take an interest in the colony. The population had by then decreased to fifteen families. About this time the name was changed to Mishmar ha Yarden (The Watch on the Jordan). Corn-growing was the principal industry, although cattle-raising was not far behind it in importance. The latter industry, however, suffered several set-backs from outbreaks of cattle disease, by which the herds suffered severely. The insufficiency of land was also always a serious handicap, and it was not until 1907 that the size of the settlement could be extended. Even then the needs of the colonists were not fully satisfied, but the holdings have since been again supplemented, and the condition of the colony now shows an improvement year by year. If only further land can be acquired, Mishmar ha Yarden should in course of time become one of the largest and most prosperous in Galilee. In consequence of the very serious difficulties with which the colonists had to contend throughout the greater part of the life of the colony, their number was never considerable. At present they amount to about 100 and occupy about 1,750 acres.

Ain Zeitun, about a couple of miles from Safed, is a colony of 1,500 acres, with a population of less than fifty. The colony was founded in 1891 by the *Dorshé Zion* Society of Minsk, Russia, but they had not the means to work it properly, and transferred it three years later to Baron de Rothschild. The settlers are for the most part labourers who cultivate corn, olives, and the vine.

Metullah, the northernmost of the colonies, is situated at the foot of Mount Hermon, not far from the ancient Dan. It is one of the colonies that were founded by Baron de Rothschild himself. It was laid out in 1896, and the original settlers were drawn from labourers or the sons of colonists in other colonies. When Metullah came under the administration of the Ica in 1900, it was decided, in view of the insufficiency of the land available per colonist, to remove some of them to other colonies. Fifteen colonists were consequently transferred to Lower Galilee. At the same time, further land was purchased and money advanced to the remaining colonists to enable them to extend their plantations. Wheat and barley cultivation, supplemented by cattle-breeding and poultry-farming, are the principal occupations. Metullah is, in fact, a typical farmers' colony. Its beautiful situation, looking towards the Lebanon, and healthy climate have of recent years made of it a summer resort to which the inhabitants of the warmer regions betake themselves for health and rest. Metullah now covers about 4,250 acres and has a permanent population of about 300. One of the conditions on which the original settlers were assisted was that when they married they should seek their brides only in the Jewish colonies in the Holy Land, so that their wives should be helpmeets, fitted to take their share in the work of the farm.

Mahanaim, the colony next to be founded in Galilee, is a short distance from Rosh Pinah. It was founded by the Galician *Ahavath Zion* Society with the aid of the Ica and the Ezra Society. Of the first colonists ten families came from Galicia and six were natives of Palestine. The population now amounts to about 100, and the colony covers about 2,000 acres, for the most part owned by the colonists in Rosh Pinah.

In the same year Sedjerah, the first of the colonies to be settled by the Ica, was founded. A site was chosen in Lower Galilee, due west of the Sea of Galilee at the foot of Mount Tabor, where a tract of 4,250 acres was acquired. At first a farm was built, wheat and barley sown, and cattle-breeding and poultry-farming undertaken. Fifty-two workmen, mostly unmarried, were brought to the farm, where they were taught suitable methods of agriculture and cattle-farming by the Arabs from whom the land had been bought, and who remained settled on their own lands in the neighbourhood. In 1900 a formal colony was established next to the farm. In this colony the Ica departed from its previous practice of supplying the settlers with farms, etc., leaving the cost to be repaid in instalments. They introduced the practice of retaining possession of the land and of giving employment to the settlers, so that before themselves becoming farmers they might serve an apprenticeship to the calling they were about to adopt. Among the settlers who were placed by the Ica were two proselytes, Russians who had adopted Judaism and had in consequence to flee from their homes. The main products of Sedjerah are grain—wheat, barley, oats, sesame—cattle, and vegetables. Tobacco is also grown. The *Agudath Netaim*, a plantation society to which the lands still worked by the Ica are about to be transferred, proposed to introduce the cultivation of the almond, the olive, and the vine. The population of Sedjerah is now about 200 and the area of the colony about 6,000 acres.

Four colonies—Jemma, Bedjen, Mesha, and Melhamieh —were founded by the Ica in Lower Galilee in the course of the year 1901-1902, and in all four the policy adopted with regard to Sedjerah was followed. Of these Jemma is close to the Sea of Galilee, Mesha is farther west, and Melhamieh is on the Jordan after it has issued from the sea. Bedjen adjoins Jemma. Melhamieh was settled by experienced labourers from Judæa and Samaria, the other by colonists transferred from elsewhere, who were required to work as labourers for a year or so before they were permitted to occupy farms. In the early years of a colony the upkeep of the communal institutions is a considerable burden, which hinders the attainment of economic independence—the aim of all the colonies. To lighten that burden at Jemma and Bedjen, which are only ten minutes apart, the experiment has been tried of having institutions in common. These two colonies have one school, one doctor, and one dispensary between them. By these economies an annual expenditure of 10,000 francs is saved. In recent years the Ica has encouraged the settlement of farmers with capital in these colonies. Having a greater stake in the land, they show all the greater zeal in attending to it.

Mesha shows an almost uninterrupted progress since its establishment thirteen years ago. Wheat is the principal product, but other cereals are also grown. The planting of olives, almonds, and vines was recently undertaken. The colonists have been able to establish a loan bank—originally helped by the Ica, but now possessing its own capital—a cattle and fire insurance society, and a co-operative society. Electric power has been installed whereby water has been brought to all the houses as well as to the fields, and the corn mill is driven. The 15,000 francs required for this purpose was advanced by the Anglo-Palestine Bank, and is to be repaid in the course of four years. The colony of Mesha extends to 4,000 acres and holds a population of about 250 souls.

Jemma's advance was slow—if there was any movement at all—until the year 1907, when with the removal of some of the colonists and their replacement by newcomers the colony made a definite move forward, a movement which has never ceased. Cereals are the principal produce; but the cattle and poultry owned by the colonists are not inconsiderable in number. Planting is about to be undertaken. Jemma extends to 6,100 acres, with a population of 250.

Bedjen, otherwise known as Delaika Sahou, resembles its neighbour, Jemma, very much, both in history and in products. It is, however, much smaller, with a population of only about fifty occupying 1,100 acres.

THE FARM OF KINNERETH

A COLONIST'S WIFE AT KINNERETH

Face p. 143

In Melhamieh also a change of colonists in 1903 led to improvement. Corn and cattle are the principal industries. Cotton was planted in the Jordan Valley, but although the results were fairly satisfactory, the cultivation was abandoned after a short time. The cultivation of bananas, early citrons, and other fruits is about to be undertaken. The population amounts to about 100, and the land of the colony to about 3,400 acres.

During the last few years five further colonies have been established in Lower Galilee: Mizpah and Kinnereth in 1908; Migdal, off the northern shore of the Sea of Galilee, in 1910; and Merchavia, the southernmost of them all, on the Haifa-Damascus railway at the junction with the branch which is ultimately to be extended to Jerusalem, and Poria, in 1911. Mizpah, otherwise Ain Kateb, was, like the others, founded by the Ica. The population numbers only forty, who cultivate 900 acres. Kinnereth has next to it the estates of Daleika and Dagania, which belong to the Palestine Land Development Company. The former was previously an agricultural school. Both Daleika and Dagania, which were founded and are conducted under Zionist auspices, are co-operative working men's settlements. The total population of the three settlements amounts to about 120. The Ica holds about 1,400 acres and the co-operative settlements about the same amount. Migdal, or Medsjdel, the property of the Tiberias Land and Plantation Company, is intended to be primarily a cotton plantation. Corn and vegetables are, however, also grown there. The population is already 100 and the settlement extends over 1,125 acres. Merchavia is also a co-operative working men's settlement belonging to the Co-operative Settlement Company. It houses 100 inhabitants on about

2,350 acres. Poria, the most recent of the settlements in Galilee, consists of about 900 acres belonging to an American Jewish *Achuza* or Plantation Company. Work in which a population of fifty is engaged has commenced on the planting of almonds and olives.

These five colonies are still in their infancy, and it would be premature to speak of their progress or prospects of success. Merchavia, which is an experiment in co-operation, has succeeded sufficiently to enable the expert directors to be withdrawn, and the management of the settlement to be entrusted safely to a committee drawn from among the working-men settlers.

CHAPTER XIV

THE COLONIES IN DETAIL—III. SAMARIA AND TRANSJORDANIA

THE story of the first settlement of Zichron Jacob has been told on a previous page. Its further history followed lines very similar to those of Rishon le Zion. With the support of Baron de Rothschild the wine industry monopolized the interests of the settlers. Large wine-cellars to serve not only Zichron, but also the other colonies in Samaria, were erected; additional land was acquired by the Baron without difficulty. Four small daughter colonies—Shefeya, Bath Shelomo (Um el Djemal), Marah, and Herbet Menshié—were also settled with selected agricultural labourers whose records promised that they would make good farmers. Cereal-growing was pursued mainly in these small settlements. The principal industry of Zichron and its offshoots was, however, still the vine.

The wine crisis was a time of great anxiety for all interested in the colony, but in due course it passed away without inflicting any enduring harm. Under the Ica administration further land was acquired, and this, as well as much of that which had previously been vineyard, was devoted to agriculture in the narrow sense. The holdings of the existing colonists were increased, and new settlers were provided with adequate land. Cattle-breeding was also followed on a larger scale, and the value of the herds owned by the colonists rose in the course of a few years to 180,000 francs. From two-thirds to three-quarters of the income of the colonists is now derived from corn-growing and cattle-breeding. The remainder is dependent mainly on the plantations, which comprise principally vines, oranges, almonds, figs, tangerines, anise, roses, acacia, and olive-trees. Silkworm-breeding, agriculture, and vegetable-growing, are also pursued.

Zichron is beautifully situated, 800 feet above sea-level, surrounded by corn-lands and orchards, with the sea within sight and almost within hearing on the west, and the mountains ending in the historic height of Carmel on the north. Dependent solely on the work of the field, Zichron should be considered a village: judging from its size, its paved streets, its substantial stone houses and its public buildings, one is justified in calling it a small town. The most prominent situation is occupied by the synagogue, the gift of Baroness Edmund de Rothschild—a spacious building, simply yet artistically decorated, with comfortable accommodation for four hundred worshippers. The Administration building, another of the public buildings, faces the small park, which on its part increases the beauty and the attractiveness of the settlement. The hospital is more than adequate to satisfy the not excessive needs of Zichron and the surrounding colonies. Other institutions are the school, the library, the baths, the aforementioned wine-cellars, and the steam-mill. Zichron is also the locale of the offices and laboratories of a Jewish Agricultural Experiment Station which was founded by some public-spirited American Jews in 1910, and has already well fulfilled their expectations. In estimating the value of this settlement it must not be forgotten that before the Jewish colonists came, the site of Zichron was a rocky, boulder-strewn wilderness that had to be cleared before it was capable of supporting a population of any size.

One of the offshoots of Zichron is the small settlement of Tantura, on the site of the Biblical Dor. The Baron established there a glass factory to supply the considerable demands for bottles on the part of the Palestinian colonies, but the sand at Tantura proved unsuitable for the purpose, and the industry had to be abandoned. The Jewish workers were, however, remarkably successful in learning the craft, and showed that, given satisfactory conditions, they had no reason to fear the competition of experienced European workers. The few colonists who remain at Tantura are engaged in raising corn and vegetables.

The population of Zichron and its subsidiary settlements approaches two thousand. The lands they occupy exceed 4,700 acres in extent.

In the year 1883 some Russian Colonization Societies purchased 6,500 acres of land at Chederah, south of the ancient port of Cæsarea. The land remained undeveloped for eight years until 1891, when a colony was established by Jews from Riga and Wilna. The situation unfortunately was very ill-chosen. The neighbouring river, overflowing its banks, caused acres of swamps, and the resultant malaria decimated the numbers of the colonists. The survivors, however, did not lose heart, but clung to their lands. " They had come to colonize," they declared, " and so long as there was still an atom of strength left to them, they would continue the struggle." The colonists unaided could never have overcome this misfortune, but here also the Baron came to their assistance. A complete scheme for draining the colony was drafted, and the means for putting it into force were

154 PALESTINE

provided by Baron Edmund. The women and children were temporarily removed from the settlement: the men remained behind until they had gathered in the harvest. Three hundred Egyptians, accustomed to drainage work and immune from malaria, were brought to perform the labour. When the harvest had been gathered, some of the colonists declined to leave, persisting in their request to be allowed to share in the unhealthy work of drainage, on the ground that they were a part of the colony and it was their duty to take their share in all the work that it required. This claim was at length recognized, and colonists were permitted to work side by side with the imported labourers, buried as far as their knees in the pestilential mud. Nine hundred acres in all were drained and 500,000 eucalyptus-trees planted as a ward around the settlement. A school was also presented to the colonists by the Baron, and the Russian *Chovevé Zion* rendered them assistance in other directions.

The sanitary state of Chederah is now quite satisfactory. Among the mainly agricultural colonies of Palestine it is one of the most successful. The colonists, who as a rule own their holdings, are of the best type of farmer. The principal product is corn, but the inferior lands on which agriculture would prove unremunerative are devoted to plantations, oranges, olives, and grapes being cultivated. The colony occupies in all nearly 8,000 acres. Its inhabitants number nearly 500 souls, a considerable proportion of whom consist of labourers, including Yemenite immigrants. For the labourers, quarters have been provided by the Jewish National Fund and the Ezra Society of Berlin, for the unmarried men as well as for the families.

At Chefzibah, close to Chederah, the *Agudath Netaim*

has acquired about 2,000 acres, which it proposes to divide into farms, which are to be sold to settlers disinclined themselves to undertake the pioneer work. Apart, however, from the employés of the Company and their families, Chefzibah has as yet no inhabitants.

Atlit, the last established of the Jewish colonies in Samaria, lies on the sea-coast, close to the picturesque ruins of the Crusading stronghold of the same name. It was one of those founded by the Baron and taken over by the Ica in 1900. It was then in the first stages of settlement. The land was not divided into separate holdings until 1908, when twelve houses were erected. This colony, whose lands extend to 1,700 acres, is still in a backward state. Its population numbers fifty.

On the other side of the Jordan, the only colony that has yet been settled is Bené Yehudah, or El Jekum, on the eastern shore of the Sea of Galilee, almost opposite to the city of Tiberias. It was originally settled in 1886 by Jews of Safed, acting on the suggestion of Laurence Oliphant. Possessed of insufficient means, these settlers were quite unable to cultivate the 2,000 acres which were at their disposal, even with the assistance of the Arabs, who were in a sort of limited partnership with them. Assistance was rendered by the English *Chovevé Zion* and other institutions, but none of them was able to make the small colony self-supporting. The number of the settlers has nevertheless increased, though very slowly, and now amounts to about ninety. When, after the political settlement, security is given to the land, and other colonies are founded in the fruitful lands of Transjordania, Bené Yehudah will doubtless take its place among the flourishing Jewish settlements of Palestine, the pioneers of the Return of the long-dispossessed heirs to the Land.

CHAPTER XV

THE ZIONIST IDEA BEFORE THEODORE HERZL

No history of the renaissance of Palestine can be complete without some chapters regarding the growth among the masses in the Diaspora of the movement for the Return, of the preservation through centuries of exile of the longing of the Jewish people for their ancestral land, and of the crystallization during the past two decades of that longing into the Zionist Movement. A history of Zionism, the movement for the Return of the Jews to Palestine, might well comprise a history of the Diaspora. The love, the longing, the passion of the Jew for his motherland, for the home of his people, was not quenched in the blood of the hundreds of thousands of followers of Bar Cochba who were involved in the failure of his rising. Exile, in fact, made it the more intense. The banishment of the Jews from their home, their dispersion among the nations, instead of leading them to forget their origin and their kindred scattered in all the countries of the known world, reminded them of their former state. The miseries of their new condition aroused hopes of a change, to be effected in their own land, with freedom to live their own life. This hope for a return to Zion, which has survived undimmed for almost two thousand years, has been due to a not inconsiderable extent to the attitude adopted towards the Jews by the nations in whose midst they have

THE PRODUCE OF THE LAND

THE WINE HARVEST

Face p. 156

dwelt. At first, for many centuries they were a people apart, entirely outside of the State organization, in the Middle Ages, secluded in ghettoes, marked by badges so that they should be recognized by all, loaded with disabilities—in fact, in many cases possessing no rights whatsoever, aliens and outlaws in every land. The Jews everywhere were driven in upon themselves. No interests were allowed to them outside of Jewry. Assimilation to the larger population was impossible. The Jew who escaped massacre remained a Jew. No third course was possible, except for a few occasional renegades, who were not only religious apostates, but also traitors to their people. The Jews, driven back upon themselves, had recourse to their vast literature, all of which, dealing with many aspects of life, was permeated with that nationalistic outlook with which Judaism as a religion is inextricably intertwined. Throughout those centuries until to-day, wherever the lot of Jewry is a hard one, Judaism is, in fact, Zionism—a longing for release from the present miseries by the restoration to the land of their fathers. It is only in those lands where the Jew is free to live as the equal of his neighbours, and where in consequence the disintegration of Jewry—assimilation— has set in, that Zionism fails to coincide with Judaism. It is there that synagogues have been founded that have no place for Zion or the Restoration in their ritual, and that other congregations are to be found which, while retaining the Zionistic prayers in their services, recite them perfunctorily—merely as an archæological survival. Among the assimilated Jews of Western Europe and America the nationalistic idea has little force. It is in the lands of oppression only, that the prayers for Zion have their full meaning.

The Zionism which has been an integral part of Judaism for the past eighteen centuries has until very recent times been a purely religious hope. Throughout those centuries the Return to Zion has been prayed for, and hoped for, and expected, but not as a result of human foresight or human exertions. It was to come as a miracle, presented to the Jews by a heaven-sent Messiah who was suddenly to appear and to lead them back to Palestine. This was the Zionism which was universal in Jewry for almost the entire period which has elapsed since the destruction of the Jewish State. This longing for Palestine, this unquenchable hope for the Messiah who was to lead them back to their land, permeates the Jewish liturgy. In the very many periods of darkness which are to be found in the history of Jewry during the past eighteen centuries this longing for Palestine is the only spark of light. If it had been quenched Jewry would have disappeared with it, and Jews and Judaism, like the other peoples and faiths of antiquity, would have belonged entirely to the realm of archæology.

Unfortunately for the peace of mind of Jewry, this ceaseless longing for the Messiah led to many false hopes and disappointments. In fact, from the days of Bar Cochba until last century, except for brief intervals, Jewry in one country or another was never without a claimant to Messianic attributes. Every one of these pseudo-Messiahs, no matter how obvious his charlatanry, has had a following. Every one has included the Restoration to Palestine in his programme. Every one without exception has brought misfortunes on his people. Moses of Crete, in the fifth century, led the Jews of the island into the sea, where many of them were drowned. Isaac ben Obadiah, of Ispahan, two centuries later, was, with many of his followers, killed in battle by the army of the Caliph. Serenus, a Syrian, not many years later, admitted when arrested that he had been deluding his followers. David Alroy, the hero of Lord Beaconsfield's Zionistic novel, was killed in battle against the Sultan. His followers had to pay the penalty for the rising. Abraham ben Samuel Abulafia in the thirteenth century actually attempted to convert the Pope to Judaism. The reaction which followed the failure of fulfilment of the prophecies of Nissim ben Abraham, of Avila, led to the adoption of Christianity by many of his deluded followers. Asher Lämmlein, of Istria, at the beginning of the sixteenth century drew disciples from among Christians as well as Jews, but his prophecies were not fulfilled. David Reubeni, the ambassador of the Jewish King of Khaibar to the Portuguese Court, had Messianic attributes thrust upon him against his will, by the suffering Crypto-Jews of Portugal. His contemporary Solomon Molcho, himself one of these Crypto-Jews, claimed to be not the Messiah himself, but his prophet. He gained widespread adhesion to his claims, and even the personal protection of the Pope, Clement VII., not only by his eloquence, his fervour, and his sincerity, but also by the fulfilment of his non-Messianic prophecies. Isaac Luria, in the same century, claimed also to be the forerunner of the Messiah, the greater office being taken to himself by his disciple, Hayyim Vital Calabrese, who had, however, to contend with a rival Messiah in the person of Abraham Shalom. Of all the pseudo-Messiahs, however, the most influential, the one fraught with the most serious consequences to the fortunes of Jewry, was Sabbathai Zevi of Smyrna (1621 or 1626-1676). His claims and adventures affected the politics of Europe. At one period of his romantic career the exchanges of Germany, Holland, and England were idle while the merchants discussed his claims and their possible authenticity. Tributes and embassies came to him from all quarters of the world. His birthday was made a day of rejoicing in the Jewish liturgy. Solemn fast days were abrogated in his honour. The Jews of the East and of the West abandoned their daily work and prepared for the Return to Zion. Prophets arose in all the Jewries of Europe and Asia, and proclaimed Sabbathai as the Messiah. Christians, both in Turkey and in Europe, also accepted his claims. The Protestants of Hamburg appealed to their pastor to direct them in their great emergency. " What will become of the Christian doctrine and the belief in our Messiah ?" they asked. The Sabbathai Messiahship, however, burst like a bubble, pricked by the threat of the Sultan. Sabbathai, in order to save his life, became a Moslem, and the number of his supporters who followed his example almost threatened Turkish Jewry with annihilation. The apostasy of Sabbathai, and even his death nine years later, did not mean the end of the Sabbathaian cult. It was claimed that his Mohammedanism was merely a necessary phase in the career of the Messiah. The controversies that surrounded him continued to divide Jewry for generations after his death, and even to-day in Salonica and Constantinople are to be found the *Dönmeh*, a sect of Moslemized Jews, descended from Sabbathai's followers, to whom his claims still hold something of the truth.

After Sabbathai came many other pseudo-Messiahs, none of whom, however, attained to anything like the notoriety of the prophet of Smyrna. Most prominent among them was Jacob Frank, of Podolia, who ultimately led his followers over to Christianity. As recently as the year 1889 one Joseph Abdallah, a Jew, appeared in Sanaa, in Arabia, and claimed that he had been sent to lead his co-religionists back to the Promised Land.

Contemporary with many of these Jewish pseudo-Messiahs were many Christian millennarians who also looked longingly toward the Restoration of Israel. Those in England during the time of the Commonwealth gave some assistance towards the readmission of the Jews into England. It is also certain that their dreams and prophecies gave some encouragement to the pretensions of Sabbathai Zevi. A few years later Holger Paulli, a Dane who believed himself to be of remote Jewish ancestry, created much excitement in both Jewish and Christian circles on the Continent. Such an one also was an Italian contemporary, Johann Peter Spaeth, who ultimately adopted Judaism.

The religious Zionist was, and is, essentially a man of hope, not of action. To him the Messiah will come and Israel will be restored to his heritage " in God's good time." To attempt to hasten that time would be ineffective; it would be an endeavour to force the hand of Providence—almost a blasphemy. The part of man in the Restoration is confined to hope and prayer. These people naturally expect the restored Jewish State to be a theocracy as in Old Testament times, governed by the Rabbinical Code. Until the nineteenth century—the era of Jewish emancipation—this point of view monopolized the field in Jewish thought. The French Revolution, which broke down the intellectual as well as the physical walls of the ghettoes of Western Europe, however, brought with it a change in the attitude of Jewish thought towards Palestine. In some quarters the result was, as has already been mentioned, to expunge Palestine altogether, either in reality or in effect, from the Jewish liturgy and Jewish thought. For the most part Zionism was quite quiescent. But when Anti-Semitism arose in the lands of the West, and the persecution of the Jews became still more intense in those of the East, the promise of Emancipation, of Liberalism, and of the era of the Rights of Man, was found not to be fulfilled, and the minds of thinkers began again to turn towards Palestine—not, however, as the fulfilment of a distant religious hope, but as a means of solving an insistent political problem, of finding a land of refuge for the victims of persecution.

The practical use of Palestine as a means of solving, or of partly solving, the question of the Jews of Europe had occurred to Napoleon. Whether or not he was sincere in his offer to the Jews of the East cannot be said: they distrusted either his desire or his capacity to fulfil his promises. In France, however, some sympathy was shown with some such project, as is evidenced in a letter to the Jews of France published by one of them, who remained anonymous, in 1798. The proposal of this writer was that the Jews of the world should appoint a representative council to treat with the French Government for the restoration of Palestine to the Jewish people. " The country we propose to occupy shall include (subject to such arrangements as shall be agreeable to France) Lower Egypt, with the addition of a district, which shall have for its limits a line running from Acre to the Dead Sea, and from the south point of that lake to the Red Sea." The writer was the first member of a new school of Zionists. He looked forward to the creation of a State economically independent. " This position," he continued, " which is the most advantageous in the world, will render us, by the navigation of the Red Sea, masters of the commerce of India, Arabia, the south and east of Africa, Abyssinia, and Ethiopia. . . . The neighbourhood of Aleppo and Damascus will facilitate our commerce with Persia; and by the Mediterranean we may communicate with Spain, France, Italy, and the rest of Europe. Placed in the centre of the world, our country will become the entrepôt of all the rich and precious productions of the earth." The writer must not, however, be considered merely a materialist, for in a burst of fervour he concludes: " Oh, my brethren ! What sacrifices ought we not to make to attain this object ? We shall return to our country—we shall live under our own laws—we shall behold those sacred places which our ancestors illustrated with their courage and their virtues. I already see you all animated with a holy zeal. Israelites ! The term of your misfortune is at hand. The opportunity is favourable. Take care you do not allow it to escape." Nevertheless, the letter met with no response. The hour had not yet struck; for Israel was either still in bondage or only just released from it, still incapable of standing upright.

Thirty years later another French Jew, Joseph Salvador, the historian and the intellectual head of French Jewry, asked for the summoning of an international congress in order to restore Jewry to its ancient home. Twelve years previously Mordecai Manuel Noah, perhaps the most distinguished Jew of his day in American public life, had first given public expression to his schemes and hopes for the Restoration of the Jews. " Never were prospects for the restoration of the Jewish nation to their ancient rights and dominion more brilliant than at present. . . . The signal for breaking the Turkish sceptre in Europe will be their emancipation . . . they will assist to establish civilization in European Turkey . . . they will march in triumphant numbers, and possess themselves once more of Syria, and take their rank among the governments of the earth. . . . Let us then hope that the day is not far distant when, from the operation of liberal and enlightened measures, we may look towards that country where our people have established a mild, just, and honourable government, accredited by the world and admired by all good men."

This was only a hope. To assist towards its realization Noah set about establishing a temporary Jewish State, of which he constituted himself " Governor and Judge of Israel," on Grand Island, in the Niagara River. The State, and also the proclamations of its " Governor " to the Jews of the world, were not taken seriously by any of them, and " Ararat," as the new " State " was somewhat contemptuously called, was soon forgotten. Later in life Noah returned to his Zionist dreams. An address on the Restoration of the Jews, which he gave in New York in 1844, he reprinted as a pamphlet the following year. Here again he affirmed his belief that the shape political events were assuming would lead to the consummation he desired. " The political events in Syria, Egypt, Turkey, and Russia indicate the approach of great and important revolutions, which may facilitate the return of the Jews to Jerusalem, and the organization of a powerful government in Judæa, and lead to that millennium which we all look for, all hope for, all pray for." Noah certainly possessed some political foresight, as the following passage—written, it must be remembered, over seventy years ago—shows: "England must possess Egypt, as affording the only secure route to her possessions

in India through the Red Sea; then Palestine, thus placed
between the Russian possessions and Egypt, reverts to
its legitimate proprietors, and for the safety of the
surrounding nations, a powerful, wealthy, independent,
and enterprising people are placed there, by and with
the consent of the Christian Powers, and with their aid
and agency, the land of Israel passes once more into the
possession of the descendants of Abraham. The ports
of the Mediterranean will be again opened to the busy
hum of commerce; the fields will again bear the fruitful
harvest, and Christian and Jew will together on Mount
Zion raise their voices in praise of Him whose covenant
with Abraham was to endure for ever, and in whose
seed all the nations of the earth are to be blessed."

Noah again, despite his earnestness and his eloquence,
failed to get a response. Even the Jews of America
remained cold. Isaac Leeser, the most prominent
American Jewish publicist of the day, discouraged the
project, not because it was impracticable, for the Sultan
would probably grant with readiness the privilege of
holding real estate "and any other requisite to carry
out colonizing Israelites in large numbers in Syria and
Palestine," but because in his opinion the European
Powers would never tolerate an independent State at
the very outlet of the commerce of the Mediterranean
and the Arabian Gulf, commanding the land routes from
north to south, and the sea routes between Asia and
Europe.

In the year 1833 Benjamin Disraeli published his
"Alroy," a Zionist romance, in which the author said
he had portrayed his "ideal ambition." Seven years
later came another call to the Jews from one of their
brethren who has succeeded in preserving his anonymity.

The writer, a German, also sees in the then apparently impending break-up of the Turkish Empire the hope of the Jews: " It needs no extraordinary effort to take possession of Syria, at least under the Egyptian supremacy. If the Servians and Greeks have found protection, why should not we ? . . . France lavishes blood and treasure to civilize Africa; India flourishes under the British sceptre; the hordes of the Mongols learn agriculture under the strong hand of Russia: shall no Government be found to rescue Syria from desolating anarchy, to erect there a school of humanity and civilization for the East ?" This eloquent appeal also seems to have fallen on deaf ears, although the American historian who published it in English a few years later mentioned a probably apocryphal petition presented by thirty thousand Polish Jews to the Czar asking for permission to proceed to Palestine to await the coming of the Messiah, and promising, if three years passed without his advent, to return to Poland and adopt Christianity.

Henceforward Zionist projects appeared more frequently. The middle years of the century saw those of Warder Cresson, the American Consul at Jerusalem, who afterwards became a Jew, taking the name of Michael Boaz Israel, and of Abraham Benisch, the Editor of the *Jewish Chronicle*, and Solomon Sequerra, both of London. Cresson, who found support in England and Germany as well as in the United States, proposed to relieve the existing distress among the Jews of Palestine by employing them on the land, and the oppression of the Jews elsewhere by enabling them to settle in the Holy Land. He was able to commence agricultural work in the Vale of Rephaim, but the support forthcoming was insufficient to put the larger plan into operation, or even to put the smaller one on a permanent basis. Cresson's projects were, however, of considerable educational value, and if they themselves withered even in his lifetime, they left seeds behind which fructified.

Benisch, when a student at the Vienna University, had been one of the founders of a Jewish Students' Society for the Furtherance of the Resettlement of Jews in Palestine, and had come to England in the first instance to gain support for that idea. In this he was not successful, but he settled in England, together with Albert Löwy, one of his colleagues in Vienna. These both in course of time attained to influential positions in the Jewish community, and were able to influence it in many directions to the advantage of their less fortunate coreligionists abroad. The project of Benisch and Sequerra had the support of a committee of English Christians which included John Mills, an author and Calvinistic Methodist minister; William Henry Black, the antiquary; and Sir Hugh Owen, the promoter of Welsh education and philanthropist. Their objects were to settle Jews in Palestine with the grant of local autonomous government, and to develop the land by means of the improvement of roads, harbours, etc. The proposed society intended to seek the support of the British and foreign Governments in their negotiations with the Porte. This project also failed through want of support.

During the following two decades suggestions for the resettlement of the Jews in Palestine were relatively frequent. In 1852 an English political writer published a pamphlet, " Remarks upon the Present Condition of the Jews in Palestine," advocating the creation of a Jewish State, partly in the interests of the British Empire, to safeguard the overland route to India. Of a different character was the advocacy of his contemporary, the great Italian Jewish philologist, poet, and Biblical scholar, Samuel David Luzzatto, who wrote: " Palestine must be peopled by Jews and tilled by them, so that it may flourish economically and agriculturally, and take on beauty and glory."

CHAPTER XVI

THE ERA OF THE " CHOVEVÉ ZION "

HITHERTO these plans and proposals, all tending towards a common object, although often by different means, had been spasmodic, unrelated to one another, even in most cases unconscious of one another's existence. They might almost be termed blind instinctive feelings towards a goal far out of reach of their outstretched hands. From this time forward, however, one begins to see some connexion between the Zionist plans and projects, which multiplied with ever greater frequency. Judah Alkalai, a Croatian Rabbi; Hirsch Kalischer, a Prussian Rabbi; and Moses Hess, a German socialist publicist—all three of whom turned their attention to the Palestinian aspects of the Jewish Question during the first years of the second half of the nineteenth century—were in direct spiritual relationship with one another. Alkalai from 1857 onwards published several treatises advocating the Restoration. His plan was to form a Jewish chartered company which should obtain from the Sultan the cession of Palestine as a tributary State, such as the Danubian principalities (Roumania) then were or the Lebanon is now. From the letters of approval from many eminent Jewish scholars which Alkalai published, the advance which Zionism was at length beginning to make in Jewish public thought was evident.

Kalischer went even further than Alkalai. In his

writings he too advocated with no uncertain note the resettlement of the Jews in Palestine. His plan was the agricultural colonization of Palestine by the wretched Jews of the East. To effect this purpose he proposed to collect funds for the purchase and cultivation of the land, to found a school of agriculture so as to supply experts for the colonies that were to be established, and to form a Jewish military guard for the protection of the latter. Directly from Kalischer's writings, which spread through Germany, came the establishment of Jewish colonization societies for the furtherance of his scheme. Among the Jews of Russia also his writings in Hebrew created for him a band of supporters. Kalischer's ideas, taken up by Charles Netter, led to the establishment by the *Alliance Israélite* of the Jewish Agricultural School at Mikweh Israel. Another fruit of his movement was the foundation of a colony by Kalischer himself near the Sea of Galilee. Kalischer had been offered the office of Rabbi of the Mikweh Israel settlement, but felt compelled, on account of his age, to decline it. His own colony was not a success, and by the short-sighted the whole of his efforts might, with one solitary exception, be considered a failure. The seed he sowed, although it failed to fructify in his own lifetime, did not die in the ground. Fragile and delicate, it yet helped to keep alive the idea which, growing with the years and gaining strength with the generations, ultimately realized the furthest ideals of which Kalischer in his most optimistic moments had dreamt.

Similar views were put forward at this time by David Gordon, the Russo-Jewish journalist—who had, it is interesting to note, lived for a few years in Liverpool— and Elijah Gutmacher. The great intellectual leader of the still inchoate movement in the early sixties was, however, Moses Hess, the socialist free-thinker, who had early abandoned Judaism as a faith, and was in most matters the antithesis of the Rabbi Kalischer. Hess owed his reconversion to Judaism, or his conversion to Zionism, like many another of the leaders of Jewish nationalism, to an outburst of persecution. The Damascus affair of 1840 awakened him to the bitterness of the Jewish agony: the shortcomings of the Liberal movement in Europe opened his eyes to the precariousness of the Jewish position even in civilized lands. At this critical moment in his intellectual career the writings of Kalischer, of Gordon, and of Guttmacher, attracted his attention. The outstanding result of these influences was the publication in 1862 of " Rome and Jerusalem: the Last Nationality Question," wherein Hess indicated his belief that the only solution of the Jewish Question lay in the Resettlement in Palestine. For by the other peoples Jews will always be considered strangers, liable to suffer from the blind prejudice which overcomes the wisest nation at times; and, on the other hand, eighteen hundred years of history and of unexampled suffering had shown that, despite inconceivable persecution, the Jewish race was indestructible. It was for these reasons that Hess saw the only solution of the Jewish Question in the reconstitution of the Jewish nation. The Jew would then still be a stranger among the peoples, but he would be a stranger with a status. And he, the former German of Jewish origin, went so far as to say that if the Jews found social and political emancipation in Europe incompatible with the preservation of their nationality, emancipation would have to be sacrificed. Hess had been settled in France for some years, and he looked to the aid of that nation for the practical solution of the problem. He relied on France to assist the Jews to colonize Palestine, remembering that France and French writers in the past had shown sympathy with such a project.

Two years after the publication of " Rome and Jerusalem," French Jewry itself produced an advocate of Jewish nationalism in the unexpected guise of a banker and politician, Lazar Lévy-Bing, who, on his part, owed his inspiration to a Protestant pastor and professor, Abraham Pétavel, whose pamphlet, " The Duty of the Nations to restore to the Jews their Nationality," created some stir in Jewish circles. Even Bismarck is stated at this time to have given some encouragement to the idea of the restoration of the Jewish State, and in 1880 to have taken some steps in that direction in his private capacity. Far more active in the same direction was Henry Dunant, the founder of the Red Cross Movement and the inspirer of the Geneva Convention, who actually founded an International Palestine Society, and a Syrian and Palestinian Colonization Society, and laboured strenuously in their interests for a period of thirteen years. But he was powerless to overcome the apathy of the Jews of Western Europe, who, immersed in an atmosphere of assimilation, considered the present of supreme importance when compared not only with the past, but also with the future.

A few years before Dunant had abandoned all hope of converting the Jews of Western Europe to his Zionist projects, Perez Smolenskin, a Russo-Jewish man of letters, commenced his literary campaign on behalf of Jewish nationalism. His " Am Olam " (The Eternal People), published in 1873, is his principal work in this campaign, and was also the first Hebrew book in which the Messianic idea was given a purely nationalistic clothing. The fire of Jewish nationalism, kindled by Kalischer and Hess, and fanned by Smolenskin's writings, burnt yet more brightly, and spread yet farther among the Jewish masses. It was still, however, but an ideal, not yet a matter of practical politics. Even in England, in a soil least suited to Jewish idealism, the Jewish national idea was not without some influence. George Eliot, in her " Daniel Deronda," made a stirring appeal to the Jews of the West to resume their duties and their privileges, to form once again a nation that shall lead the van of civilization as their ancestors did of yore. " Let the torch of visible community be lit ! Let the reason of Israel disclose itself in a great outward deed, let there be another great migration, another choosing of Israel to be a nationality whose members may still stretch to the ends of the earth . . . but who will still have a national hearth and a tribunal of national opinion. . . . Let the central fire be kindled again, and the light will reach afar. The degraded and scorned of our race will learn to think of their sacred land . . . as a republic where the Jewish spirit manifests itself in a new order founded on the old, purified, enriched, by the experience our greatest sons have gathered from the life of the ages. . . . The Messianic time is the time when Israel shall will the planting of the national ensign. . . . Let us help to will our own better future and the better future of the world—not renounce the higher gift . . . but choose our full heritage, claim the brotherhood of our nation, and carry it into a new brotherhood with the nations of the Gentiles." But George Eliot was still in advance of the times.

Laurence Oliphant and Edward Cazalet, of whose schemes

mention has been made in a previous chapter, were a little nearer, but an impetus was necessary in order to introduce the spark of actuality into all these Zionist visions, to bring the dreams of the dreamers into relation with life. This impetus was given by the Russian massacres which appalled Europe in the years 1881 and 1882. Incidentally this orgy of barbarism sent back voluntarily into Jewry thousands of her sons, who, warmed by the sun of temporary freedom, had wandered far from her temples, and had been considered by their mother-people as practically lost. Directly or indirectly Leo Pinsker, Moses Lilienblum, Lev Levanda, Asher Ginzberg, Nathan Birnbaum, and, on another plane and in a different hemisphere, Emma Lazarus, were all, as leaders of Zionist thought, products of the atrocities of that terrible year, or owed much of their development to them. The *Chovevé Zion* Movement was born of the same agony of Russian Jewry. Pinsker, a Russian physician and Jewish leader, lulled by the humane government of Alexander II., had trusted to the era of Liberalism, in whose guarantees he believed the future of the Jews of civilization secure. But the year 1881 was a rude awakening for him. Previous to that year Pinsker's public labours had been directed towards the emancipation of the Jews of Russia. Henceforward he recognized that the hope of Jewry rested rather without than within the Russian Empire. His " Auto-Emancipation," published anonymously, crystallized the opinions which circumstances had developed. He did not ask for a Jewish State, but for a " home " for the Jewish people, for Jewish ideals. At first the locale of this home was almost immaterial. It was Judaism and the Bible that had made Palestine

holy, and would make any other land equally holy. He
was soon, however, convinced that Palestine was the only
possible home. He looked to the organization of the
Jewish people to obtain for them a home there. His
first expectation was that the Jewish organizations of
France, Austria, and England would take the lead, but
on second thoughts he considered a body of representatives of Jewry chosen for the definite purpose the more
suitable. Above all, he emphasized the necessity for
a *modus vivendi* with the Porte. The results of Pinsker's
efforts did not fully realize his anticipations. Unable
to attain his larger objects, he contented himself with less.
Out of his teachings grew the *Chovevé Zion* Movement, of
which he became the head in Russia. Compared with
his own schemes, the realization was almost parochial, but
it served to keep alive the Zionist idea, and to prepare
the way for the greater movement which was to follow.
Pinsker died in 1891.

Moses Lilienblum, a Russo-Jewish litterateur, also owed
in effect his conversion to the pogroms of 1881. The
mental course he followed was very similar to that of
Pinsker. As early as 1876 Lilienblum had written in
favour of the acquisition of Palestine for Jewry. The
appearance in the Zionist field of Pinsker definitely
brought Lilienblum under his influence. The latter's
Zionism was more of the heart than of the mind. He
hoped and strove for a mass migration of Jews into
Palestine. Beyond that, to the political and social
problems of the movement, he did not look. Like Pinsker,
Lilienblum became absorbed in the *Chovevé Zion* Movement. He was the secretary of the first Russian committee of which Pinsker was the chairman.

Lev Levanda was also a Russo-Jewish writer, who at

first pinned the whole of his faith to assimilation. He was awakened by the same causes as were Pinsker and Lilienblum, and with them turned to Palestine as the land of hope for Jewry.

Isaac Rülf was another disciple of Pinsker. He was a German Rabbi and author who had been educated at German Universities, a type very different from that of his three contemporaries, and the first non-Russian to come under the influence of the new movement. This was probably due to his residence at Memel, the German window which looked on to the miseries of Russian Jewry. The Jews of Russia had been fired by the writings of Pinsker and Lilienblum. Their hopes had once again been rescued from the depths of despair. But the emotion which swept through Jewry was confined to the Russian dominions. Several causes contributed to this. The writings of Lilienblum were in a language practically unknown to the Jews of Western Europe, and therefore did not touch them. The latter also, having enjoyed political and social freedom for a generation or more, were already on the road to assimilation. For the Jews of Russia they recommended the political panacea which seemingly had solved their own troubles. To them the ideal was to turn the Russian Jews into Russians of the Jewish persuasion. In such a solution Palestine has no place. Above all, the acquaintance of the Western Jews with Jewish suffering was for the most part only theoretical, and as the Russian Jews well knew, " Things seen are mightier than things heard." Thus the teachings of " Auto-Emancipation " had not yet penetrated into Europe. Rülf, whose circumstances were exceptional, was the first channel through which they were to do so. Nathan Birnbaum was the founder of the " Kadimah," a Jewish nationalist society, among the Jewish students at Vienna University. It was the first outpost of the movement outside of Eastern Europe, and served to form a direct connexion between the Zionism of the early eighties and the later Zionism which Theodore Herzl was to bring into existence.

One seed of the Russian movement was caught up by the wind and wafted across Europe and the Atlantic, to drop in New York, there to sprout and blossom. Emma Lazarus was an American poetess of some success, who, in consequence primarily of her home surroundings, was practically estranged from Judaism, or, rather, had no interest in it. In this condition she continued until the age of thirty-two. The arrival in America of the first batches of Russo-Jewish refugees, however, aroused a consciousness that after all had hitherto only been dormant. In helping to receive on American soil the wretched fugitives, and in tending those of them who were weak and fainting, she discovered her kinship with Jewry. Henceforth she abandoned all other subjects than Jewish for her pen. She turned to the Bible, to the Hebrew language, to Judaism, and to Jewish history, and although she lived only another five years, those years were filled with the Jewish spirit. Her transition into Jewish nationalism was easy, and not surprising, and in a series of " Epistles to the Hebrews " she openly advocated an independent Jewish nationality and the re-settlement of the Jews in Palestine.

Of the coterie of Jewish thinkers who led the van in the Zionist revival of the early eighties, the last place has been kept for Asher Ginzberg, better known under his pen-name of Achad Ha'Am (One of the People), not because he was the least important of the company, but,

on the contrary, because in foresight and in statesmanship
he towered over almost all of his contemporaries, and
above all because, being younger than his fellow-workers,
he survived them all and is to-day one of the leaders,
although he holds no office, of the Zionist Movement.
His Zionist activities date from a somewhat later period
than those with whom he first co-operated. In 1884
Ginzberg first joined the committee of the *Chovevé Zion*.
After a few years' experience of this body he became
convinced that it did not altogether fulfil the objects
which he had in view. It was degenerating into a mere
colonization society, and gradually losing that spirit
which had originally inspired it. In order to restore
the ideal to the higher level which its founders had
given to it, Ginzberg formed the " Bené Mosheh," or
" Sons of Moses," an association of men who were to be
trained to become leaders of the Palestinian Movement,
who were to be an inspiration to one another "and a
help in communicating their own feelings to the people,"
so that in the course of time they might succeed in " in-
fusing their spirit into the people at large, and in restoring
those moral qualities to it without which a people cannot
exist as such."

The " Bené Mosheh " were never many in number, and
they did not succeed in their principal intention of raising
the *Chovevé Zion* Movement as a whole to a higher plane.
Their influence, if not immediate, was perhaps all the
surer on that account. The Association existed for eight
years, until 1897. During that period from the " Bené
Mosheh " came the inspiration for several of the most
useful and permanent institutions that the *Chovevé Zion*
produced. The model colony of Rechoboth, the Carmel
Wine Company, a school at Jaffa, the Hebrew Publication

Society " Ahiasaf," and the Hebrew periodical *Ha Shiloach*—all owe most, if not all, of their usefulness and success to Asher Ginzberg and those who gathered round him. In the meanwhile, by means of his Hebrew writings, he was rising to the forefront among Hebrew men of letters, and ultimately to the position of the foremost master of living Hebrew—a position which he has held for years. He soon acquired, too, a leading position among Jewish philosophers, and in the Zionist Movement he has for long been the greatest thinker. His subsequent history, however, belongs to the period of Herzl's Zionism.

From this period until the advent of Herzl, the history of Zionism is practically the history of the *Chovevé Zion* Movement, of which a sketch has already been given. The recrudescence of intense Jewish suffering in the East of Europe in 1890 was one of the principal causes that led to the presentation of a memorial to the President of the United States by many of the leading citizens of that country, asking him to use his influence with the European Powers so that an international conference to consider the condition of the Jews in Eastern Europe, and the expediency of creating a country and a home for them in Eastern Palestine, might be convened. But the condition of the Jews of Eastern Europe was then outside of the purview of diplomacy, and of course nothing resulted. Five years later, almost simultaneously with the publication of Herzl's epoch-making " Jewish State," Holman Hunt, who had himself lived in Palestine and was intimate with its Jewish inhabitants as well as with many Jewish friends in Europe, issued an appeal to the Jews to recover the Holy Land and to inhabit it. He advocated no conquest, but the purchase of the land from the Sultan.

He looked forward to the time when, under Jewish auspices, " the places desolated by bad government should be restored, aqueducts rebuilt, the land made fruitful, harbours constructed, new appliances used to develop riches, and all intelligent energy exercised, and this revivifying should be carried on to such perfection that all other well-ordered territories, grand with beautiful cities, should be in comparison the work of mere apprentice hands, while the principles of morals and religion should be so perfected that previous systems should seem but the scattered pieces of a puzzle—put together at last to show the hitherto unguessed harmony of the pattern."

Holman Hunt advocated the acquisition of Palestine by the Jews, not only in their own interest, but also in that of Europe and of civilization. Writing twenty years ago, he foresaw that " left as it is, Palestine will soon become a direful field of contention to the infernally armed forces of the European Powers, so that it is calculated to provoke a curse to the world of the most appalling character. Russia and Greece will contend for the interests of the Greek Church, France and Italy for the Latin, Prussia and Austria for the German political interests. . . . In addition to the above-named certain contenders for Palestine, there would be England, for I have been assured by military authorities that our Government could never consent to the land going into the hands of the other Great Powers, since this has, during all its history, been essential to the holders of Egypt." Anglo-Jewry as a whole was deaf to this appeal, and once more no visible result was forthcoming.

CHAPTER XVII

THEODORE HERZL

SUCH was the position to which the Zionist idea had arrived when a new era opened with the publication of " The Jewish State " by Theodore Herzl. Herzl, an Austrian journalist, Parisian by domicile, was apparently, both by birth and education, almost as far removed from Judaism and Jewish ideals as it is possible to be without formally abandoning all connexion with Jewry. He was the supreme type of the assimilated Jew who holds back only from the last step of baptism. To no man better than to Herzl before 1896 was the designation Austrian or Parisian of Jewish race more appropriate. Apart from the accident of ancestry, a matter in which he was merely a passive force, until 1896 Herzl was in no sense a Jew.

The cause of the sudden awakening of the Jewish spirit in the popular Parisian feuilletonist is uncertain. It was, of course, always within him, although latent. No member of a people with three thousand years of heroic history behind it can ever be devoid of that race consciousness, of that pride in the past and corresponding hope in the future, which together go to make up the indefinable feeling of nationality. It may be latent: in most Jews, especially those who live under conditions of freedom, it is latent; in many it has been deliberately suppressed in the mistaken idea that it is incompatible with loyalty to the State and country to which they belong, in which their homes and interests lie. Jewish nationalism is in reality in no sense incompatible with, for instance, the loyalty of the English Jew to England, any more than, as has been aptly pointed out, the loyalty of a Scotsman to Britain is suspect because of his devotion to his own particular portion of the United Kingdom. Against the Jewish nationalist less than against any other description of nationalist can the suggestion of disloyalty to the object of his allegiance be brought with propriety. His nationalism is in no sense aggressive : it seeks no political independence : it covets no territory : all it asks is freedom to live its own life, to develop on its own lines. But it is essential that the Power which shall include Palestine within its dominions shall understand the Jewish ideal and be sympathetic towards it; that it shall leave the Jew free to fulfil his own destiny in Palestine, while it protects him against all external aggressors. The Jewish people, for its part, living once again as a people in its own land, will continue its Divinely appointed work, which, although impeded and sorely threatened with destruction many a time during the past twenty centuries, has never ceased since the Jewish people were first driven into exile. The destruction of Judaism or Jewry in one centre has merely led to the creation of a centre in another land.

Herzl himself said that the Judaism that was innate in him, as in all other Jews, was awakened when his boy began to pass out of childhood. For himself the problem of Jewry was not a living one, nor did it become so even when his child was born. But when he saw that child growing towards manhood, he began to see also that the future of his child was involved in the future of their people.

It has also been suggested that the wave of active anti-Semitism which overran Liberal Austria in the nineties of last century reacted on Herzl, who, like many another assimilated Jew overtaken by similar circumstances, found himself brought much closer to his distressed kinsmen. The orgies of anti-Semitic prejudice which centred around the figure of Captain Dreyfus in that democratic France which had been the pioneer of Jewish emancipation in the modern world, were also not without their influence on the detached thinker who was living in the midst of them. It is probable that all these forces combined to make of Herzl a Jewish nationalist and the founder of a new school of Zionism.

While the idea which afterwards crystallized into " The Jewish State " was agitating Herzl early in 1895, he sought an interview with Baron de Hirsch, the great philanthropist who had created the Jewish Colonization Association and endowed it with millions for the purpose of relieving the misery of the Jews of Eastern Europe, for the most part by means of emigration. But Herzl's proposal for the creation of a Jewish self-governing colony did not find any sympathy with Baron Hirsch. No locale for the desired settlement seems to have been decided at the time of this interview. Four years previously, however, in negotiations with the *Chovevé Zion*, Hirsch had offered his services in any negotiations that might be opened with the Turkish Government in the direction of the systematic Jewish colonization of Palestine; but he gave the representatives of the *Chovevé Zion* no room for misunderstanding that his own colonies in South America had the first and by far the greatest claim on his interest.

Herzl at first did not admit any particular claim on

the part of Palestine to be the new Jewish land. The locale was to him an open question. It might be in Palestine and it might just as well be in South America or elsewhere. With him the great point was that if Jewry was to continue to exist, there must be a Jewish State somewhere. The only alternative was complete assimilation, and the Jews did not desire assimilation, nor would it be permitted by the nations. The creation of a Jewish State was the programme put forward in " The Jewish State," in which the scheme was elaborated in such detail that even the particulars of the national flag were given. Jewry was to be organized through a " Society of Jews," the instrument of which was to be a chartered company, founded in accordance with the laws of England. It is probable that Herzl was unacquainted with the writings of Hess, Pinsker, Lilienblum, and the other pioneers of Zionism: otherwise his own proposals would have shown their influence. Moreover, when he sat down to write his " Jewish State," and even when he published it, it does not seem that he had any intention of leading a practical movement.

Events were, however, stronger than he had anticipated. Within a few months of the publication of the book he happened to be in Sofia, where he was welcomed by deputations of the local Jews, who hailed him as a leader in Israel. Almost simultaneously the Viennese Students' Society, the *Kadimah,* which had been founded by Nathan Birnbaum, approached him with a direct offer of support, and proposed the foundation of a Society of Jews such as he had sketched. The headquarters of the Society were to be in London, almost the only great European capital which was free from the poison of anti-Semitism, in whose Jewish population it was thought a ready adhesion to the new nationalism would be obtained. Even before that Herzl had seen the Sultan, by invitation, and had submitted his proposals to the Porte. His scheme was not unfavourably received. The position in Constantinople was then somewhat critical in consequence of the recent massacres of Armenians which had re-echoed far and wide throughout Europe. The Sultan apparently felt the necessity for rehabilitating himself in the sight of Europe, and, independently of his conversations with Herzl, had sent an emissary to London to secure the supposed influence of the Anglo-Jewish leaders with the British Government in return for the grant of considerable concessions in Palestine. The British Jews, however, apart altogether from the question of approving any Palestinian project, declined any such bargain with the Sultan.

Meanwhile a direct invitation to put his views before the Anglo-Jewish public had been conveyed to Herzl by Mr. Israel Zangwill, on behalf of the *Maccabæans*, a society of Anglo-Jewish professional men. Herzl addressed the *Maccabæans* early in July, 1896. His reception was disappointing. The welcome accorded to the man was enthusiastic; but the enthusiasm was not extended to his proposals, although they were generally supported by Holman Hunt in London and by Max Nordau in Paris. A meeting of the Jewish masses held a week later in the East of London, under the auspices of the *Kadimah* and other Zionist societies, gave a far heartier welcome to the project. Nevertheless, Herzl was deeply disappointed with the results of his visit. He had sought the co-operation of the leaders of Anglo-Jewry. With very few exceptions they held aloof.

Incidentally the rise of Herzl's movement led to the

absorption of the *Chovevé Zion* in England, and, in fact, everywhere but in Russia. The principal function of the *Chovevé Zion* had been the gradual colonization of Palestine without much heed to the political conditions. The outstanding feature of Herzl's movement was, however, political, and in his view, until political security was forthcoming there should be no question of further colonization. The land certainly needed development, but all development should be stayed until the charter which Herzl sought, and which would secure to the colonists the fruits of their labours, was forthcoming. The new movement was therefore regarded as antagonistic to the old. Nevertheless, the *Chovevé Zion*, in England at any rate, might have continued its activities as a separate organization, if its supporters themselves had not split into two parties. Of these the one, composed for the most part of the larger foreign element, gave their adherence at once to the movement at whose head Herzl was. The other, representative of the native and wealthier section in the community, dismayed by Herzl's political schemes, abandoned all connexion with work in or on behalf of Palestine.

The *Chovevé Zion* organization did not succumb immediately after Herzl's visit to England. It lingered for yet another two years, but from the day of that visit its days were numbered. In common with its allied societies in France and Germany the English *Chovevé Zion* felt compelled to refuse Herzl's invitation to the Congress of representatives of Jewry which he convened in the spring of 1897. It did so with sincere regret, for it felt that the objects of the two organizations were one, even though their means differed. It felt the attraction the new Movement had for its adherents, and seems to have recognized the perilous condition into which it was passing. It did not, however, allow itself to pass out of existence without an effort to survive. In order to retain the interest of its members, the English *Chovevé Zion* decided to hold half-yearly conferences. The first of these, with an extensive programme, was held in March, 1898. At its conclusion the meeting, contrary to the wishes of its conveners, resolved to combine with Herzl's movement, and with that resolution the *Chovevé Zion* in England came to an end.

This is, however, anticipating somewhat. Long before the end of the year 1896 the schemes promulgated in the " Jewish State " had spread far and wide throughout the Diaspora, and had everywhere secured the adhesion of a people eager to become converts. During the quarter of a century since the day of Pinsker and his colleagues a great change had come over the Jewish situation. In their time persecution of the Jews had been practically confined to the backward lands. In Central and Western Europe the Jew was, except for a few isolated instances, as little subject to danger or discomfort as his Christian fellow-citizen. There was then some justification for the contention that Parliamentary government and anti-Semitism are incompatible, and if that had been so, the solution of the Jewish Question in Eastern Europe would have been only a matter of time. During the last three decades of the nineteenth century, however, anti-Semitism had flourished and spread throughout Europe. A democratic form of government had proved itself no bar to the adoption and diffusion of the prejudice. In Germany, Austria, Hungary, and France, active anti-Jewish prejudice had become a living and apparently permanent feature in social and political life. Those who despaired of solution by means of civil emancipation had also, therefore, some justification. And many of those who despaired turned to Herzl as the leader of the new exodus. The new Movement did not make, however, only friends. As its objects crystallized, so did its critics grow in number. There were the assimilated in Western Europe who clung to the belief that political emancipation was the only solution of the Jewish Question, and in whom the fear was aroused that the proposal to establish a Jewish State would endanger the security that the Jews of the Diaspora already possessed. There were the extreme adherents of traditional Judaism who prayed night and day for the restoration to Zion, but awaited the bidding of the Messiah before they were willing to take the first step. To them the Zionist Movement was almost blasphemous; its wickedness was, if possible, enhanced by Herzl's proposal to create a secular State, whose inhabitants would be free to adopt whatever form of religion they preferred. There were also the Reform Jews, who had carefully excised all references to the Messiah and the Return to Zion from their ritual, who lived in the present and perhaps the future, but to whom the past was entirely blotted out. To them Germany or America, never Palestine, was Zion. Above all, there was that school of Jewish thought which held the view that the mission of Judaism can be performed only by Jews scattered among the nations, and that a concentration in Palestine or elsewhere would tend to retard rather than to forward that mission. Among none of these did Herzl find adherents. On the other hand, opposition was encountered from all of them in turn.

The Zionist Movement with Herzl at its head was now

well under way. A Press organ, *Die Welt*, had been
established in Vienna by Herzl at his own expense, but
the movement had neither organization nor funds. The
necessity to meet and consult with representatives of
his adherents scattered throughout the countries of the
civilized world was obvious. It was first intended to
hold a Congress at Munich, but the local Jewish leaders
were so hostile to the proposal that the project was
abandoned and Basle was chosen instead as the scene of
the first gathering of Zionists from all parts of the world.
The first Zionist Congress opened on the 29th of August,
1897, when two hundred and four delegates were present.
They came from almost every country in Europe, as well
as from the United States and Palestine. The best-
known of them were Max Nordau, from Paris; Mr.
Zangwill, from London; M. Ussischkin, a prominent
member of the Odessa Committee; Professor Mandelstamm, of Kieff; and Dr. N. Birnbaum, the founder of
the *Kadimah*. A few non-Jews, including M. Dunant,
the founder of the Red Cross Society, were also present.
The Government of the Canton of Basle extended its
hospitality to the Congress, which was attended by a
representative of the Turkish Government, who had been
instructed to submit his report to Herzl before forwarding
it to Constantinople. The enthusiasm of the gathering
was tumultuous. Strangers embraced one another.
Strong men shed tears of emotion at the thought that at
length, after the lapse of nearly two thousand years,
Jewry had once again gathered together in preparation
for the march home to Zion. No hero ever received a
greater ovation than did the leader of the new movement.
At the conclusion of the meetings the parting between
him and many of his newly-found followers and friends was

most affectionate. Delegate parted from delegate with the time-honoured Jewish wish—" Next year in Jerusalem."

At this Congress a Zionist organization was duly constituted. The government was to be vested in a congress representative of shekel-payers—*i.e.*, supporters of the cause who contributed at least a shekel* (in England a shilling) a year. The Congress was to elect an Executive Committee to carry out the resolutions of the Congress, to conduct the business of the movement until the next Congress is held, and to make the preparations for that Congress. The Executive Committee was to be representative of all countries, but it was to act for the greater part through a committee of five residents in Vienna, who were to be elected by the Congress. The outstanding result of the Congress was the adoption of the following programme:

> Zionism strives to create for the Jewish people a home in Palestine secured by public law. The Congress contemplates the following means to the attainment of this end: (1) The promotion, on suitable lines, of the colonization of Palestine by Jewish agricultural and industrial workers. (2) The organization and binding together of the whole of Jewry by means of appropriate institutions, local and international, in accordance with the laws of each country. (3) The strengthening and fostering of Jewish national sentiment and consciousness. (4) Preparatory steps towards obtaining Government consent, where necessary, to the attainment of the aim of Zionism.

It will be noticed that, advancing on Herzl's original proposals, the future home for the Jewish people was fixed definitely in Palestine. The Congress also declared

* The unit of coinage in the Jewish State.

the necessity of creating a Jewish National Fund, and appointed a committee to consider the position of Hebrew as a living language.

The Congress at Basle gave a great impetus to the movement for the re-creation of a centre of Judaism in Palestine. The adherents of the movement increased manifold. New societies sprang into existence in all parts of the world. Within a few months every country of Europe had its Zionists organized in societies. Every town in Galicia had its separate society. Roumanian Jewry also counted its Zionist societies by the score. In New York the fifteen Zionist societies had already formed a federation, and steps were immediately taken to federate all the societies in the United States. Before the end of the year three other subsidiary conferences had been held, one at Frankfurt, a second at Kieff, and the third at Lemberg. In Canada, even in Australia and India, Jewry was engaged in forming Zionist societies. Almost equal interest was being aroused outside of Jewish circles. The Congress at Basle was noticed, in most instances sympathetically, by the Press of the entire world. Important English papers even suggested the convening of an international congress to consider the Jewish Question.

Ten Congresses have since been held, of which six were at Basle. The fourth, in 1900, was held in London; the eighth, in 1907, at the Hague; the ninth, in 1909, at Hamburg; and the eleventh, in 1913, at Vienna. At the second Congress the number of delegates was double that at its predecessor. The Rabbis, who had for the most part kept aloof from the earlier meeting, were now represented, having in many instances been satisfied that the new movement contained nothing contrary to the traditional teachings of Judaism. More of the representative men of Jewry also attended this Congress. These new-comers included Bernard Lazare, the French publicist; Dr. M. Gaster, Chief Rabbi of the Sephardi Jews of England; Rabbi Isaac Rülf, one of the pioneers of the eighties; and Professor Richard Gottheil, of New York. All the countries of Europe again sent delegates, and in addition South Africa, Egypt, and South America were represented. The number of societies represented at the Congress fell just short of a thousand. At this Congress it was decided to establish a financial instrument of the movement. This took the form of the Jewish Colonial Trust, a foreign banking business, with headquarters in London.

During the subsequent years Herzl continued his diplomatic activities with a view to securing a charter guaranteeing the rights of autonomy to a Jewish settlement in Palestine. In 1903 he was in St. Petersburg, where he obtained from the anti-Semitic Minister of the Interior, Plehve, a promise to withdraw the prohibition on Zionist activities in Russia. The previous year he had been in London, where, as a witness before the Royal Commission on Alien Immigration, he diagnosed the ills from which Jewry was suffering. He was received with much, real or apparent, sympathy by the German Emperor during his visit to Jerusalem in November, 1908, and by the King of Italy and the Pope some years after. Throughout this period he had repeated interviews with the Sultan, which are believed to have been replete with promises, but lacking in performance.

The fourth Congress was held in London in August, 1900, partly with the intention of interesting the leaders of the Anglo-Jewish Community in a Movement which had by now become a part of life to a large portion of the

Jewish population of the Continent. The English leaders, however, kept carefully aloof from it. Their view of Zionism may be summed up in the words of the *Jewish Chronicle*, their press organ, as " ill-considered, retrogressive, impracticable, and even dangerous." If the movement failed to attract the leaders of Anglo-Jewry, it secured the adhesion of the masses in the poorer districts, most of whom had either themselves come as refugees from the Continent or were in close communication with relatives and friends who had not been able to escape. It moreover attracted favourable notice in far more influential circles, not directly as a consequence of the London Congress, but undoubtedly partly in consequence of the trains of thought that that Congress excited. In the first place Lord Rothschild, the head of the Anglo-Jewish Community, whose heart was ever ready to melt at the sorrows of his widely-scattered people, failing to foresee any benefit to them from Herzl's proposals, had declined to give him the slightest encouragement. Personal contact with the magnetic personality of the Zionist leader, which the Aliens Commission of which Lord Rothschild was a member had given, was not without its effect on Lord Rothschild's attitude towards the man, even though his attitude towards his policy remained apparently unchanged. Shortly after Herzl's evidence had been given before the Royal Commission, he again returned to England as the guest of Lord Rothschild, but social intercourse did not soften the host's opposition to the political schemes of Zionism. In the years that intervened between those meetings and the end of the life of the leader of Anglo-Jewry, the Zionist Movement itself underwent a great change. External and internal circumstances combined to push the political aspect farther and farther into the background—in fact, ultimately almost to deprive the movement of its political complexion. At the same time Lord Rothschild appears to have grown more and more sympathetic towards the Zionist ideals. When at length he died in 1915 almost suddenly, but full of years, little indeed still separated him from those into whose hands the anxious heritage of Herzl had passed.

Lord Rothschild, influential as he was, was by no means the most influential of English public men on whom the Zionist hopes and efforts had some effect. The influence, possibly unconscious, of six years of the Zionist Movement, and perhaps the more insistent influence of Herzl's appearance before the Royal Commission, gave to the suggestion, which was made to the British and the Anglo-Egyptian Governments towards the end of the year, of a Jewish autonomous settlement in the district of El Arish in Egyptian territory on the Asiatic side of the Suez Canal—in effect, in the southernmost portion of Palestine—a reality that might otherwise have been wanting. The two Governments were quite agreeable to the proposed form of government if a settlement should ever eventuate. In the meanwhile an exploring commission on which the Egyptian Government was represented was sent to El Arish by the Zionist headquarters. The report of the commission was never published, and no action was taken upon it. It was said that the land was found unsuitable for an agricultural settlement of any size. It is also possible that the British and Egyptian Governments, for strategic reasons, preferred to retain a desert as a barrier between the Turkish and the Egyptian dominions, and the settlement of the El Arish district by a population likely to restore it to civilization was discouraged so long as Palestine remained in possibly hostile hands. The El Arish project failed to materialize, but it led direct to the offer to Jewry, as represented by the Zionist organization, of a territory in British East Africa for a self-governing Jewish settlement, the first occasion in modern history on which the Jews have received official recognition as a national entity by a European Power.

Before this time had arrived, although the number of supporters of the Zionist Movement had grown from year to year, the enthusiastic devotion with which the leader had at first been hailed was no longer unanimous. Criticism, assisted somewhat by the impatience of those who had expected the Return to Palestine to start from the first Congress at Basle, found its tongue. The apparent failure of Herzl's original project led to the suggestion of alternatives, such as Cyprus, which on their part led to opposition. The cessation of all activity in Palestine, pending the granting of a charter by the Sultan—for Herzl was opposed to the development of the country until its occupation by Jews was secure—annoyed the *Chovevé Zion*, who were still strong, especially in Russia. On the other hand, there was still a party, which shared the original views of the author of " The Jewish State," to which the locale of the State was for the most part a matter of indifference, and to whom the form of government was the chief concern. This party, also disappointed at the failure to secure any tangible concession from the Sultan, was believed to be not indisposed to negotiate for a land outside of Palestine. To their views the orthodox Zionists showed a passionate opposition. There were thus parties and cross-currents in the Zionist Movement, and in the meanwhile the first exuberant optimism had passed away.

CHAPTER XVIII

THE EAST AFRICAN PROJECT, AND AFTER

THE offer of a territory in British East Africa for a self-governing Jewish State was made on the direct initiative of Joseph Chamberlain, then Secretary of State for the Colonies. He had been acquainted with the El Arish project, with which he had every sympathy. The abandonment of that project came immediately before his visit to South Africa, on the way to which he turned aside to traverse Uganda. On the journey from the coast to that Central African territory Chamberlain passed through a region, part of the British Empire, apparently well adapted for European settlement and yet practically uninhabited. With the Jewish Question fresh in his mind; anxious, on humane grounds, to assist in relieving the misery of the Jewish people; and doubtless desirous also of identifying the British name with a departure that might well prove a turning-point in human history; above all, with true statesmanlike instinct, wishing to incorporate into the mosaic of the British Empire an element whose prospective value would be so considerable as that of a Jewish dominion—the idea of including in the ultimate British Federation a Jewish state seized his heart, his imagination, and his sense of statesmanship. British East Africa did not fall within the sphere of the Colonial Office. It would not therefore fall to Chamberlain to translate his idea into formal proposals.

He referred the matter to the Foreign Office, at the head of which was Lord Lansdowne. There the proposal met with as much sympathy as if it had remained in the hands of Chamberlain himself.

The East African project formally entered the sphere of practical politics on the 14th of August, 1903, when a letter was sent by the Foreign Office to Mr. L. J. Greenberg, a prominent English Zionist, who had been closely connected with the El Arish negotiations. This letter, after stating that Lord Lansdowne had " studied the question with the interest which His Majesty's Government must always take in any well-considered scheme for the amelioration of the position of the Jewish race," proceeded to lay down in general terms the conditions of the offer of a territory. Lord Lansdowne " would be prepared to discuss . . . the details of a scheme comprising as its main features the grant of a considerable area of land, the appointment of a Jewish official as the chief of the local administration, and permission to the colony to have a free hand in regard to municipal legislation, and as to the management of religious and purely domestic matters, such local autonomy being conditional upon the right of His Majesty's Government to exercise general control."

Herzl was in a difficult position. His efforts had resulted in an offer by the British Government of everything for which the organization of which he was the head was striving, except that the land which was offered had neither religious nor historical sentiment behind it. Herzl had long before been educated by his associates into the opinion that the soul of the Zionist Movement was the craving of the Jewish people for Palestine. He had once looked at the question as little more than one of

social economics, and the offer of the British Government
then would, to his mind, have solved the whole problem.
Lord Lansdowne and his colleagues were, in fact, in 1903
in the mental position which Herzl had occupied when
eight years earlier he wrote " The Jewish State." Herzl
therefore knew that the acceptance of the East African
offer would mean no settlement of the Jewish Question.
On the other hand, the need of the Jewish people was
urgent. The sixth Zionist Congress was held in the
midst of a period of externally induced suffering for the
Jewish people. The offer was so generous, so unprece-
dented, that one would well hesitate and hesitate again
lest its rejection might not prove an act of treason to
the Jewish people. Herzl decided to accept it, subject
to the territory being found suitable for European
settlement, a condition which the British Government
had already accepted, not as the end of the Zionist efforts,
but as a half-way house, a stepping-stone to Palestine, a
land in which the Jewish people might serve the apprenticeship of self-government, preparatory to entering
into their ancient heritage. This was the proposal
which he hoped to persuade the Congress to accept.

Herzl did not, however, even yet realize the strength
of the Palestinian sentiment among his followers. All
were unanimous in their gratitude to the British Government, but the opposition to the proposed abandonment, even only temporary and partial, of the Zionist
ideal was keen. The Russian delegates, who, one might
have expected, would have welcomed almost any land of
refuge, were practically unanimous in their opposition
to the proposal. The parties among the other national-
ities were more evenly divided. In England Dr. Gaster
and Dr. Weizmann were pure Zionists. Mr. Herbert

Bentwich, who thought with them, carried the Order of Ancient Maccabæans, one of the two principal English Zionist institutions, with him. On the other hand, Mr. Zangwill and Mr. Greenberg were in favour of the acceptance of the offer. Max Nordau agreed with Mr. Zangwill. Ultimately a compromise resolution, which in effect committed no one to any decision, was adopted, but the opposition of a large section of the Palestinian party even to this was intense. The resolution was to the effect that a commission of investigation, as suggested by the British Government, should be sent to East Africa to ascertain whether the country was suitable for the purpose to which it was proposed to devote it; that the cost of the commission should not come out of Zionist funds, but should be specially provided from private sources; and that on the presentation of the Commission's report to the next Congress, to be expressly convened for the purpose, a decision should be taken whether to accept or decline the British offer. This Congress was held in the following year, but in the meanwhile Herzl had died, a self-sacrifice to the cause of his people.

Theodore Herzl, the re-creator of Jewish nationalism, one of those very occasional leaders whom the Jews of all lands accept, died on the 4th of July, 1904, at the premature age of forty-four years. He was the one universal Jew of his age, the unique personification of the Jewish spirit that it had possessed since the death of Sir Moses Montefiore. Half of the Jewish race called him Master and owed to him the revival of the Jewish hope. Thousands of Jewish homes, the humblest in the Diaspora, in Russia, in Roumania, in Galicia, in the United States, and in a score of other countries, possessed and treasured the portrait of the Viennese journalist. Into these dwellings, the abodes of the most wretched of God's creatures, Herzl came with a message that lit up the gloom and replenished the oil in the lamp that was about to perish of exhaustion. The cumulative pressure of two thousand years of persecution and of oppression had almost extinguished the last glimmer of the brilliant light created by Israel's prophets and tended by the Jewish poets and prophets of succeeding generations. So many centuries had passed since the Restoration to Zion was first promised, the experiences of the Wandering Jew had been so bitter throughout that long-drawn agony, that history was beginning to merge into legend; and the reality contrasting so painfully with the hope, the annual cry at the celebration of the Passover, " Next year in Jerusalem !" had become more and more a mere formula. It was at this juncture that Herzl arose and gave to the eternal movement for the Return to Zion a strong practical impulse. It was he who brought Israel back into the family of the nations. Out of a number of widely scattered fragments, sundered one from another by distance, by interests, by culture, by surroundings, by sentiment, he formed again a nation. He re-created the Jewish consciousness and made every Jew feel his kinship with his fellow-Jews. The Zionist Movement has been great enough to bring into its fold Jews of every complexion, religious and physical. From every corner of the earth, in innumerable garbs, Jews of every country made the annual pilgrimage to the Congress over which Herzl was wont to preside, and where he was accustomed to conduct the deliberations of a cosmopolitan gathering three-quarters of whom were often totally unacquainted with the language in which they were being addressed, and for whose benefit every speech had to be translated into four languages. With him year after year, they repeated the abjuration of the psalmist: " If I forget thee, O Jerusalem, may my right hand forget its cunning !" Jews of every variety of belief and want of belief ranged themselves around him. The superstition-tinged extremists of the East and the assimilated Sunday-service Jews of the West, the Karaite rejectors of traditional Judaism—representatives of the earliest schism in Jewry in the Christian era—and the Talmudolaters, joined with the agnostics of the Jewish race, all imbued, however, with the Jewish spirit and brought together in the furtherance of the one ideal. In the course of eight years Herzl created the Jewish nation and secured its recognition by the rulers of most of the Great Powers of Europe, and then he died at the age of forty-four, sacrificing his life as he had already sacrificed his fortune, to the Cause the furtherance of which was his legacy to the Jewish people.

The *Chovevé Zion* element in the Zionist Movement was very prominent in the opposition to the East African project. They had become restless even before the British offer was known, and simultaneously with the holding of the sixth Congress at Basle, there was held in Palestine a *Chovevé Zion* Congress, under the chairmanship of M. Ussischkin, a Russian Zionist leader, who had been prominent in the counsels of the *Chovevé Zion* before the advent of Herzl. This Palestinian Congress recommended the formation of a permanent body, representative of Palestinian colonization interests, Zionist and non-Zionist, which would in effect have been a rival to Herzl's organization. To these Palestinian enthusiasts the colonization of Palestine, not the political and tactical movements which Herzl favoured, was both

the means and the goal. A few months after the holding
of the sixth Congress, the majority of the prominent
Russian Zionists convened a Russian Congress at Charkow,
which formed an organization of their own within the
movement, designed to safeguard the Palestinian ideal.
This Charkow conference threatened a sort of revolt
against Herzl's rule. It helped to organize the forces
which were opposed to the East African project, and
might ultimately have acquired a commanding position
in the general Movement if events had not marched into
quite an unexpected direction. In January of 1905
another conference of Russian Zionists, held at Wilna,
strongly supported the platform which the Charkow
Congress had adopted.

The seventh Congress, the most historic in the history
of the movement, was held at Basle at the end of July,
1905. The report of the commission which had been
sent to East Africa was not altogether favourable, as the
question whether the region was suitable for agricultural
as distinct from pastoral settlement remained in doubt.
The suitability of the offered territory, however, scarcely
came into consideration at the Congress. The question
that arose for settlement was whether the Zionist Organization was to confine its efforts to securing the creation
of a Jewish autonomous State in Palestine or in the neighbouring lands or not. From the opening of the Congress
there could be no doubt as to the views of the majority
of the delegates. In fact, at a meeting, at which they
numbered six hundred, a resolution was adopted, *nemine
contradicente*, reaffirming the fundamental principle of the
movement as adopted at the first Congress, rejecting
either as an end or a means, all colonization outside
of Palestine and the adjacent lands, thanking the British

Government for its offer and declining it, but expressing the hope that the further good offices of that Government would be available "in any matter it may undertake in accordance with the Basle programme." The numbers of the advocates of East Africa were relatively so small that they abstained from voting. The breach between them and the majority was, however, impassable. Under the leadership of Mr. Zangwill and Professor Mandelstamm they seceded from the Zionist Movement and founded the Jewish Territorial Organization (the Ito), whose object is the creation of a Jewish autonomous settlement, without any limitation of locality.

The rejection of the East African project was the last outstanding feature in the Zionist Movement. Its subsequent history was relatively humdrum and attracted little attention outside of Jewry or even of Zionist circles. Max Nordau was offered the formal succession to Herzl, but, entirely on personal grounds, was unable to accept it. No president of the organization was thereupon elected by the seventh Congress. Instead an executive committee representative of all parties in the Movement, and consisting of David Wolffsohn and Professor Otto Warburg from Germany, Heer Jacob Kann from Holland, Dr. Kohan-Bernstein and M. Ussischkin from Russia, Mr. L. J. Greenberg from England, and Dr. Alexander Marmorek from France, was appointed. This committee chose Wolffsohn, one of Herzl's immediate followers, who had been prominent in the movement since its inception, as its chairman, and he became the nominal head of the Zionist Organization. The seventh Congress marked not only the concentration of Zionist energies on Palestine. It went farther and reacted from Herzl's policy of making practical work subservient to political

languages of the Congress, but it was given no priority over any of its fellows. The eighth Congress, however, held at the Hague in 1907, made Hebrew the official language. Another decision of this Congress was to form a special department for work in Palestine, and in particular for the encouragement of Hebrew education, and the establishment of agricultural and urban credit banks there. The opening of a permanent office of the organization at Jaffa was also decided upon. The importance of the Palestine Commission, as the Palestinian department of the organization was known, grew continually, and in the end it practically monopolized the whole of the movement. At its head was Professor Otto Warburg, a distinguished German botanist, who had for long been deeply interested in Jewish agricultural efforts in Palestine and other regions of the Near East, and who had been one of the most prominent members of the *Ezra* Society. Under his direction practical work in Palestine marched with relative rapidity. The many enterprises which came into being attracted interest and support without as well as within the Zionist ranks, for many Jews who had always felt attracted by the idea of the re-creation of Jewish life in the Holy Land had, on account of its apparently exclusively political character, been hostile, or at best frigidly neutral, towards the organization founded by Herzl. They were the Moderates of Zionism, who felt that the immediate task, sufficient for the present generation, was the planting of a healthy Jewish life in Palestine. The ultimate consequences of the growth of that life did not concern them, but a future generation.

The immediate fruits of the new direction the movement was taking showed themselves in several organizations, constituted for work in some definite field in Palestine. There were the Hebrew Higher Grade School at Jaffa, founded in 1907, and the David and Fanny Wolffsohn Fund for the Erection of Workmen's Dwellings, constituted in the same year. In 1908, the year in which the Palestine office at Jaffa was established, the Palestine Land Development Company and the Anglo-Levantine Banking Company, an offshoot of the Jewish Colonial Trust, were founded. At the ninth Congress at Hamburg in 1909 it was decided to found a society for the encouragement of co-operative agricultural settlements in Palestine. At the last Congress held, that at Vienna in 1913, the establishment of a Hebrew University at Jerusalem was decided upon. Particulars of the work of these institutions will be given later.

Wolffsohn remained the head of the movement until 1911, when his place was in effect taken by Professor Warburg. By this act the control of the organization passed nominally as well as actually into the hands of the " Practical Work " party. The control of the movement was placed in the hands of a small Executive Committee, which was re-elected with the addition of Dr. E. W. Tschlenow, an eminent Moscow physician, by the eleventh Congress. The headquarters of the movement had by then been removed to Berlin, the residence of Professor Warburg. When it was under Wolffsohn's control, its centre was at Cologne. The outbreak of the War threatened the disintegration of the organization, composed of elements emanating from all the belligerent countries, as well as from many of the neutral ones. To avoid this, strenuous efforts were made. For a time it was thought that the centre of the movement would shift to the New World, and that all Zionist

activities would radiate from New York, where one
member of the Executive Committee happened to be at
the time of the outbreak of the War. The American
Committee, under the chairmanship of Mr. Louis, afterwards Supreme Court Judge, Brandeis, that was formed
did much to safeguard the interests of the movement in
that time of crisis. The unity of the Zionist Organization was, however, secured by immediate transfer from
Germany to neutral lands—the Jewish National Fund to
the Hague, the Zionist Organization itself to Copen-
hagen. At the same time the Executive Committee
deputed its authority to two of its members, Dr.
Tschlenow, the Vice-President of the organization, and
Mr. Nahum Sokolow, of Warsaw, who were free to move
in all the allied and neutral lands.

The development through which the Zionist idea has
passed during the twenty years since the appearance of
Herzl as the leader of his people has owed more to Mr.
Asher Ginzberg (Achad Ha'Am) than to any other individual. Nevertheless, he has never held office either
in the organization or at any of the Congresses, nor has
he sought or obtained any prominence in the deliberations
of the latter. Achad Ha'Am was one of the inspirers
of the *Chovevé Zion* Movement. To him, however, that
movement was at fault in absorbing the whole of its
energies in " practical " work, to the neglect of what was
to him of at least equal moment—spiritual Zionism, or
the rehabilitation of the Jewish consciousness; and in
order to keep this aspect of Zionism in the forefront,
the *Bené Mosheh* was founded by him. Herzl's movement
in its earliest stages, in Achad Ha'Am's opinion, erred
equally, although in a different direction, for the spiritual
and practical aspects of Zionism were neglected and sub-

ordinated to the political aspect. The colonization of Palestine was no longer the main object of the movement. The securing of political guarantees was the goal to which all energies were to be devoted. The *Chovevé Zion* and Baron Edmund wanted to use an existing population as an instrument towards gaining further benefits. Herzl thought it wiser not to sink a penny in Palestine until guarantees had been sustained for the security of the investment. Achad Ha'Am felt no less strongly than his colleagues the necessity for a centre of Judaism and of Jewry in Palestine, but he felt just as urgently the necessity for preparing the Jewish people for their inheritance. Otherwise there was a risk that when Palestine was ultimately obtained as a centre, there would be no Jewry to take possession of it.

The state of Jewry, and with it Judaism, during the latter decades of the nineteenth century and in the opening years of the present one, has been very critical. One-half of the Jewish people has been groaning under a relentless persecution which has been gradually destroying it in body and soul. The other, but recently escaped from the confines of the Ghetto, has found a new world opened before it. Into the pleasures of newly-found liberty it has rushed headlong at the great risk of losing itself entirely there. The Jew, having discarded his Jewish culture, assimilates rapidly to the surrounding, numerically overwhelming population, and so far as Jewry is concerned this assimilation means annihilation. It is the assimilation of the wineglassful of wine with the basin of water. As a consequence it is exceptional for the third generation of assimilated Jews to be Jewish even nominally. If it had not been for immigration from Eastern Europe during the past half-century,

14

Judaism would have been practically extinct to-day in such countries as England, France, and America, where the Jew has been free for the course of three generations. In fact, the Jewish communities of these countries contain very few members whose ancestors were in the land a century ago.

The danger which this tendency meant has always been very present to Achad Ha'Am. Only those who consider the mission of Israel to be fulfilled can be satisfied with such a consummation; and current events must convince the shallowest thinker that the mission of Israel among the nations is still far from fulfilment. To Achad Ha'Am it is as evident as to anyone that only with a centre in Palestine, untrammelled by all external influences, is it possible for Judaism—which, it must be recognized, is more than a form of religion: it is a civilization—to develop naturally on its own lines. But he never forgets that the creation of a Jewish centre in Palestine is a means, not the end. The end which he keeps before him is the preservation of the soul of the Jewish people. There are twelve millions of Jews in the world to-day. In the most favourable circumstances, after perhaps a century of preparation, Palestine cannot hold more than a sixth of this number. There are six million Jews to-day living in a termless agony. If by a miracle Palestine were made immediately capable of receiving a population as large as that which it will be able to hold after generations of normal preparation, two-thirds of these sufferers would still have to remain without. It cannot therefore ever directly solve the problem of the Jews who are persecuted or of those peoples who wish to eject their Jews. Both problems, which are in fact parts of one, will remain or be solved elsewhere. The mission of Zionism, as interpreted by Achad Ha'Am, is higher even than to bring relief to the suffering, to provide a land of refuge to the terrified fugitives: it is to preserve alive in spirit as well as in body the people which has already provided the world with its system of morality, with the best elements which modern civilization contains, and whose mission he does not believe to be completed. To Achad Ha'Am, in fact, the re-creation of the Jewish people is more important than its part—the restoration of the Jews to Palestine. The first essential of a people is its tongue. The rehabilitation of Hebrew as a living language is therefore an essential part of Achad Ha'Amism (as Achad Ha'Am's philosophy has come to be called). The extent to which this has proceeded will be shown in a later chapter. From this has sprung naturally the educational revival in Palestine, equally essential to Achad Ha'Amism, which also is dealt with later. But Achad Ha'Am does not neglect the resettlement in Palestine in the physical sense. In his own words, " On one side we must work for the creation of an extensive and well-ordered settlement in our ancestral land; but, on the other side, we are not at liberty to neglect the effort to create there, at the same time, a fixed and independent centre for our national culture, for learning, art, and literature. Little by little, willing hands must be brought into our country, to repair its ruins and restore its pristine glories; but at the same time we must have hearts and minds, endowed with knowledge and sympathy and ability, to repair our spiritual ruins, and restore to our nation its glorious name and its rightful place in the community of human culture."

Three men in the present generation have been in the

van of the movement for the re-creation of the Jewish people in Palestine, and all three have their monuments. The colonization of Palestine by the Jews will for all time keep green the memory of Baron Edmund de Rothschild, who, if he did not initiate it, tended it and cared for it as if it were his own flesh and blood during its years of infancy. Whatever the future will bring forth, on the pages of Jewish history which relate to our own times the name of Theodore Herzl will stand out in letters of gold as that of one who gave his whole life in order to lead his people back towards Zion. Achad Ha'Am's memorial will be the spiritual rebirth of the Jewish people.

CHAPTER XIX

In reviewing the institutions that have been formed for the development of Palestine, it is possible to adopt two methods of classification. One may divide them into those which owe their genesis to the influence of Herzl's organization and those which do not ; or one may classify them as institutions belonging primarily to the Diaspora, or primarily to Palestine. Neither classification is entirely satisfactory. Some of the pre-Herzl institutions have become in course of time tinged with Zionism. In many cases it is difficult to classify an institution as belonging to the Diaspora or to Palestine. If one attempts to deal with these many institutions in the order of their foundation, the result is not satisfactory, nor can they be dealt with properly in their order of importance. The most suitable method of dealing with them is to group them according to activities, after taking all other circumstances into consideration.

The oldest of the existing institutions that operate in Palestine for its benefit is the *Chalukah*, some account of which has been given in an earlier chapter. For the most part, the *Chalukah* is not organized. The funds of which it is composed are collected by messengers sent from Palestine into the lands of the Diaspora, who, after deducting their expenses and a liberal commission, hand the balance to the Palestinian Rabbis by whom they are commissioned. This system is of considerable antiquity and is, it is presumed, generally found satisfactory. The German and Dutch supporters of the *Chalukah*, however, broke away from it more than a century ago. In 1809 they founded a definite administration with headquarters at Amsterdam and a representative in Jerusalem. The costs of administration were thereby much reduced, and the funds devoted in the first place to the support of needy families who have migrated to Palestine from Holland and Germany; secondly, to promote the economic, hygienic, and religious welfare of the Jewish population in Palestine; and, finally, to further the study of Rabbinic literature in Palestine. The administration—whose income in normal times, derived entirely from voluntary contributions, amounts to about £8,000 a year—was reorganized in 1906.

The non-Zionist institution whose activities in Palestine are the most considerable is the Jewish Colonization Association (or Ica), which was endowed by Baron de Hirsch with a fund which fell not far short of £10,000,000. The Ica's principal objects are the assistance and promotion of the emigration of Jews from the lands of oppression, and their settlement in colonies in North and South America; and also the preparation of such Jews for colonization by means of the establishment of educational and training institutions, model farms, loan banks, industries, factories, etc. But a relatively small portion of the Ica's activity lies in Palestine. North and South America and Russia are the centres of its labours. The Ica's main work in Palestine has been the administration and encouragement of the colonies transferred to it by Baron Edmund, and also of those which it has itself founded. In particular it gives encouragement to settlers with a small capital. If the prospective settler is able to produce about £200, the Ica will put him in possession of a holding of some 60 acres, build a house, outhouses, etc., for him, and allow the cost to be repaid in small instalments spread over forty years. Closely related to the colonization work is the model farm established by the Association at Sedjerah.

Apart from its work in the colonies, the Ica has devoted much attention to the town populations in Palestine. Two of the new quarters of Jerusalem have been built with its assistance. The Ica supplies the money required for the erection of the buildings, on easy terms of repayment, to artisans, small shopkeepers, etc. The tenants by this means obtain, as soon as the houses can be erected, comfortable dwellings which in course of time become their own property. In Jerusalem the Ica has also established a silk and woollen mill and a dyeing industry in connection with it. One of its subsidiary institutions supplies knitting-machines to Jerusalem families, who pay for them in instalments. Artisans who have been trained under its auspices are given loans to enable them to open business on their own account, and a loan bank has been established. This bank lends money on security, at moderate interest, to artisans, labourers, manufacturers, and small shopkeepers. Finally, the Ica grants subventions to the *Alliance Israélite* to assist it in its educational work in Palestine.

The *Alliance Israélite* of Paris, the *Hilfsverein der deutschen Juden* of Berlin, and the Anglo-Jewish Association of London, confine their work in Palestine entirely to education. The institutions of the *Alliance* include the Agricultural School at Mikveh Israel, which has become the nucleus of a colony, and also manual training schools in most of the cities of Palestine.

The *Lemaan Zion* Society of Frankfort-on-the-Main maintains a public hospital, an ophthalmic hospital, and a dispensary in Jerusalem; grants assistance to the sick poor, lends medcial accessories, assists students and apprentices, and grants loans without interest to artisans.

The Union of Jewish Women, also a German institution, but with branches in all parts of the world, devotes most of its attention to the employment of girls in the manufacture of lace both in its workrooms and in their homes, and to its girls' agricultural school at Kinnereth. A subsidiary work of the latter institution is the training of Palestinian Jewish girls to be fitted to become the wives of farmers. The object of the Union of Jewish Women— or, to give it its full title, the Jewish Women's League for Cultural Work in Palestine—as stated in its statutes, is " to induce all Jewish women to work in common for the improvement of the social conditions of the Jews in Palestine. This work is more especially intended for the benefit of Jewish women and children." The Union also gives some attention to health conditions in Palestine. Directly and indirectly it assists in the fight against the two scourges of Palestine, malaria and trachoma. It contributes largely towards the support of a hospital at Haifa and maintains a nursing service.

In commemoration of the sixtieth birthday of Dr. Max Nordau a fund was raised for the establishment of an Hygienic Institute in Palestine. Several well-known scientists, including the world-renowned Paul Ehrlich and Professor Jacques Loeb, of the University of California, interested themselves in the project. The institute has not yet been established, but when it is in existence its purpose will be to devote itself to the suppression and prevention of contagious diseases, to enlighten the people on the most important hygienic questions by means of popular leaflets, and to act as an advisory centre to the Government and municipal authorities in regard to all problems of sanitation. In the meanwhile Mr. Nathan Straus, an American-Jewish philanthropist, has himself established and maintained a Health Bureau at Jerusalem. The work of the bureau is much assisted by the Society of Jewish Doctors and Scientists for Sanitary Improvements in Palestine.

Another American-Jewish institution operating in Palestine is the Jewish Agricultural Experiment Station. It was incorporated in New York City in 1910 for " the establishment, maintenance, and support of agricultural experiment stations in Palestine and other countries; the development and improvement of cereals, fruits, and vegetables indigenous to Palestine and neighbouring lands; the production of new species therefrom and their distribution elsewhere; the advancement of agriculture throughout the world; and the giving of instruction in new and improved methods of farming." The headquarters and laboratories of the station are at Zichron Jacob, where also are situated the scientific museum and library. Atlit, near Haifa, on a large estate placed at its disposal by the National Fund, is the scene of the experiments and demonstrations. The period of activity of the station has necessarily been very brief. Yet it may be said to have already justified its existence. Its director, A. Aaronsohn, has discovered in Palestine primitive wild wheat. A new form of sesame, twice as valuable as that hitherto cultivated, has also been discovered.

Five new species of wheat and barley, specially adapted for growth under the conditions to be found in Palestine, have been created. A variety of table grape, ripening three weeks earlier than those of Smyrna and Cyprus, which have been to a large extent exported to Egypt, has been acclimatized. The superiority of the olive of Palestine over that of all other varieties has been demonstrated. The station has effected great improvements in the cultivation of the mulberry-tree, which provides food not only for silkworms, but also for Lebanon cattle. It has improved and developed the cultivation of the native spineless cactus, from which fodder can be provided. In other directions also has the Jewish Agricultural Experiment Station conferred great benefits on the land.

Although the Central Committee of the *Chovevé Zion* Movement at Paris, as well as most of the national societies, especially in Great Britain and the United States of America, speedily succumbed to the competition of Herzl's movement, in Germany and Russia, where the *Chovevé Zion* were far more strongly rooted, the organizations survived, and after a time renewed their activity, but in a direction different from that of actual colonization. The German society, the " Ezra," now devotes itself especially to the establishment of Jewish labourers in the colonies, and to the erection of dwellings for them. The Russian Society, the " Odessa Committee," which has larger means at its disposal, works on a somewhat more ambitious programme. By resolution 25-30 per cent. of its total expenditure must be devoted to educational purposes in Palestine. It spends a large portion of its income, which amounts to about £16,000 a year, in founding workmen's colonies and in the provision of houses and small holdings for labourers, who pay for them by instalments. The Committee also assists commercial enterprises in the colonies, and provides grants for doctors, chemists, watchmen, etc. It encourages the laying out of gardens. In the educational field it supports the secondary school for girls at Jaffa, together with a Teachers' Seminary and a Kindergarten. It also subsidizes schools in many of the colonies, and its services in the rehabilitation of Hebrew as a living language are incalculable.

The headquarters of the Zionist Movement were at Vienna under Herzl, at Cologne under Wolffsohn, and at Berlin under Professor Warburg. The seat of the financial institutions of the Movement has, however, been uninterruptedly in London. The Jewish Colonial Trust, which is the financial instrument of the Movement, is an English limited liability company operating as a bank. Its nominal capital is £2,000,000 in pound shares, but only a little more than a quarter of a million has been paid up. There are over a hundred thousand shareholders scattered in almost every country of the civilized world. Both in regard to the number of shareholders and their distribution, the Jewish Colonial Trust is unique among limited companies.

Herzl founded this bank with the intention of using it to finance the chartered company which he hoped to form with the approval of the Sultan. In the event the Trust itself has been unable to act in Palestine, but it has established a subsidiary institution, the Anglo-Palestine Company, which is also an English company with its headquarters in London, and has become one of the financial instruments of practical Zionism. The task of the Anglo-Palestine Company has been very much more complex than that of any bank or banking company elsewhere.

When it commenced operations thirteen years ago there was practically no system of credit in existence in Palestine. It had almost to initiate banking business in the country, and also, in the absence of other agencies, to enter into business which was not strictly within the objects for which the company was founded. Its main purpose is the strengthening of the economic position of the Jews in Palestine. The interests of the Jews are, however, closely intertwined with those of the other productive classes of the population. Thus the economic strengthening of the Jewish element has resulted also in the benefit of the more valuable of the Christian and Moslem elements. That these latter recognize the benefit the Jewish immigration and the institutions it has brought with it are to the land, is shown by the large number of Christian and Moslem merchants, shop-keepers, professional men, and officials who utilize the company as an ordinary bank.

At the outset of its activity the company had to overcome very considerable difficulties, some deliberately placed in its way by the local authorities, others inherent in the laws of the land, which did not provide facilities for a business of this kind. The local officials were at the best suspicious of the newly-arrived organization and in many cases hostile. In fact, so great were the difficulties placed in the company's way, that it was found necessary to appeal to the good offices of the British Minister to the Porte. These were readily forthcoming and succeeded in their object. When the Constantinople Government gave written instructions to its local officers, forbidding all hindrance to the activities of the company, the hostility of the local authorities ceased. A fresh difficulty, however, arose. The local authorities came with repeated requests for loans which it was not politic to refuse, although the available funds of the company were by no means excessive even for the furtherance of its primary objects. The loans were repaid, but only after much trouble and delay. These incidents relate to the early times. The local authorities in due course came to recognize the great value of the work which the company was performing, and the relations with them have for several years been most cordial.

A large portion of the company's business consists of short-term loans to colonists, merchants, and manufacturers on the security of growing crops, accruing rents, merchandise on the seas, etc. By means of the system of short credits, a whole class of Jewish merchants has been built up in Palestine. There was only one such merchant when the company commenced operations. The entire absence of bad debts in this branch of the company's business, as well as in the others, is noteworthy. For the granting of long-term credits at first no means were available, but when money was deposited at the bank by the Jewish National Fund and other institutions for this purpose, it was possible to enter into this business on an adequate scale. Long-term loans have been made, especially for building purposes, and among the improvements which have been rendered possible by this means are the garden suburbs at Jaffa, Jerusalem, and Haifa. Similar loans have also been made for the extension of plantations, and for the erection of workmen's dwellings in the colonies. In the same category come the loans to the administrative bodies of the colonies to enable them to carry out necessary public works. By means of loans, also, these bodies are enabled to farm their own State taxes and thereby save their constituents about 50 per cent. of the amount.

The system of mortgage was, until a few years ago, unknown to Turkish law, and although now legal is not yet adopted to any extent. That of raising public loans for municipal purposes is still unknown. These loans were therefore beset by legal difficulties, which have been overcome partly by confidence in the company's clients—a confidence that has never been abused.

It has been the policy of the company to encourage the formation of co-operative societies and to grant them loans on favourable terms. As a consequence many such have been formed, greatly to the benefit of their members and indirectly to that of the community as a whole. The Palestinian Jewish Co-operative Movement includes societies for the disposal of the produce of the colonies, for the supply of water to groups of colonists, for the formation of workmen's colonies, for the securing of supplies of artificial manure, and in one instance for the establishment of a new agricultural school. Some of these local co-operative societies have developed into regular branches of the company. The company also makes loans to educational and philanthropic institutions whose income is reliable, but comes at long intervals. When the company first entered upon its activities there were no Zionist institutions engaged in land purchase transactions in Palestine, and it therefore entered also on this branch of business. Since that time institutions have come into existence for that specific purpose, and the company has consequently turned its energies into other directions.

The Anglo-Palestine Company now has branches in all the principal towns of Palestine as well as in many of the colonies. Its business has increased year by year, and its annual turnover amounts to about £6,000,000.

The Jewish National Fund, also an English company,

is raised by means of donations, and is intended for the purchase of land in Palestine, to be held as the inalienable possession of the Jewish people. Legal difficulties have, however, prevented it from carrying out this object to the full, and some of its means have been devoted to subsidiary objects which indirectly serve the same purpose. These subsidiary objects include the establishment of model farms, reafforestation and the advance of money through the Anglo-Palestine Company for the building of Jewish quarters in the towns. The land held by the Fund in Palestine has been leased to other institutions working for the welfare of the country. Thus it is on National Fund land that some of the co-operative colonies have been established. The Hebrew secondary school at Jaffa and the technical college at Haifa have also been built on land belonging to the Fund.

Affiliated to the Jewish National Fund are the David and Fanny Wolffsohn Fund and the Olive Tree Fund. The former is devoted to the erection of workmen's dwellings in the colonies. The latter was raised for the reafforestation of Palestine. The profit derived from the plantations is to be devoted to the furtherance of education in Palestine.

The Palestine Land Development Company is an English company formed for the purpose of enabling private owners to acquire land in Palestine. Its business is to buy estates and to sell them in smaller plots either before or after development. Large tracts of land have been purchased in conjunction with the Ica. This company cuts roads through its estates, distributes water over them, and, in fact, performs all the preliminary work before the purchaser-occupier arrives. It even looks after the interests of absentee owners. In order to keep a steady

flow of purchasers the Palestine Land Development
Company encourages the formation in Europe and
America of *Achuzahs*, or land plantation societies, conducted on lines similar to those of building societies.
These societies are specially popular in the United States
and in Russia. In England the Order of Ancient Maccabæans, a large Zionist friendly society, has formed the
Maccabæan Land Company, Limited, on similar lines.
Some of these societies have already acquired land
preparatory to founding colonies in Palestine. A development of the *Achuzah* movement in the United States is
the Zion Commonwealth, whose ambitions are greater than
those of the more modest *Achuzahs*. This organization
has acquired 400 acres in the Valley of Jezreel, with an
option on 3,000 more, and proposes to form a settlement
there on a combined individual and co-operative owner-
ship system.

There are many other smaller organizations created for
the encouragement and development of the settlement
of Jews in Palestine. The *Erez Israel* Colonization
Society was formed for the establishment of co-operative
agricultural workers' colonies. Two such have been
established—at Dagania and Merchavia respectively. If
the experiment proves successful, it cannot fail to have
far-reaching influence on social and industrial conditions,
not only in Palestine, but throughout the civilized world.
The Sir Moses Montefiore Testimonial Fund, created in
commemoration of Montefiore's many missions on behalf
of his people, advances money for the erection of houses
outside of Jerusalem. The *Agudath Netaim* is a Turkish
Plantation Company which has acquired a number of
sites and laid them out, partly on its own account and
partly on that of others for whom it acts as agent. The

Palestinian Real Estate Company of Berlin buys urban sites, especially in Jerusalem and Haifa, and, after breaking them up, resells them.   The Jewish Colonization Society of Vienna proposes to found an urban settlement in Palestine.   The object of the *Moria* of Hamburg is to promote the colonization of the land on an orthodox Jewish basis.   The *Geulah* is a Russian company formed originally for the purpose of buying and selling land in Palestine.   It soon discovered that it was advisable to develop the land before attempting to sell it.   It operates in the neighbourhood of existing settlements, urban as well as rural.

The Tiberias Land and Plantation Company owns land at Migdal, where it engages in cotton-growing.   The Palestinian Plantation Society plants fruit-gardens in Palestine on behalf of owners resident in Europe.   The Baroness Cohn-Oppenheim Olive Grove, on the shore of the Sea of Galilee, is extended by 25 acres every year by the Jewish community of Dessau.   The Palästina Irrigation Society, a German company, constructs, acquires, manages, leases, and sells irrigation works in Turkey, and especially in Palestine.   The object of the General Jewish Colonization Organization is announced as " Agricultural colonization in Palestine, Syria, and the Sinai Peninsula, upon a humanitarian basis and without any political aim."   Its financial instrument is the Orient Colonization Company. an English limited company.   The Moscow *Kadimah,* a society for the purchase and settlement of land in Palestine, acts in co-operation with the Orient Colonization Company.

The foregoing list, although lengthy, does not by any means exhaust the record of the activities in Palestine of the Jews of the Diaspora.   Educational and kindred activities have been deferred for consideration in the next two chapters. The many hospitals, orphanages, and other benevolent institutions have been omitted from a record intended to deal only with the regenerative forces that are at work. They, as will be expected, are very numerous, for Jewish charity, in Palestine as elsewhere, never fails.

CHAPTER XX

THE history of the development and progress of Jewish education in Palestine falls into two distinct parts, which correspond roughly with the two colonization periods, and the two Jewish populations—the old and the new. The older population has always provided, with and without external assistance, those schools and colleges of Jewish learning which are an integral part of orthodox Judaism and form the most important part of the synagogue itself. No synagogue in any part of the world is complete without its school of *Torah* (the Bible), and these are lacking no more in Palestine than elsewhere. All these institutions, from the college of Jewish learning to the elementary religion class, may be classed together as institutions of religious education. For the most part they are similar in organization to those of the Diaspora. There is nothing peculiar about them, and a chapter devoted to this system of education in Palestine would be little more than a catalogue of institutions. On the regeneration of Palestine in the sense in which the term is at present employed they may be said, with justification, to have had no effect.

For the present purposes the Jewish secular educational system is the one that merits attention. This, in its beginnings and until the last few years, has come entirely from without. The schools have been established and

supported by foreign agencies, at first entirely in a
spirit of philanthropy. Gradually some of them, for
a time at least, acquired a political complexion, and took
their places among the weapons used by the nations from
which they sprang in the contest for political influence
in the Near East. None of these or of the other of the
earlier schools was founded with any thought for the
revival of Palestine or of the Jewish people. The highest
ideal of most of these schools, it is to be feared, was the
training of the Jewish youth of Palestine so as to fit
them for emigration to Europe and America. With the
revival of Jewish nationalism, when the sleeping spirit
of the Jewish people once again began to stir, a new type
of school arose, one intended to train the Jewish youth of
Palestine to remain in the land and enrich it. Schools
of this type have even attracted Jewish parents in
Europe and the other Continents to send their children
to Palestine to be educated there. As this new type has
advanced, the older one has receded. Some of the older
schools have been absorbed into the new: the others
without exception have shown evidence of the new influence. These new schools have all been raised on a basis
of Hebrew as the language of instruction and everyday
use. They are Jewish schools, whereas the older ones
were, and still to a considerable extent are, English,
French, or German Jewish schools.

The movement for bringing facilities for a European
education to the Jews of Palestine commenced about the
middle of the nineteenth century. The pioneer was Albert
Cohn, an Austrian Jew settled in Paris, who was sent
by the Jews of France to the East to investigate the conditions of the Jews there. He had the implicit confidence of
the French and Austrian Rothschilds, and it was with

means supplied by them, that in the course of his five visits to the Holy Land during the years 1854 to 1869, he founded schools and other institutions at Jerusalem and Jaffa, as well as in other cities outside of Palestine. Great difficulties were, however, placed in the way of his educational programme by reactionary Rabbis who considered all secular knowledge heretical. About the same time Sir Moses Montefiore, in the course of one of his several visits to the Holy Land, established a school for girls in Jerusalem where, in addition to the ordinary subjects, dressmaking, embroidery, and domestic economy were taught. Want of funds compelled the closing of this school after a few years. After the lapse of a decade another Anglo-Jewish Girls' School, now one of the most valuable Jewish educational centres in the East, was established, and one is almost justified in considering the present school, the Evelina de Rothschild, as a revival of the earlier one founded by Sir Moses Montefiore.

A third Jewish school founded in Jerusalem about the same time was the Edler von Lämel School, which has had an uninterrupted career until the present day. Ludwig August Frankl, the Austrian Jewish poet and man of letters, visited Jerusalem in 1856 to arrange for the establishment of a school which Elise von Herz-Lämel wished to endow. The reactionary Rabbis opposed him also, but he was able to overcome them with the support of the Austrian Consul and the Turkish statesman Kiamil Pasha, who was at that time governor of Jerusalem. In 1865 a Jewish manual school was founded in Jerusalem by Baron Franchetti, of Turin. Three years later the Evelina de Rothschild School for girls was founded by Baron Lionel de Rothschild, of London, in memory of his daughter. It was entirely supported and managed by

the Rothschild family of England until 1894, when its
administration was transferred to the Anglo-Jewish
Association, the Rothschild family continuing their
generous support. In 1899 the school was reorganized,
and Miss Annie Landau, the present head-mistress,
appointed to that office. With her advent the language
of the school became English instead of French, as it
had hitherto been. Under Miss Landau's direction the
school has reached the foremost rank of similar institutions. It is the finest type of English girls' school,
above the rank of elementary, but somewhat lower than
that of secondary. At the same time, it has managed
to secure a thorough Jewish atmosphere. The position
it has attained is shown by the support and approval
given to it by the best Turkish families in Jerusalem,
who send their daughters to be educated there. The
school is attended by children of all classes, but only from
the more prosperous are fees required. The accommodation has on several occasions been enlarged, but on none has
it been able to keep pace with the demand. Educationally
the school is above reproach. The institution is, however,
far more than a school. At times of epidemic it is
partly a hospital, partly a place of refuge for the avoid-
ance of contagion. It is always a centre for the distribution of relief, with discrimination. The position to which
the Evelina School has attained could never have been
reached if it had not been for the personality of Miss
Landau and the devotion of her staff. She has made for
herself, and incidentally for the school, a position of great
influence in Jerusalem. That this position is recognized,
and that this influence is beneficial, is shown by the
continuance of the school undisturbed on its usual course,
but under the special protection of the Turkish Govern-

ment and the local authorities. Although Britain and Turkey had been at war for more than a year, Miss Landau still remained at her post, with the full approval of the British Foreign Office.

When Graetz, the Jewish historian, and Gottschalk Lewy, of Berlin, were in Jerusalem in 1870, they were touched by the deplorable condition of the Jewish orphans there, and on their return to Germany founded a society for their relief and education. This also came under the ban of the obscurantists. Neverthleess, a school in which a modern education was given was established for the orphans.

Montefiore, on the occasion of his last visit to Jerusalem in 1875, was too feeble to do much visiting, but he requested his friend and travelling companion, Dr. Louis Loewe, to inspect the educational institutions and report to him upon them. The two with which he was most impressed were the *Doresh Zion* for boys, which had been established ten years previously, and the von Lämel School. The former had been founded by Joseph Blumenthal, of Paris, and was then under the management of a committee of Austrian Jews. It had fifty-four pupils drawn from all classes. They were taught Hebrew in all its branches, Talmud, Arabic, and arithmetic. The von Lämel School had forty pupils, who were taught Hebrew and Arabic. The Evelina de Rothschild School had 119 pupils who were instructed in Hebrew, religion, arithmetic, and needlework. Loewe also visited several Rabbinical schools where the Talmud and kindred subjects only were taught, and the head-mistresses of several girls' schools, where instruction was given in Yiddish, brought parties of their girls to be received by Montefiore. Within a few years of Montefiore's visit, German was added to the curriculum of the von Lämel, and French to that of the Evelina School.

The educational activity of the *Alliance Israélite* in Palestine commenced outside of Jerusalem. The first of their schools was one for girls at Beyrout, opened in 1878. In the following year a boys' school was opened in the same city, and a trade school at Haifa. In 1881 an ordinary boys' school was opened at Haifa. The boys' school and the manual training school at Jerusalem commenced work the following year. In 1888 a manual training school for girls was opened at Beyrout. Since that year boys' schools have been established at Jaffa, Acre, and Safed; girls' schools at Jaffa, Haifa, and Safed; and manual training schools for boys at Jaffa, Beyrout, and Safed. In most cases the funds have been supplied by the Jewish Colonization Association. The *Alliance* also controls the agricultural school at *Mikveh Israel*, where, in addition to the special instruction, a good general secondary education is given. The schools at Jerusalem and Haifa receive some assistance from the Anglo-Jewish Association. At all these *Alliance* schools the standard of education given is relatively high. The language of instruction is as far as possible French, which language receives every encouragement. Arabic is also taught, but Hebrew only as a dead language.

At Beyrout there was also at the beginning of the last quarter of the nineteenth century an excellent private school for boys founded and kept by a local resident, Zaki Cohen, who felt that the Jews of the town should have educational facilities equal to those of their Moslem and Christian neighbours. At first he lost heavily on his undertaking, and although previously a man of means, was for a time in danger of becoming impoverished, but the fortunes of the school took a favourable turn, and when the school was visited by Colonel (then Captain) A. E. W. Goldsmid in 1883, he found children attending who had been sent from communities as distant as those of Constantinople and Asia Minor. The school was entirely a private venture, but the proprietor made it a rule for every nine paying pupils to admit one orphan or child of destitute parents without charge. Hebrew, Arabic, French, English, Turkish, and German, were all taught at the school.

The Manual Training School at Jerusalem is a memorial to Baron Lionel de Rothschild, of London, and is generously assisted by members of the Rothschild family. A number of trades are taught there with much success. The pupils come from all parts of Turkey, from Egypt, Russia, Roumania, Greece, and the Balkan States, and when they have become efficient craftsmen, they settle in all parts of Palestine and the Near East, and follow the trades which they have learnt. Moslems and Christians as well as Jews attend the school, which is free; but those, mostly Moslems and Christians, who can afford to pay, do so. There is apparently no maximum limit of age, for men as well as boys attend the classes. In the Boys' School English is among the languages taught, at the express desire of one of the Pashas of Jerusalem, who sent his son to the school. The artisans trained at the school are in great demand even while they are still pupils, and much of the best work in sculpture, carving, and metal performed in Jerusalem in recent years has been produced by pupils of the Lionel de Rothschild School.

CHAPTER XXI

EDUCATION IN PALESTINE—THE NEW

THE foregoing describes the educational facilities available in Palestine when the new Jewish population began to enter. The tendencies of which this new immigration was a symptom in due course revolutionized the educational system of the country, just as in another direction they created a new centre for Palestinian Jewry. The European schools which the *Alliance* and other organizations had founded were excellent of their class, and, as European schools, had no need to fear comparison with any others. The reports on their work, given repeatedly by competent authorities, were such as any body of managers might justifiably envy. From the wider Jewish point of view, however, one essential was missing. They contributed nothing towards the future of the Jewish people: they benefited Jews only as individuals, and counted themselves the more successful if they fitted a young Palestinian Jew to succeed in his chosen calling in France rather than to contribute towards the rebuilding of the Jewish people in Palestine, or even to support himself as an Occidentalized Jew in the land in which he was born. For the new outlook, the new national consciousness, which the immigrants of the past thirty-five years have brought with them, a different educational atmosphere was needed. This has been provided for the most part by an entirely new educational system, but partly also by a modification of the old—a modification

THE HERZL GYMNASIUM *EN FÊTE*

A WORKSHOP AT THE BEZALEL

Face p. 234

due not so much to any conscious effort as to the insistent yet perhaps hardly noticeable influence of the new conditions.

The pioneers of the new educational movement in Palestine were undoubtedly the Odessa Committee, who, acting mainly under the influence of Achad Ha'Am, decided to devote a very large proportion of their activity in Palestine to education, and to encourage by every means in their power the spread of Hebrew as a living language. It was well recognized that the only means of dealing satisfactorily with a heterogeneous mass of children coming from all points of the compass and speaking a score of tongues, all of which, so far as they were concerned, belonged to the past rather than to the future, was to give them a common language. Although these children understood nothing of one another's everyday talk, there was one tongue with which they all had some acquaintance, which, moreover, was indigenous to the land in which they lived, and was closely connected with all that was best in the past of the people to which they belonged. Of the languages spoken by the children there was no justification for giving one any preference over the other. The choice of Hebrew as the common language, however, even on practical grounds, had much to commend it. This was the narrow case for Hebrew in Palestine. The wider case was that that language alone could be the language of the Jewish people: all other tongues were proper only to Jewish communities.

The first school in which Hebrew was used as the language of instruction in all subjects was the Higher Grade Girls' School in Jaffa, one of the worthiest monuments of the activity of the Odessa Committee in Palestine, by which it is entirely supported. The work commenced in this institution has spread in many directions. The Hebrew Gymnasium (Higher Grade School) at Jaffa, the most important of the new class of school in Palestine, owes much to the Committee, as does also the similar institution which has been established more recently in Jerusalem. The Odessa Committee also maintains and subventions Hebrew kindergartens and schools in all the towns and in several of the colonies. It has penetrated into many of the *Talmud Torahs* or Rabbinical schools, where it has influenced the introduction of modern subjects. It assists the *Bezalel* School of Arts and Crafts of Jerusalem, and subsidizes libraries, Hebrew newspapers, and publishers, especially of educational works. It was the Odessa Committee that, under the leadership of M. Ussischkin, in 1903 convened a conference of Palestinian teachers and formed of them an organization for the development of Hebrew education in Palestine, and for the improvement of the position of the Hebrew teachers there. The Odessa Committee continues to support this organization in every possible manner. The latter has been continually gaining in influence on the education of the growing generation, and has gradually become an authoritative centre for the consideration of educational questions. The Teachers' Union has elaborated a uniform system for Palestinian elementary schools; it inspects and makes appointments to the staffs of the schools, examines candidates for appointments as teacher, and has codified and elaborated a Hebrew educational terminology. It has held summer courses of lectures on subjects such as physics, botany, geology and school hygiene, using on all occasions Hebrew as the language of instruction and intercourse. The Union has its special periodical, *Hachinuch* (Education).

Another institution that has conferred great benefits on the cause of Jewish education in Palestine is the *Hilfsverein der deutschen Juden*. With objects somewhat similar to those of the *Alliance Israélite* and the Anglo-Jewish Association, the *Hilfsverein*, coming later into the field, after the new Hebrew Movement had commenced, was able to adapt its organization to the new conditions more easily than was the case with the other institutions which had been founded and had grown up under the older régime. Thus, from their establishment the schools of the *Hilfsverein* accepted Hebrew as the language of the new Palestine. That language, as a living tongue, therefore from the first occupied a very prominent position in its school system. As formally stated, the *Hilfsverein* exists, so far as Palestine is concerned, " to train the Jewish youth in the Orient to have a love for its home, to remain permanently settled on the land, and to earn its own living." But political motives are not altogether wanting, and the *Hilfsverein*, like the *Alliance* and the Anglo-Jewish Association, was also at one period of its career intended to further the interests of the State from which it emanates. Consequently German occupies an important position in the curriculum of its schools.

Although the last comer in the field, the *Hilfsverein* has constructed a network of excellent schools all over Palestine. They range from kindergartens up to a teachers' seminary and a seminary for Rabbis. In Jerusalem it has three kindergartens, a course for kindergarten teachers, a girls' school, an evening school for adults, a commercial school in addition to the two seminaries, and the von Lämel School for boys, the administration of which has been transferred to it. The *Hilfsverein* also subventions several other educational

institutions in Jerusalem. That city is the centre of the
organization's activity, but it does not monopolize the
whole of it. At Jaffa it supports three kindergartens
and a boys' school; at Haifa a kindergarten and a higher-
grade school; at Safed, Beyrout, and Tiberias, kindergartens. At Rechoboth it helps to support a kindergarten
and a school for boys and girls, at Katrah a school. It is
interested in thirty schools in all in Palestine, and has
3,000 children under its influence.

The *Alliance* is concerned with the education of about
2,200 children. Its schools for boys and girls are to be
found in all the cities of Palestine. In addition there are
the great technical school at Jerusalem, technical schools
at Jaffa, Haifa, and Safed, and the Agricultural School
at *Mikveh Israel.*

There is no Jewish colony in Palestine, except perhaps
the very smallest, that does not supply facilities for the
education of its children, and in every case the school
is well equipped and staffed by teachers zealously devoted
to their profession. Besides the schools in the colonies
supported by the *Hilfsverein*, the Ica—that is to say,
the Baron—pays the expenses of a large number. The
management of these schools, however, remains with the
colonists, the Ica contenting itself with supplying the
funds. In several of the larger schools there is also a
Talmud Torah or school of the *Torah* (the Bible) supported
by the Frankfort Union for the Interests of Orthodox
Judaism. These schools combine an agricultural education with that more usually given in schools. At Petach
Tikvah, also, the Union has arranged courses for the
training of teachers. The language difficulty which sometimes arises among the mixed populations of the towns
does not exist in these colonies. There there is, practically

speaking, one language only—Hebrew. Consequently
without exception the language of the schools of the
colonies, no matter by what organization they may be
supported, is Hebrew.

Apart from the schools supported by these European
organizations, there are other educational institutions,
several of them of the most important in the country,
which are independently managed and supported, or at
the most receive assistance from the *Hilfsverein* or the
Odessa Committee. The Theodore Herzl Hebrew Gymnasium at Jaffa, a secondary school for boys, was founded
in 1907 by an association of Palestinian teachers, who
were determined to create a secondary school on a Hebrew
basis. The difficulties in their way were many. There
were not even textbooks in Hebrew for many of the
subjects without which the school would have failed
of its purpose—to make itself equal to the best of
its class in Europe. The enthusiasm and zeal of the
founders, however, overcame all difficulties. The hundred
pupils, boys and girls, with whom the school opened,
increased sevenfold in the course of seven years. The
experiment in its first year attracted the attention of
Mr. Jacob Moser, of Bradford, who was travelling in Palestine, and he generously defrayed the expense of erecting
a suitable building. The fame of the school spread
across the continent of Europe, and before long Jewish
families in Europe sent their sons to Jaffa to be educated
at the Hebrew Gymnasium. The usual secular subjects
are taught, and also the Bible and Talmud, all through
the medium of Hebrew. Instruction is also given in
Turkish, Arabic, French, and German. In the upper
classes the school separates into classical and modern
sides. The leaving certificate is recognized as an equiva-

lent of matriculation at several European and American Universities, and pupils have passed direct to the Universities of Constantinople, Berlin, Paris, and New York. In 1909 a similar Hebrew Gymnasium was founded in Jerusalem, where it has progressed towards a similar success.

The Jaffa Gymnasium has no religious basis. It is Jewish only in the national sense. Its pupils and staff are drawn from all schools of thought in Judaism, and in order that offence shall be given to none of them, positive Judaism is not taught there. This did not satisfy the orthodox section among the Zionists, who, in 1909, opened another Hebrew higher-grade school at Jaffa, the " Tachkemoni," which is on a " religious basis, adapted to Palestinian conditions." A reading-room and continuation classes for ex-pupils who have passed through the school are connected with it. The school is for boys only, but the establishment of a similar school for girls is in contemplation.

The success of these schools in Jaffa and others of modern character in other parts of Palestine turned the attention of the organizers of Hebrew education in Palestine to the necessity for preparing the next step in the educational ladder. The desirability of a technical institute was manifest if the best was to be obtained from the material which the new educational institutions were forming and developing. To found such an institution, if it were to be of value, a large sum was needed. The success of the Jaffa Gymnasium had, however, gained friends from unexpected quarters, and it was not long before a sum of £60,000 was available for the new institution. The nucleus was provided by a legacy of £10,000 bequeathed by Wolf Wissotzky, a Russo-Jewish philanthropist who had been greatly attracted by the *Chovevé*

Zion Movement.   Twice that amount was presented by
Mr. Jacob Schiff, of New York, the leader of American
Jewry in all works for the benefit of his people, who had,
however, not hitherto displayed any special interest in
the Jews of Palestine.   The Baroness Cohn-Oppenheim
Foundation, which is connected with the *Hilfsverein*,
contributed £15,000, and £4,000 came from the Jewish
National Fund.   With such support the project went
forward.   A site was obtained at Haifa, building operations commenced, and it was expected that the Middle
School connected with the college would have been
opened in April, 1914.   The governing body was representative of the principal donors, but in the absence of
the American members, the power rested with the members
of the *Hilfsverein*, who formed the working majority.

Some six months before the date appointed for the
opening a crisis arose in the *Hilfsverein* schools in Palestine
which quickly spread to the projected polytechnic also.
The German institution had accepted the new Hebrew
movement with apparent cordiality, and its schools had
become, with the full sanction of the governing body in
Berlin, strongholds of the new movement.   Apparently,
however, while the principal object of the *Hilfsverein*
remained the benefit of Palestinian Jewry and the
development of the new Jewish life, the interests of
Germany also were not forgotten.   As a means of supporting these the propagation of German in the Near
East was very important.   The *Hilfsverein*, it seems,
was willing that Hebrew should be a language of instruction in its schools, but it was also anxious that German
should occupy a position little if at all inferior to it.
Hebrew, however, seemed to be about to monopolize the
schools of the *Hilfsverein*, and in order to preserve the *status*

16

quo the Berlin committee decreed that in future certain subjects were to be taught in German. The result of this decision was unexpected, for few, if any, knew the strength that the Hebrew movement had acquired. A strike immediately spread among the teachers and pupils of the *Hilfsverein* schools. Under the leadership of Mr. David Yellin, one of the most prominent of Palestinian Jews, new schools on a Hebrew basis were set up in all parts of the country for the accommodation of the pupils who had seceded from the German ones. The task which Mr. Yellin had undertaken was a very heavy one, but the Zionist Organization quickly came to his assistance. Whether this new network of schools would have continued its activity, or whether a *modus vivendi* with the *Hilfsverein* would have been found, cannot be said, for before any opportunity for development was given, Europe, and shortly afterwards Western Asia, was plunged in war.

The struggle between German and Hebrew in the *Hilfsverein* schools at once spread to the Haifa Polytechnic, whose building was on the point of completion. At a meeting of the governors, at which the Germans were in a majority, it was resolved that the Polytechnic should have no official language, but that in its classes, as well as in those of the secondary school which was to be attached to it, the sciences were to be taught in German. As a consequence the Zionist members of the governing body immediately resigned. The wave of indignation that spread through the Jewries of the Continent reached the United States and influenced the American members of the governing body to intervene. A new arrangement was made whereby some of the excluded subjects were to be taught in Hebrew immediately and the others after the lapse of four years. This delay was to give the professors who had already been chosen time to make themselves masters of modern Hebrew. In this position the matter stood when the clouds of war descended in the summer of 1914.

The leaders of the Hebrew movement in Palestine allow no lethargy or indolence to envelop them. They are always looking ahead and make plans for the next step but one, even before the next is taken. Beyond the Polytechnic was the Hebrew University, but the Polytechnic did not have to get to work before plans were laid for the establishment of such a University at Jerusalem. The University project was approved by the eleventh Zionist Congress, where it was pressed by Dr. C. Weizmann, of Manchester, as the spokesman of its advocates. It gained adherents in quarters where they might least have been expected. Although launched under Zionist auspices, it drew enthusiastic supporters from the ranks of confirmed opponents of the aims of the Zionist Movement. Baron Edmund de Rothschild, of Paris, as is not surprising, promised valuable assistance towards the realization of the scheme. In England Sir Philip Magnus, always a consistent opponent of Zionism, addressed public meetings in its support. In Germany it gained the assistance of Paul Ehrlich, the greatest pathologist of his generation. In the meanwhile funds were being obtained for the establishment and endowment of a Hebrew University which should be worthy of the genius of the Jewish people. A suitable site was purchased on the Mount of Olives. And then the War intervened.

Outside of the direct line from the kindergarten to the University there are other educational institutions in Palestine of the new type. The girls' farm and lace-making schools of the Union of Jewish Women, have already been mentioned. Conservatoires of music have been established at Jaffa and Jerusalem. The Hebrew Art School, however, which has acquired the widest reputation, in both Jewish and non-Jewish circles in Europe and America, is the Bezalel School of Arts and Crafts in Jerusalem, which is maintained by the *Bezalel*, a German society for the promotion of artistic crafts and domestic industry in Palestine and neighbouring countries. Under the direction of Professor Boris Schatz, a distinguished Bulgarian Jewish sculptor, a school of a distinctively Jewish art, not an imitation of European schools, has grown up. The aim of the *Bezalel* is, however, not merely to create a school of fine art. The principal object is to train its pupils in a handicraft or profession which will enable them to earn their living. The pupils get the whole of their education inside the school. In addition to the ordinary subjects they are taught drawing, painting, and modelling, and as they advance they are instructed in the principles of decorative art.

The *Bezalel* is not only a school: it is also a manufacturing centre. Among the subjects which it teaches are carpet-weaving, filigree work, wood-carving, inlaid work, lace-making, copper-work, lithography, metal-chasing, and ivory-carving. The products of its workshops are sold not only in Palestine. By a series of exhibitions in most of the principal cities of Europe and the United States, they have been brought under the notice of a wide public, and leading firms in several of the Western capitals act as the agents of the *Bezalel*. Connoisseurs say that the *Bezalel* carpets are equal to the famous products of

Turkey and Persia. Yet the *Bezalel* School is only ten years old, and when Professor Schatz first entered on his work there his pupils had not even attempted to draw. In the year 1913, despite the depression caused by the wars through which Turkey had just passed, the income from all sources amounted to a quarter of a million francs, more than half of which was expended in wages. There were in that year 500 pupils and workers in regular attendance. A branch of the *Bezalel* has been established in the colony of Ben Shamen, where a group of Yemenites has been provided with cottages and plots of land as well as a workshop. There they engage in carpet-weaving and filigree work, supplemented by market-gardening and poultry-rearing. Other extensions were in prospect, and if misfortune had not overtaken Palestine in common with the greater part of civilization, it is probable that by now *Bezalel* workshops would have been open at Safed, Tiberias, and Hebron, to the great benefit of the local populations.

Professor Schatz is an enthusiast who has devoted his life to the service of his enthusiasm. His ideal he has himself described in these words: " The erst barren hills are covered again with plantations, the valleys are decked again with flowers; a new and healthy life is again awakening, a new life without any smoky chimneys above and grimy labourers below. The labourer is free—he creates only things in which his intelligence and individual taste can find expression, things which assume ever new and more beautiful forms. The women are famous for the carpets, lace, and embroideries which they make. The Palestinian faience, majolica, glass, carvings, and the beautiful copper and silver work, enjoy a renown throughout the world. They have a specifically Jewish Palestinian style, which reflects the beauty of the Biblical age and the fantasy of the Orient. Our workman in Palestine has become an ideal for his comrade in civilized Europe. He knows nothing of barrack-like dwellings, without light or air, in which the European workmen with their families pine away. He has his bright cottage in a green garden, and his secure employment in the co-operative society to which he belongs." This is the end towards which the gifted Principal of the *Bezalel* School is striving.

In all these institutions Hebrew is the only language in use.

The foregoing catalogue, although a long one, does not exhaust the list of Jewish educational institutions at work in Palestine. In fact, so numerous, and in many cases so self-contained, are they that no list could exhaust them. There are, however, yet a few others that ought not to pass without mention. At Jerusalem the German-Dutch Chalukah Administration has opened a manual school, the *Darche Chayim*, to train the boys who leave the orthodox Rabbinical schools in a handicraft, and at the same time to continue their religious studies. In 1910 a German committee was formed for the founding of popular schools and domestic economy schools in Palestine. Its object is to train Jewish girls to fulfil the rôle of farmers' wives in the colonies. The first school was opened at Petach Tikvah, where the subjects of instruction are gardening, farming, Hebrew as a living language, Arabic, Jewish ethics and history, gymnastics, and domestic economy and hygiene.

Formal education in the best of circumstances is only a means, and not the final means. This is clearly recognized by those by whom the regeneration of Palestine is being directed. The provision of books was early

A GROUP OF PUPILS OF THE BEZALEL SCHOOL

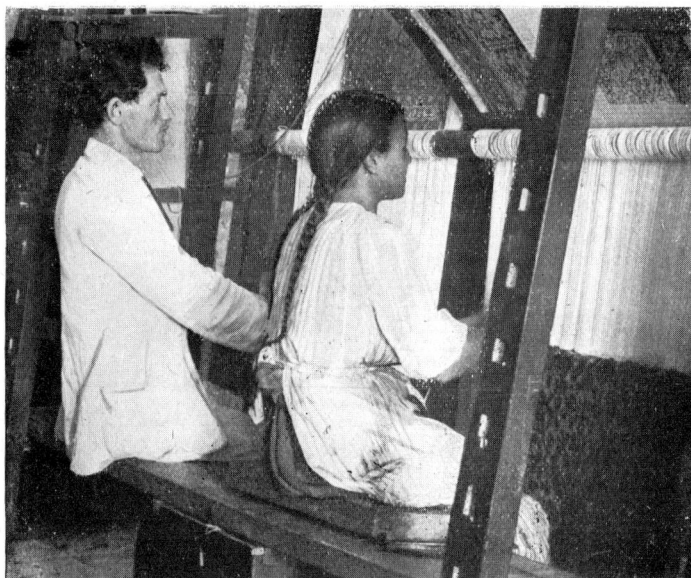

WEAVING CARPETS IN THE BEZALEL

Face p. 246

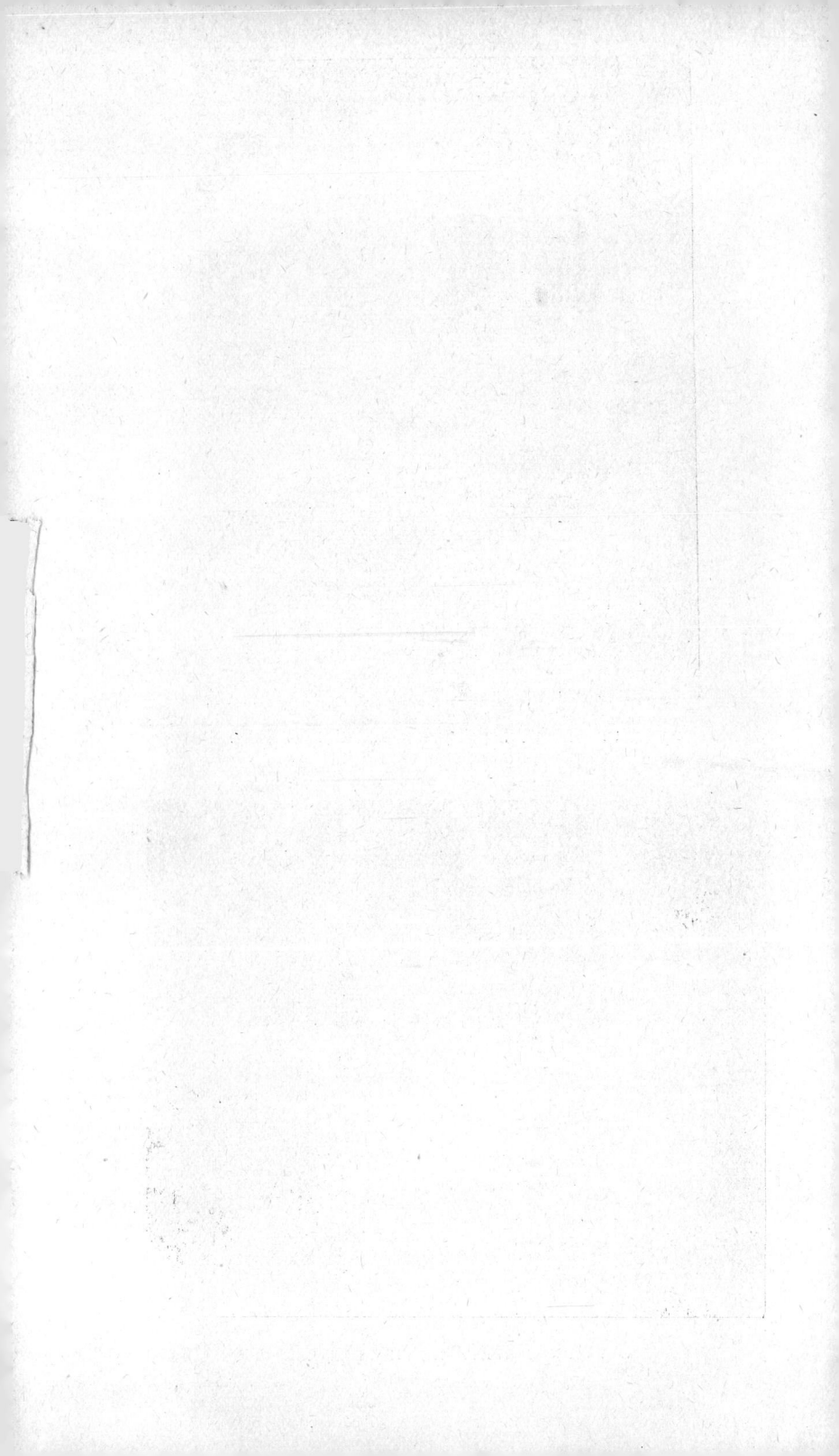

taken into consideration.   There are very few settlements of Jews in Palestine or elsewhere that have not their collections of books for general use.   In the colonies, therefore, a library almost invariably ranks among the communal institutions.   In Jerusalem and the other towns also the many learned and religious institutions all have libraries, but in most cases these are limited to Talmudical and cognate literature.   A library of a different character is the Central Library at Jerusalem, founded in 1892 by Dr. Joseph Chasanovitz, of Bielistock, in commemoration of the four hundredth anniversary of the arrival in Palestine of the refugees from Spain.   It contains about 35,000 volumes, somewhat more than half of which are in Hebrew.   In addition to being a library, this institution is an intellectual centre for the new population of the capital.   Another Jerusalem institution of the same character is the People's Institute, which was opened in 1908.   The Workmen's Club has also a library and reading-room.   The *Shaare Zion* at Jaffa, founded in 1891 by the *Chovevó Zion* in memory of Levanda, is of the same character as the National Library of Jerusalem; and at Jaffa also the Workmen's Club contains a library, reading-room, and lecture hall.

Among the other Jewish learned and scientific societies and institutions in Palestine are the Society for the Exploration of Palestine (a German society founded in 1910); the Jewish Medical Society of Jaffa for the discussion of medical questions, for research, and for hygienic improvements, which publishes quarterly transactions in Hebrew; the Society of Jewish Doctors and Scientists for Sanitary Improvements in Palestine (also a German institution); and the Society of Lovers of the Hebrew Drama, of Jaffa, established in 1906 to create a Hebrew drama in Palestine, which proposes to build a national theatre. By means of this society and through private endeavours, a Hebrew drama is gradually coming into existence. A neo-Hebrew literature also is being produced in the new Palestinian conditions, the most important production of which is the *Millon*, the monumental lexicon of the Hebrew language, ancient, medieval, and modern, on which Mr. Elieser Ben-Jehuda, of Jerusalem, has been engaged for several years.

This educational and literary activity has given rise to two or three Hebrew publishing firms, which devote most of their attention to educational works. The granting of a Constitution to Turkey resulted immediately in great activity in Hebrew journalistic circles in Palestine. Previously there had been two Hebrew periodicals, but neither reached the European standard. There are now several daily and weekly papers as well as four monthly periodicals, one for children, all in Hebrew.

CHAPTER XXII

THE REHABILITATION OF HEBREW

THE story of the rebirth of the Jewish people and of the opening stages of its return to its ancestral land which has been told in the preceding pages would not be complete without some mention of the restoration of Hebrew, the ancient language of the Jews, to its due place as a living language. Not that there is any justification for the widespread belief that Hebrew is or ever was a dead language. From the day on which it ceased to be the common everyday language of the Jews, in consequence of their dispersion among the nations and the practically compulsory acquisition and use of the languages of the lands in which they dwelt, until the present day, Hebrew has never ceased to be the language of Judaism and of Jewish learning. It has not only been the language of prayer and as such familiar in some degree to every Jew; it has been the ready medium of communication between Jewish scholars in all lands, who in their homes and their everyday life spoke the local vernacular. It is the language in which until a century ago almost the whole of Jewish literature was written, and in a few isolated communities in the East it has even remained throughout the centuries of exile a living language of everyday intercourse.

Nevertheless, Hebrew cannot be said to be the Jewish language. Until a generation ago it had hardly secured a claim, so far as the common people are concerned, to be recognized as a Jewish language except for special purposes. The Jewish languages, the languages peculiar to, current among, and used every day by, the Jews of the Dispersion are Judæo-German, or *Jüdisch;* Judæo-Spanish, or *Espagnol* or *Ladino;* and Judæo-Persian: the first a corruption of the old German of the Rhinelands which the survivors of the widespread massacres by the Crusaders brought with them when they fled to Poland; the second closely akin to the old Castilian brought by the fugitives from Spain to the Moslem lands in the fifteenth century; the third the language of the Jews of Persia. It is only in the course of the past generation that Hebrew has taken its place among these as the language of everyday intercourse by any considerable number of Jews. In the future, unless the justifiable anticipations of those who are qualified to judge are belied, it will be *the* Jewish language, for, although it has a much smaller circle than any one of the other three, it is the only language of the four that is advancing. The others are losing adherents every day.

It is not much more than a century since the first attempts were made to popularize Hebrew among the Jews. It was then a part of the Mendelssohnian movement to introduce European culture among the Jews of Germany who were still prisoners in their *Judengassen.* The object of Moses Mendelssohn and his school was to Germanize the Jews and at the same time to give them German as their mother-tongue. Hebrew was used as a means to this end, as an opportunity for bringing modern thought and modern views to the Jews of the eastern provinces. The Hebrew writings of the *Meassefim,* as this school of writers came to be called, were, as a rule, intended only to be ephemeral, to be read only until their readers were able to read German. Their influence on the development of Hebrew and its approaching rebirth was consequently insignificant. The most prominent of the *Meassefim* was Naphtali Hartwig Wessely, who wrote essays, poems, and grammatical works.

The next movement in the quickening of Hebrew came from the other side of the Russo-German frontier, and from Galicia. The *Maskilim*, the promoters of the *Haskalah* or " Enlightenment," had objects very similar to those of the *Meassefim*. Theirs were also to introduce Western culture into the confines of the ghetto. The results in Russia and Galicia were, however, very different from those in Germany. In the first place, the reformers met with an adamant opposition from the upholders of rigid orthodoxy in Jewry. To them all reform or movement was anathema. Above all, to use Hebrew, the sacred tongue, for secular purposes was blasphemy. This intense opposition to the secularization and vulgarization of Hebrew was paralleled later by the opposition which came from the same quarters to practical Zionism, on the ground that it was attempting to force the hands of Providence, to anticipate the Millennium. The other point of difference between the two movements was that whether the *Haskalah* succeeded in its object or not, the walls of the Russian ghetto would remain standing and the Jew would not be allowed to leave it. Germany was ready to welcome the Jew once he had become occidentalized: Russia was not.

The *Haskalah* movement lasted much longer than the *Meassefim*. In a sense it still survives, although the massacres of the early eighties of last century turned it in a new direction and ultimately merged it in the Zionist Movement. Of the writers whom the *Haskalah* movement produced, the most prominent were Isaac Erter, the satirist; Solomon Judah Rapoport, one of the founders of modern Jewish historical scholarship; Nachman Krochmal, a pioneer of modern Jewish philosophy; Meir Letteris, the poet, who translated " Faust " into Hebrew; Kalman Schulman, who translated Eugène Sue into Hebrew, and thus introduced Western romanticism to the Jewish masses; Abraham Mapu, who wrote original novels in Hebrew; and Judah Leon Gordon, the poet and novelist, the greatest of them all.

A decade before the death of Gordon the first phase of the *Haskalah* movement ended. The period of ruthless persecution that opened in Russia with the accession of the Czar Alexander III., persecution of the mind as well as of the body and the soul, brought home to most of the leaders of " Enlightenment " the hopelessness of the Jewish future in Russia. In the despair of Russia, the hope of Zion was born, or rather reinvigorated. The leaders of the old movement became the leaders of the new. Henceforth the *Haskalah* had a new meaning. It meant not only the enlightenment of the Jewish mind, but also the redemption of the Jewish people. The principal writers of the *Haskalah* since 1880 have already been mentioned among the leaders of the *Chovevé Zion*. Smolenskin was a political philosopher and a novelist; Lilienblum wrote on a variety of subjects, but always with Palestine before him. Of them all, the greatest in his influence both on Jewish thought and on the development of modern Hebrew, is Achad Ha'Am, a little later than the others in time, who is still in the plenitude of his powers, and from London, where he took up his residence a few years ago, exercises a silent but deep influence over modern Jewish thought in all the countries of the world.

The present generation has produced a considerable harvest of Hebrew writers, with very few exceptions Russian or Galician in origin. Mr. Nahum Sokolow is foremost among these contemporary men of letters. Mr. Elieser Ben-Jehuda has, by his lexicographical work, made Jerusalem once again a centre of Jewish scholarship. Mr. David Yellin, also of Jerusalem, is a master of Hebrew style. Mr. A. L. Ben-Avigdor has, by means of his publication societies, enabled Hebrew writers to reach their public. Constantin Shapiro, Menahem Dolitzki, and Mordecai Zebi Manne, are poets, as was also Naphtali Herz Imber, the national poet of the new Palestine. S. Tchernichovski is also a poet; but the greatest of them all, a sweet singer in Israel, is Hayyim Bialik, " a Hebrew with an Hellenic soul." Solomon Jacob Abramowitsch (" the Jewish Cervante "), Isaac Löb Perez, Reuben Brainin, David Frischmann, and Ben-Avigdor are favourite novelists. Brainin is also the historian of modern Hebrew literature, and Frischmann a translator of scientific books. In other branches of literature, also, Hebrew writers are to be found, and Hebrew by its breadth as well as by its depth has now, although only a few decades old, secured its position among contemporary literary languages.

The new Hebrew movement has gradually come almost to dominate Jewish nationalism. It supplies the essential without which the reconstitution of the Jewish nationality would be impossible, for who can conceive of a people without a common language ? The sympathetic interest in the Hebrew revival has spread far outside of the formal ranks of the Zionists; but in the larger sense all these Hebrew enthusiasts, no matter how moderate may be their enthusiasm, are Zionists, although they may be quite unconscious of it. Classes for the study of Hebrew as a living language, Hebrew lecture and debating societies, Hebrew periodicals, have sprung up in scores of centres of Western Jewry. At the eighth Congress the Zionist Organization made Hebrew its official language. At the time this was merely a compliment, for to the great majority of the delegates to that Congress an address in that language would have been unintelligible. The decision, however, did not remain merely a compliment. At the last Congress the discussion on one motion—that advocating the establishment of a Hebrew University—was conducted entirely in Hebrew, and speeches in that language were also interspersed throughout the proceedings. Nevertheless, outside of Palestine the revival of Hebrew is necessarily merely an academic movement. In everyday life, in the midst of a population which must necessarily in all circumstances be non-Hebraic, it is impossible for it to exist unsupported, to grow of its own accord. In the new Palestine, however, Hebrew has its opportunity.

Palestine is a land of all peoples and of all tongues. The Jews hailing from twenty countries have brought twenty languages with them. In the consequent babel the Jew from one country was unable to understand his co-religionist from another. In language the Jew from Roumania and the Jew from Persia were as far removed as their respective countries. If the Jews of the Holy Land were ever to come into contact with one another, to coalesce, to form again one people, a common language was a necessity. Arabic and Hebrew were the only languages

possible for this purpose, and of these two Hebrew had
the undoubted advantage. Although a living language
to but a very few of the Jews of Palestine, it was a language with which all of them had a considerable acquaintance. By sentiment and by history, the people, the land,
and the language all belonged to one another. Hebrew
and Palestine are almost two forms of the one idea. For
the Jews of Palestine only one language was possible.
In the Russian Pale of Settlement *Jüdisch* might be the
language of the Jews; in the Balkans, *Ladino ;* in Paris,
French; in London or New York, English; but in Jerusalem and the Holy Land, Hebrew only. All languages
are still spoken there, but they are the languages of the
past—dying languages so far as Palestine is concerned.
The new generation, the children, the youths and maidens,
speak Hebrew as their mother-tongue, the language which
has been a part of life since the kindergarten age. The
other languages they speak are foreign to them. The
children play in Hebrew and learn in Hebrew. The
young men and girls make love in Hebrew. In the new
settlements all conduct their business, perform their
ordinary work, and enjoy the common pleasures of life,
in Hebrew. The new Jews of Palestine think and
dream in Hebrew: Hebrew is their language, is a part of
themselves.

Although it is only in the course of the present generation that Hebrew has come to be spoken at all generally
in Palestine, there have for generations been Jews in the
country to whom it has been a living tongue. James
Finn, the British Consul in Jerusalem and protector of
the Jews of Palestine, who himself spoke Hebrew, mentioned in his diary that that language was sometimes
used in his office for the transaction of business with

Jews. As an instance of the usefulness of the language as a means of communication between Jews from different countries, he also mentioned that a Jew from Cabul met a co-religionist from California in his office in Jerusalem, and they were able to converse with one another by means of Hebrew. In his day Hebrew was certainly used in Palestine as a conversational language. Evidence to the same effect is to be found in the diaries of Sir Moses Montefiore. The *Chovevé Zion* encouraged the spread of Hebrew in Palestine which had commenced under their régime. As the Palestine Movement grew, so the impetus towards Hebrew became stronger. The growth of Hebrew in the schools has already been sketched.

The Hebrew Movement in Palestine was indigenous, not exotic. The scholar Ben-Jehuda was the first of the modern Jews to introduce it into his household. From private houses it soon passed to meetings of societies, in particular those of the B'nei B'rith Order. Then it passed to the schools, conquering one after the other, until those of the *Alliance* alone stand out, and they are not unaffected. The children brought the language home from the schools, and taught it to their parents, and now the mothers and the fathers speak it as their own tongue. So strong has the language become in Palestine that, as has already been related, it was able to meet German in battle and to vanquish it. In the course of a few years Hebrew has become one of the languages of Palestine. If the present course continues, without either deterrent or special incentive, the next generation will see the innumerable languages of Palestine reduced for practical purposes to two— Hebrew and Arabic.

CHAPTER XXIII

THE ECONOMIC PRESENT AND FUTURE

THE narrative in the foregoing pages marks the point which has been reached in the regeneration of Palestine, a region which has lain waste for centuries, and in the reoccupation by the Jews of the land which belonged to their ancestors. It must not be forgotten, however, that the regeneration is still of the nature of an experiment. It has occupied but the period of a generation, a moment in the history of a country. The revival cannot be said to have been spontaneous, for it has been in almost every detail initiated from without. The older Jewish population of Palestine would never of itself have made any effort towards the rehabilitation of the land, nor was there any other class in the population, until the new Jewish immigration commenced—with the exception, perhaps, of the few German colonists at Haifa and Jaffa—that gave any promise for the future. Without the Jewish immigrants Palestine would have remained in the condition in which it had been for centuries—that of a desert.

It is in this state that Palestine is still generally believed to be by those who have some slight interest in the land, but have never seen it, or if they have, have done so only from the railways and the high roads. Their information is based on writers who knew the land before the beginning of the new era, or who base their writings on the reports of those who visited it before the last decade of the nine-

are secure. All other industries — commerce, mining, manufactures—are less vital. A State can exist without them, but without agriculture death is inevitable. In the national economy agriculture occupies the position of bread in domestic economy. It is the very basis of life. In the past—in Biblical, in Roman, and in later times—the abundance of the productions of Palestine was proverbial. But we are concerned with the present. And there is plenty of evidence that the land is still as it was. The deterioration is due to no more than the neglect from which it has suffered for centuries, and human care can remove the effects of human neglect. Colonel Claude Conder, than whom no one knew Palestine better, was always impressing on his hearers and readers that Palestine was not desolate; that the forests of the land had not been destroyed, as is generally supposed by those who have never been there; that the seasons rotate still as in Bible times; that the innumerable springs and streams mentioned in the Bible still flow; that the rainfall is quite sufficient if only it were stored—and the ancient cisterns in which it was formerly stored can easily be repaired; and that the climate could easily be improved by drainage and the planting of trees. Colonel Conder knew Palestine before the new immigration had commenced: he died before it had been long in motion. If he had been living to-day he would have been glad to recognize how the lines of progress that he had indicated were being followed. The excess of water in the winter is being retained for use in the summer; the land is being drained and the climate improved by means of afforestation. For the regeneration of the land, however, these improvements must be conducted on a much larger scale.

Another authority who knew the country well, the Rev. G. E. Post, writing still later, expressed the opinion that the climate of Palestine was adapted to the existence of a large population. "Those plants which require moisture," he wrote, "find it. Those which flourish best without it are also suited. Hence almost every foot of land not actually rock, produces something directly or indirectly useful to man, and even the clefts of the rocks furnish pasture of no little value to sheep and goats. . . . Given a carefully prepared soil and sufficient water, there seems no limit to the agricultural possibilities of this land of fertilizing sunshine."

The agricultural possibilities of Palestine are, in fact, exceptional. Inland from the coast, from south to north runs a series of plains, every one with better capacity for production than its predecessor. That around Gaza grows the finest barley the world produces. Inland from Jaffa lies the Plain of Sharon—a land of orchards and of vineyards: to the north is the Plain of Esdraelon, famous for its crops of sesame; and also the Plain of Beisan, the land of wheat. The Mountains of Judah were in the past covered with olive groves and vineyards, and there is no reason why they should not be restored to their ancient state. The so-called Desert of Judæa is capable of supporting innumerable flocks of sheep and goats. The great fissure of the Jordan Valley, known as the Ghor, has, on account of its depth below the sea-level, a tropical climate, and with it, a luxuriant tropical vegetation. Beyond the Jordan stretch the steppes of Moab, a vast district which is described as desert only because it has no inhabitants to develop its agricultural possibilities. To the north of Moab are the Mountains of Gilead with their forests of oak and pine; and farther north still, the wheat-lands of the Hauran, once one of the granaries of the world.

The foregoing estimate of the agricultural possibilities of Palestine if the present conditions were changed may seem extravagant, but it is not so. At least, one can say that it has plenty of unbiassed authority behind it. The luxuriant growth of trees in Gilead and elsewhere, despite any protection from the destructive ravages of the wandering Bedouin, is a standing evidence of the natural fertility of the soil. The crops that respond to the primitive Arab methods of cultivation are another. In some parts—for example, in the districts of Gaza and Siloam—the land already yields a hundredfold. The irrigated districts produce four crops in the year, giving at the same time the products of England and of Italy. Lucerne, under irrigation, produces ten crops in the year; without irrigation, in the valleys, three. In 1915 the agriculturists of Palestine, relatively few in number and for the most part primitive in their methods, despite a plague of locusts more terrible than any in the memory of living man, were able to supply the country with sufficient corn to keep the people alive while it was closed by the War to the outside world. The Rev. F. A. Klein, writing in 1883, said: "The fruitfulness of the land when irrigated is really astonishing." The Rev. G. E. Post, the botanist, testified that in flora Palestine is the richest country of its size in the world. It includes more than three thousand species of flowering plants.

Just as agriculture is the basis of the State, so is the cultivation of cereals the basis or kernel of agriculture. The first test of the prospects of the future of the land is therefore its capacity for producing wheat and other cereals. From such a test Palestine has no need to recoil.

PACKING ORANGES FOR EXPORT

LOADING WINE AT JAFFA

Face p. 262

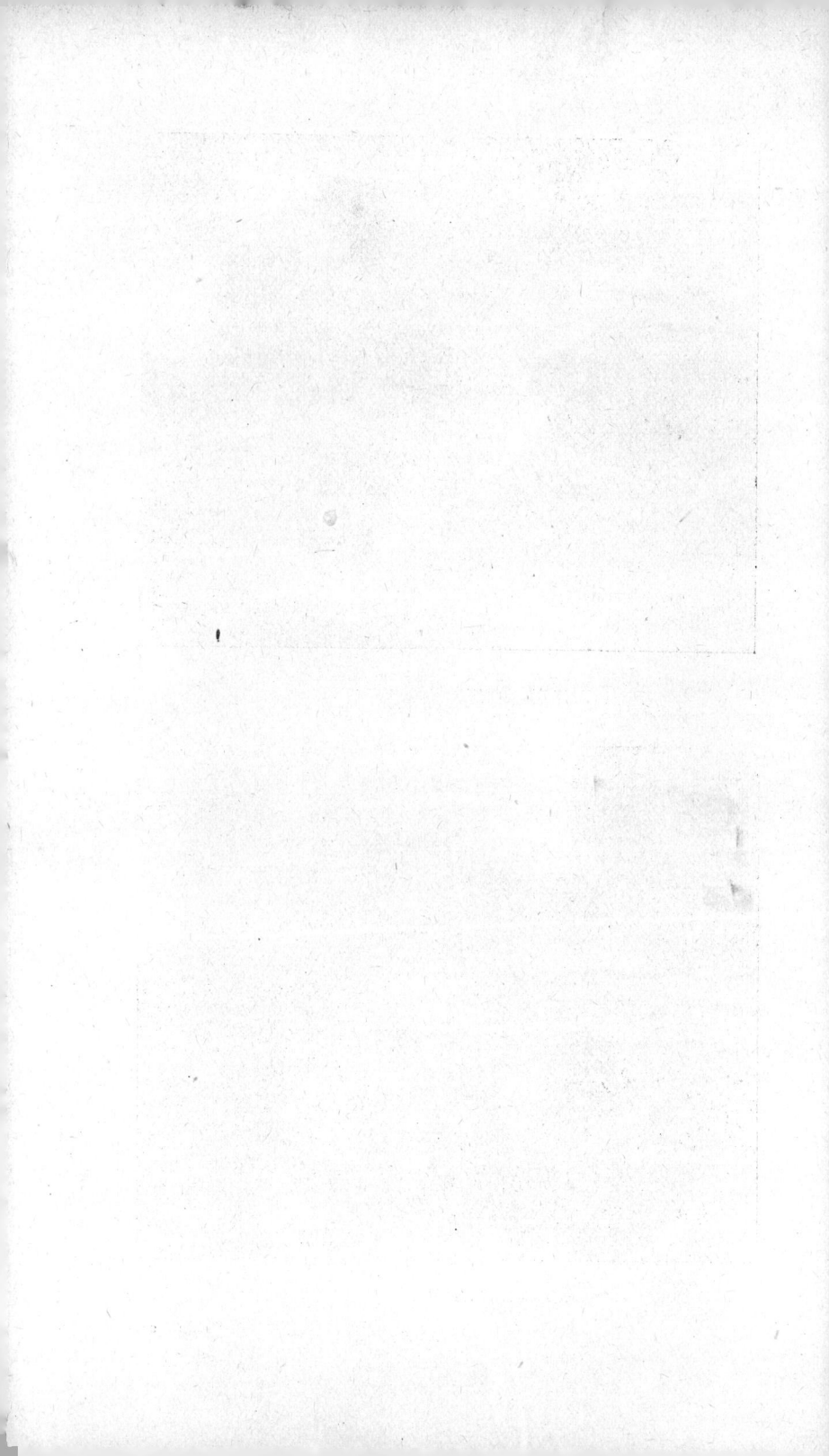

In ancient times it included within its confines one of the granaries of the world; and in modern times it has shown that, given satisfactory conditions and a little encouragement, it can fulfil the promise given by its history.   The whole of the land east of the Jordan, from Moab to Hermon and the Hauran, has been described as a wheat country which cannot anywhere be surpassed in excellence.   The wheat of the Hauran is famed throughout the East.   Other rich wheat-fields are in the Gaza region, in the Plain of Esdraelon, and in the Mukhneh to the east of Nablous.   Barley, durra (or millet), sesame, lupin, oats, and maize, also flourish.

The oranges, the olives, the grapes, and the almonds that are grown in such profusion give evidence of the capacity of Palestine as a fruit-producing country. Sir George Adam Smith describes the region as " a land of orchards."   With one exception, that of chestnuts, all the fruit-trees of the temperate zone— apples, pears, cherries, apricots, figs, walnuts, peaches, mulberries, almonds, blackberries, plums, quinces, etc.— flourish there.   In addition there are the fruits of the warmer climes—the banana, the mandarin, the lemon, the citron, the date, the medlar, and the carob, or locust bean.   The flora and also the fauna of Palestine, in fact, range from the tropical up to the Alpine classes.   The sugar-cane, tobacco, cotton, rice, camphor, laurel, papyrus, are all to be found and could be grown with profit.   The Valley of the Jordan is one huge hothouse. Indigo, sorghum, pine-apples, yams, and sweet potatoes could be cultivated without difficulty.   In other districts, aralia or the castor-oil plant, flax, melons, gourds, cumin, coriander, anise, brinjals (or egg-plant), and pomegranates, could be cultivated without trouble.   The pistachio, jujube, balsam, pine, maple, ash, and beech-trees, artichokes, and asparagus, grow wild in profusion. All varieties of vegetables—onions, carrots, beetroot, cauliflowers, potatoes, garlic, pumpkins, cabbages, turnips, pepper, radishes, and peas—thrive in irrigated gardens; gherkins, vegetable marrows, and tomatoes, even without irrigation. Unlimited riches of the earth are there, but for the most part go to waste for lack of development.

All this wonderful fertility, existing and prospective, is of course dependent on water, of which, despite many a statement to the contrary, there need be no scarcity in Palestine. The average annual rainfall at Jerusalem exceeds that at Athens, Vienna, and Paris, and equals that of London. Farther north, in Galilee, the average is higher. All the rain, however, falls in the course of one half of the year, and the problem is how to store the excess so as to distribute it over the dry season. For this purpose the means are ready to hand in the wonderful series of ancient aqueducts and cisterns, which need comparatively little in the way of repair in order to restore them to their former usefulness. New works in addition would increase the productiveness of the land manifold. Both east and west of the Jordan there are several perennial rivers and far more springs and streams. The lake of Merom and the Sea of Galilee are great reservoirs from which miles of neighbouring land could be irrigated. " Few countries," says the Rev. G. E. Post, "have a more admirable provision for the collection, storage, and distribution of water than Syria and Palestine." The constitution of the Mountains of Lebanon and Anti-Lebanon is admirably suited to supply the country to the south with all the necessary water. By digging copious supplies of potable water can be found at a depth of from 10 to 80 feet almost anywhere in the plains. The Plain of Sharon seems to cover a subterranean lake. Even without irrigation there is very seldom a dearth of water. The drought of summer is compensated by the rains of winter, which is the period of the growth of vegetation. The dews of summer itself are sufficiently heavy to ripen the summer crops, and to give such trees as the mulberry, the vine, the fig, the almond, and the olive, all the moisture they require.

Land not suitable or not required for cultivation is, or could be, devoted to pasturage. As it is, large herds of sheep and goats find sustenance in the wild, unsettled lands to the east and the south-east, and in the more settled regions, herds, and also flocks, are fed on mulberry-leaves as well as on the fodder more familiar to Western stock-breeders. Poultry-farming in Palestine is an advancing industry, and the export of eggs from Haifa and Akka (Acre) is growing. Situated where the flora of three different continents meet, Palestine is an ideal country for bee-keeping. The Baldenspergers, a Swiss family which has been resident in Palestine for half a century, have achieved wonderful results with their bees. They made it a practice to move from district to district during eight months of the year, pursuing the spring and its flowers from the lowest to the highest levels. They were thus in the course of one season able to produce several varieties of honey which they labelled, " Orange Blossom," " Thyme," etc. By means of the care they devoted to their pursuit they obtained six tons of honey from a hundred hives in the course of the eight months, or 120 pounds per hive. In other successful bee-keeping lands the maximum per hive is 50 pounds and the average 30. Experiments have already been made in ostrich-breeding by a South African farmer, while the breeding of Arab thoroughbreds, mules, and the caracul sheep of Turkestan, should have good chances of success.

The products of the soil lead direct to certain classes of manufacture which belong rather to agriculture than to urban industry. Several of these have already been acclimatized in Palestine, and wait only for the development of the form of agriculture on which they depend for expansion. The manufacture of wine and brandy has already been mentioned. Almost a part of it is the establishment of cask factories. The mulberry-tree has led direct to silk-weaving, the olive to the manufacture of olive-oil and soap. The flower-gardens of Galilee have given rise to the manufacture of attar of roses and other perfumes. From durra spirit is distilled and starch is made. Starch is also made from wheat, while Palestine wheat is specially adapted for the manufacture of macaroni, which is exported to Egypt and Syria. The olives of Palestine produce the finest olive-oil of the world: even the refuse, jift, makes excellent fuel. There is also material for the manufacture of cochineal. The sugar factories of the Middle Ages could be rebuilt, and resume activity not only with the produce of the sugarcane, a native of Palestine, but also with that of the beetroot, which could easily be acclimatized. For the kindred preserving industry all the materials would also be to hand. With tobacco grown in Palestine, cigarette-making could be undertaken, and from the papyrus which could be cultivated there the best qualities of paper could be made. Palestine was of old a centre of tanning. At present the country exports hides and imports leather. With not much capital, assisted by suitable labour, the hides could become leather without leaving the country.   The carob, or locust bean, excellent for fodder and also for human food, is too valuable to be devoted to such purposes.   It is exported to Europe, where the demand for it, as one of the essential ingredients of cheap chocolate, can hardly be supplied.   Of the motive power for factories—electricity—the innumerable waterfalls of the land furnish an inexhaustible supply.

If the foregoing list exhausted the possible productions of Palestine, the land would well be able to support a people many times larger than at present, in comfort and in happiness.   The catalogue of natural productions has, however, by no means been completed.   Those that remain to be mentioned, if properly developed, would bring far more than comfort—prosperity—to the land. The mineral and chemical resources of Palestine are very considerable.   The Dead Sea and its shores alone are a veritable mine of precious products.   The supply of chlorate of potassium there is practically inexhaustible. In the same region are to be found bitumen, bromides, asphalt, salt, pottery clay, sulphur, and petroleum.   The Sinai Peninsula contains copper and granite.   At Ma'an, in the south-east, there are said to be large coal and iron deposits.   Near Sidon, iron, red and yellow ochre, and coal exist.   In Trans-Jordania and especially at Es-Salt, phosphates can be found in large quantities.   In the Mountains of Judah and in the Valley of the Jordan there are deposits of chalk and of plaster.   The neighbouring land of Midian, whose mines were famous in ancient history, contains gold, silver, copper, turquoise, sulphur, rocksalt, gypsum, and alabaster.

Another path towards prosperity that Palestine, under a reformed government, would possess lies in its attraction as a health resort, by means of which it might well rival Egypt, and for the countries of Eastern Europe, the Riviera. The climate of the coastal regions is, indeed, similar to that of Southern France, and Jaffa, Haifa, and other towns that would come into existence could without much difficulty be made to compete with the best attractions of Nice and Bordighera. The settlements on the shore of the Sea of Galilee and on the lower slopes of Mount Hermon have already become spring and summer resorts, and, developing with the general progress of the country, should in due course attract larger and larger gatherings of seekers after health and recreation. The Jericho region, which is already almost within a week's journey of London, was in the time of Herod a magnificent winter resort. It would not be difficult to restore to it its former functions. The hot mineral springs in its neighbourhood, at Tel-el-Hammam and Calirrhoë, would increase its attractiveness. The hot sulphur springs of Tiberias are mentioned in the Talmud. Their valuable medicinal qualities were appreciated in medieval times, and from those days to these the stream of visitors seeking relief from physical ills, although perhaps never considerable, has been practically continuous.

Hitherto we have dealt with the natural wealth of the land. Without the aid of human agencies it is, however, of little value. The wheat-fields of the Hauran may teem with their produce, but if the means whereby to distribute it are lacking, they might as well be barren. The shores of the Dead Sea may be studded with petroleum springs, but if there is no one to gather the bountiful harvest and to husband it, it will run to waste, and so far as humanity is concerned the mineral wealth of the region might well have never been. Essentials preliminary to the prosperity of the land, to its capacity to support an adequate population, are suitable and sufficient means of communication, both from one part of the country to another, and also with the outside world. The roads of Palestine at present are both bad and insufficient, but it would not be very expensive to remedy this defect. The existing roads could be improved and the old Roman roads, long ago passed into neglect and almost into disuse, could be restored. So thoroughly did the Romans build, that it is apparently impossible utterly to destroy, even deliberately, their handiwork.

In the course of the past couple of decades Palestine has been provided with a nucleus railway system which, when extended, should go far to restore the country to its ancient position as the high-road between Europe and Asia on the one hand, and Afiica on the other, and also as the bridge connecting, by means of a railway to the Persian Gulf, Europe and the East. The port of Jaffa is already connected with Jerusalem, and those of Akka and Haifa with Damascus and the Hedjaz railway, which in due course will lead to Constantinople in the one direction, Mecca and Southern Arabia in another, and Bagdad and the Persian Gulf in a third. This railway brings the rich Trans-Jordania region into touch with the outer world. At Merchaviah, half-way between the Jordan and the sea, a branch railway to Jerusalem has been built, and half of it, to a point beyond Nablous, had been opened to traffic before the outbreak of war. Damascus is connected with Haifa and Akka by two lines, one of which, the Hedjaz railway, running near the easternmost boundary of Trans-Jordania, is continued into Arabia. Since the War broke out a few miles of the railway from Jaffa have been torn up, probably in order to create difficulties for a possible hostile army landing at Jaffa. On the other hand, railways have been built from the Jerusalem-Jaffa line to the south as far as the Egyptian frontier and to the north, the latter connecting with the line to Haifa and Damascus. As the land develops, many other small railroads will be constructed, every one, in the benefits which it will bring to the land and to its inhabitants, returning the cost of construction manifold. Two, however, supplying links now missing from the chain, will help to make Palestine the railway centre of the world, a position for which geography has already qualified it. Some day or other, perhaps not very distant, the railway from Haifa will continue due east until it crosses the Tigris and the Euphrates. There it will meet lines which are already in part under construction or which circumstances will make inevitable, running to the Persian Gulf, across Persia to India, and northwards to the Russian dominions. When that day arrives, when those railways are in existence, Palestine will be in railway connection with the greater part of Asia, and for the greater part of Europe the quickest route to the East will be through the Holy Land. From the Jerusalem line a railway already stretches towards the south. Some day, when it has been made permanent, it will be continued through Gaza, across the El-Arish, the River of Egypt, the Wilderness of Zin, and the Suez Canal. Once in Egypt it will link up with the Egyptian railway system and the Cape to Cairo line, which by then will have been completed. With the completion of this link the junction of Africa with Asia and Europe will be complete. It will be possible to travel from Calcutta or Calais to Cape Town, from Siberia to South Africa, by rail all the way, and in that day Palestine will again, but in a new sense, be the centre of the world.

Railways and railways alone can connect Asia with Africa, but railways alone are not sufficient to bring Asia into close relationship with Europe over a Palestinian route. Between Europe and the East railways would be the roads, but the gates, the ports, must be open. At present Palestine, with a coast-line the whole of her length, has no ports. Jaffa and Haifa are spoken of as ports, but they are without harbours, and as a consequence, when the weather is rough, it is impossible for vessels to discharge their cargoes or land their passengers there. Beyrout is then the first landing-place, and passengers must get thence to Palestine by a circuitous railway journey or by road. Merchandise must follow a similar inconvenient and expensive course or await a favourable wind. Given sufficient resources, harbours can be constructed anywhere. On the Palestinian coast no considerable difficulties would be interposed by nature between the engineer and his goal. Jaffa is certainly not the most suitable situation for a harbour, but at Haifa the natural features are ideal. The Bay stretching from Akka, to the north, to Haifa, to the south, would form a harbour three miles broad by eight long. On the south and the east it would be protected by the mountains and promontory of Carmel. Inland easy roads and a railway, from both Akka and Haifa, lead to Damascus and all the regions which are connected with that city by rail. In its course the railway passes through the rich lands of Galilee and of the Hauran. Radiating north, east, and south, roads lead to Beyrout, the settlements in Galilee and Samaria, Nablous and Jaffa. Jerusalem is already in railway connection with Haifa, although the connection is still somewhat precarious. The richest portions of Palestine lead direct to Akka and Haifa.

To the far south-east is the derelict port of Akabah, the Ezion-Geber of Solomon's kingdom, at the head of one of the arms of the Red Sea. To Arabia, the neighbouring land, it is useless. To Palestine, its value would be above price. From Ezion-Geber the ships of Solomon sailed for Ophir and the East. From Akabah a restored Palestine might trade with East and South Africa, with the Persian Gulf, with India and the Far East. Akabah is at present isolated, deserted, a place of no consequence or value. But the railway from Damascus runs not far away. A branch from this railway to the sea would restore Akabah once more to civilization.

For the regeneration of Palestine, roads, railways, and harbours are required. But these are not all. If they were provided, the great essential would still be missing. Palestine might be like a beautifully decorated and furnished palace, fitted with all the most up-to-date contrivances intended to minister to the comfort and the pleasure of its inhabitants. But if the inhabitants were lacking, all the costly provision would be as nought. Roads, railways, and harbours may be provided by outside means, but if they are not to decay and fall into ruin, a population capable of utilizing them and anxious to do so must also be provided. Such a population cannot come from the East, for it is not of the genius of the Asiatic to regenerate a land. The new Palestine needs a new population—a population of the character of that of which a nucleus has already settled in Jaffa and in the newly founded villages of Judæa, of Samaria, and of Galilee. For the European colonist Palestine has no attraction.   It cannot compete with the call of America, of Canada, of Australia, or of South Africa.   The Jew alone feels the call to the Holy Land, to the home of his ancestors, to the region where the supremest fruits of his genius were produced for the eternal benefit of mankind.   The Jew has been entrusted from his creation as a people with the mission of interpreter and mediator between the East and the West, but it is only in his own homeland that he can properly fulfil his mission.   The Jew alone can once again make the land blossom as a rose and flow with milk and honey.   The Jew alone can make the land which has been accursed ever since his ancestors were driven out of it nearly nineteen centuries ago once again a blessing to mankind.   But it is only with the assistance of Christendom that he can do so. Roads, railways, and harbours are necessities for Palestine, but, above all, an industrious intelligent population and a just and stable government.   Only by the safeguard of a European guarantee can these be provided.

" Given a strong, wise, just government," said Colonel Conder, " and the country may be trusted to assert its ancient reputation for fertility. . . .   The only radical change required is the total abolition of the present official staff, from the pasha down to the lowest mudir or kaimakam. . . .   Palestine requires nothing but good government, an increased population, and civilized cultivation to restore its prosperity."   Mr. John B. Hay, for many years United States Consul at Jerusalem, expressed the opinion that " a European immigration on a large scale would be a valuable means of regenerating Palestine."   Sir Richard Burton, another considerable authority on the Asiatic Near East, held similar views. " The Holy Land, when provided with railways and tramways, will offer the happiest blending of the ancient and modern worlds. It will become another Egypt with the distinct advantage of a superior climate and far nobler races of men." Again, " Syria and Palestine, I may safely prophesy, still awaits the hour when, the home of a free, a striving, and an energetic people, it will again pour forth corn and oil, it will flow with milk and honey, and it will ' bear,' with proper culture, almost all the good things that have been given to man." Again quoting Conder: " The Hills of Palestine might be covered with vines and the valleys run with oil; the plains might be yellow with corn and the harbours full of ships. . . . Palestine might become the Garden of the World, situate as it is in so accessible a position, with the great Mediterranean waterway so close to its corn plains and olive yards."

CHAPTER XXIV

THE POLITICAL FUTURE

THE story has now been told of the vicissitudes which Palestine and its peoples have undergone since its subjugation by the Romans. Conquest has followed conquest from that day almost to this. Roman, Byzantine, Frank, Saracen, Turk, have all held sway for long periods. For shorter ones other conquerors have had possession of the land. In all ages Palestine has been an object of desire and of contention. Ruler has succeeded to ruler, but seldom have the subjects benefited by the change. With the exception of the period of Frankish domination, Palestine has always been governed in the interests not of its own people, but of those of another land; and even under the Franks the interests of the indigenous populations were invariably made subservient to those of new-comers. The history of Palestine during the past eighteen centuries has been bounteous in incidents. In prosperity, however, it has shown an almost uninterrupted degeneration. The Romans found the country thickly inhabited by a population generally prosperous. The forthcoming congress for the settlement of the affairs of civilization will look upon it as almost a desert land inhabited by a sparse and on the whole poverty-stricken population.

The purpose of this volume is not merely to give a history of the degeneration of Palestine. It looks toward

the future as well as back to the past. It attempts to
extract from the experience of history the lesson out of
which profit may be obtained in the future. To a large
extent it deals with the dry sticks of the dead, but it
also finds and turns the light upon the green shoots of
the living. The story of eighteen centuries of retro-
gression has been told, but in far greater detail has been
described the revival which is not yet more than a generation in age. For the promise of the past thirty or thirty-
five years is of more account in the history of Palestine
than the performance of the preceding eighteen centuries.
During this brief period of thirty-five years, difficulties
which to those of less faith or less hope would have
appeared insuperable have been overcome, and the
foundations of a new Palestine and a new Jewry have
been laid. Only the foundations, and foundations as
yet by no means too secure. The new-comers have come,
urged by no political motives, the emissaries of no foreign
state. Whole-heartedly they have given their allegiance
to the existing government of the land in which they
settled, and in normal circumstances their children born
in Palestine would have been—as are their kinsmen in
all other lands—among the most loyal of the elements
in the population. The highest ambition of the Jew in
Palestine was, and is, to live in peace—free, in a Jewish
atmosphere amid Jewish surroundings, to follow his
unaggressive callings, instinctively and unconsciously to
fulfil the mission in the world which has been entrusted
to his people—the mission of civilization. If circumstances
had followed a normal course, more and more Jews would
have settled in Palestine and been born there. Further and
further tracts would have been brought under cultivation.
Education and true civilization would have gradually

permeated the whole of the people. Palestine would once again have become a land flowing with milk and honey, bringing material and intellectual as well as spiritual benefits to humanity. In the Turkish Empire a rich province would have taken the place of a derelict land. The Jews of Palestine, the one progressive element in the population, would have benefited greatly and would in course of time have acquired an overwhelming influence in the local government, but their prosperity and happiness would have been shared by the other inhabitants. In no land does the prosperity of any considerable part of the population fail to react on that of the whole. In no land does the presence of Jews fail to spread benefits. This is true even in the poverty-stricken towns of the Pale of Settlement and in the formerly vice and crime infested slums of East London. Its truth is proved by a comparison between the condition of the people in those Russian provinces from which Jews are excluded with that in the others in which they are herded together. The history of Spain and Portugal tells of the loss brought upon a country by the expulsion of its Jews.

The Turkish Government has given no help to the Jewish regeneration of Palestine. On the other hand, it cannot be said to have impeded it very seriously. The Jews, in fact, are for the most part left to work out their own material salvation. The Turkish Government benefits from a larger revenue from taxation derived directly and indirectly from the Jewish settlements, and from greater ease in obtaining payment. In return it neglects to fulfil many of the functions proper to governments in other lands, but it grants to the Jews a large measure of freedom to manage their own local affairs. The functions which the Government neglects are performed as far as possible by the Jews themselves. The great disadvantage is the feeling of insecurity general under Oriental Governments—a feeling more active outside of Palestine than within, more powerful in deterring European Jews from entrusting their liberties or property to Turkish law, than in affecting those who are already settled in the country. Above all, the great disadvantage of the present system is the consciousness that it offers no safeguard against a possibly aggressive foreign Power. Nevertheless, despite these drawbacks, Turkish rule is by no means unfavourable to the Jewish development in Palestine, and a change may very well be for the worse.

When the representatives of the Powers of Europe meet in congress, it may well be that the destiny of Palestine will come up for consideration, and as a consequence another government will be given to it. If this be so, the fate of the new Palestine and of the new Jewry will at the same time be decided. The interests of Europe in the Holy Land, religious, historical, commercial, archæological, and strategic, are so many that every one of the Powers will be able to make out a case for consideration. Fortunately—as, for instance, in the religious sphere—some of these claims neutralize one another. Strategically, commercially, archæologically, and from the point of view of the present inhabitants, Moslem, Christian, and Jewish almost without exception, the interests of the Power that now holds the neighbouring Egypt are overwhelmingly the strongest. For the greater part of history Palestine and Egypt have been closely connected, for the smaller state is in effect a shield to the larger on its only vulnerable side. The religious interests of England may be less than those of other

Powers, but this renders the presence of England in Palestine—if it is necessary to find a substitute for the Moslem—all the more essential. To keep the peace between the Latin and Greek, and to prevent the Holy City from becoming a perpetual shambles, the Moslem soldiery has hitherto been on guard. If it is withdrawn its place must be taken by another neutral—Protestant or Jew. The latter has no desire for any such office, and would not for many years—until the new nation has passed out of infancy—have the strength to hold it. The Protestant, as the guardian of the Holy Places of Christendom, is at present the only possible alternative to the Turk. If the Turkish sway passes from Jerusalem, the Moslem Holy Places, second in importance only to those of Mecca, will also need a protector. For such an office the Great Power which counts its Mohammedan subjects by tens of millions seems indisputably marked out. Thus the security of the one weak link in the chain of empire, the religious rivalries of Christendom, the interests of the Moslem world and the desires of the many peoples of Palestine, all combine to invite that Power to extend its invincible protection to the Holy Land.

From the point of view of the Jews already settled and to settle in Palestine, such a solution of the problem already opened is practically the only possible one, if the newly risen hopes are not to be dashed to the ground. The possibility of an independent Jewish State cannot be discussed in the course of the present generation or at any date which either the writer or the reader can expect to see. Local autonomy is all that the Jews of Palestine ask—the development of the system which has already been inaugurated, and whose success has been proved by experience. The Jews desire no favour as compared with the other inhabitants of the land. They are willing for all the advantages of a free and liberal government to be enjoyed by all equally. Thus if Palestine ultimately becomes entirely—that is to say, overwhelmingly—Jewish, it will become so, not by artificial means, but as a consequence of natural growth. The function of the protecting Power would be to see fair play between the different elements in the population, to protect them all equally against outside aggression and threat of aggression, and to educate the people in the science of self-government. At first, at any rate, as in Egypt, in the native states of India, and elsewhere, the administrative body of the Government would have to be recruited to a large extent from outside. The choice of these administrators would rest with the Imperial Government, which would have the interests of Palestine and its peoples always foremost in its mind, and would select men known to be in sympathy with the ideals of the land which they would have to administer, who would go there not merely as civil servants, but as settlers determined to make their homes and their children's homes in the new land. The Power to which would fall the task of protecting the new Palestine while it recovered its soul would attract to itself the blessings promised to those who befriend the Chosen People in their adversity.

BIBLIOGRAPHY

THE following list of works on different aspects of the subject with which the foregoing pages deal is not exhaustive. It contains only English books and those which are readily obtainable, the intention being not to compile a bibliography, but to furnish the English reader who may have found an interest in the subject with a hand-list of books which will enable him to go more deeply into it.

HISTORICAL.

LE STRANGE, GUY: Palestine under the Moslems. (London, 1890.)

BESANT, WALTER, and PALMER, E. H.: Jerusalem, The City of Herod and Saladin. (London, 1899.)

CONDER, C. R.: The City of Jerusalem. (London, 1909.)

WATSON, SIR C. M.: The Story of Jerusalem. (London, 1912.)

PATON, L. B.: Early History of Syria and Palestine. (London, 1902.)

CONDER, C. R.: Latin Kingdom of Jerusalem. (London, 1897.)

SMITH, SIR GEORGE ADAM: Jerusalem. (London, 1908.)

MODERN PALESTINE.

GOODRICH-FREER, A.: Inner Jerusalem. (London, 1904.)

TRISTRAM, H. B.: The Land of Israel. (London, 1865.)

TREVES, SIR FREDERICK: The Land that is Desolate. (London, 1912.)

THE JEWISH SETTLEMENT.

SZOLD, HENRIETTA: Recent Jewish Progress in Palestine. (Philadelphia, 1915.)

COHEN, ISRAEL: Editor, Zionist Work in Palestine. (London, 1911.)

ADLER, E. N.: Jews in many Lands. (London, 1905.)

JANNAWAY, F. G.: Palestine and the Jews. (Birmingham, 1914.)

PALESTINE, MISCELLANEOUS.

SMITH, SIR GEORGE ADAM: The Historical Geography of the Holy Land. (London, 1910.)

HUNTINGTON, ELLSWORTH: Palestine and its Transformation. (London, 1911.)

POST, G. E.: Flora of Syria, Palestine, and Sinai. (London, 1896.)

TRISTRAM, H. B.: The Fauna and Flora of Palestine. (London, 1884.)

HULL, E.: The Geology of Palestine and Arabia Petræa. (London, 1886.)

ZIONISM.

HERZL, THEODORE: A Jewish State. (London, 1896.)

SACHER, H.: Editor, Zionism and the Jewish Future. (London, 1916.)

GOODMAN, P., and LEWIS, ARTHUR D.: Editors, Zionism—Problems and Views. (London, 1916.)

GINZBERG, A. (Achad Ha'Am), Translated by Leon Simon: Selected Essays. (Philadelphia, 1910.)

GOTTHEIL, RICHARD: Zionism. (Philadelphia, 1914.)

THE RENASCENCE OF HEBREW.

SCHLOUSCHZ, N.: The Renascence of Hebrew. (Philadelphia, 1909.)

RAISIN, JACOB S.: The Haskalah Movement. (Philadelphia, 1913.)

WALDSTEIN, ABRAHAM S.: The Evolution of Modern Hebrew Literature. (Oxford, 1916.)

INDEX

BILLING AND SONS, LTD., PRINTERS, GUILDFORD, ENGLAND.

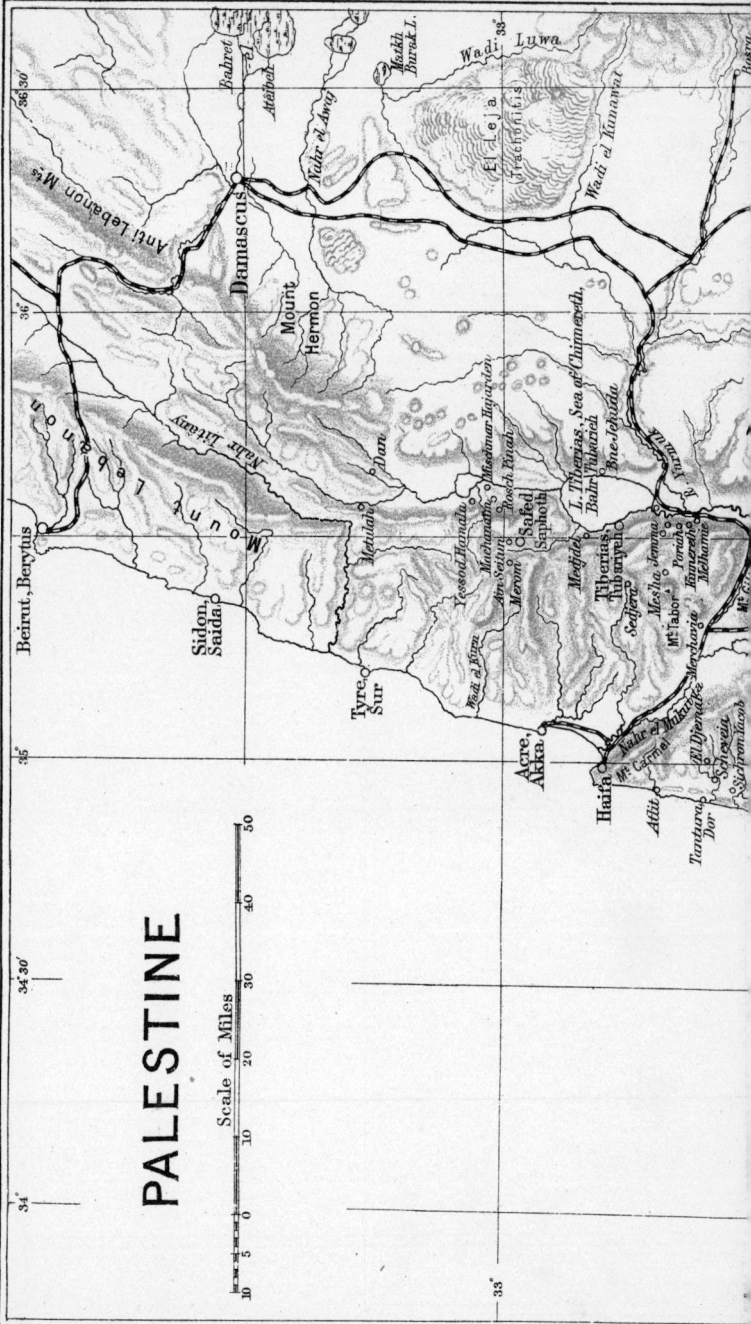

32°30'

32°

31°30'

31°

R. Jabbok

Mᵗˢ Gilead

Es Salt

Mᵗ Pisgah Mᵗ Nebo

R. Jordan

R. Arnon

Jenin En Gannim

Nablus Shechem

Mᵗ Ebal

Mᵗ Gerizim

Eriha Jericho

JERUSALEM

Dead Sea, Bahr Lut
1292 ft. below
the Mediterranean Sea.

Hebron El Khalil

Kerkur Qadirah

Kefr Saba

Ain Ghazal

Ain Baram

Petah-Tikwah

Judeideh

Wadi Hawarith

Beni Shamen

Rishon-lezion

Ekron

Rehoboth

Beer Jacob

Mozah

Zahovia

Hulda

Artuf

Katamon

Kastinieh

Juffa, Joppa

Nahr el Aujah

Mikveh Israel

Pisobano

Wadi el Chanin

Kiamm

Tjemama

Beersheba

Wadi es Seba

Gaza Ghuzzeh

Wadi Ghuzzeh

Rafa

El Arish

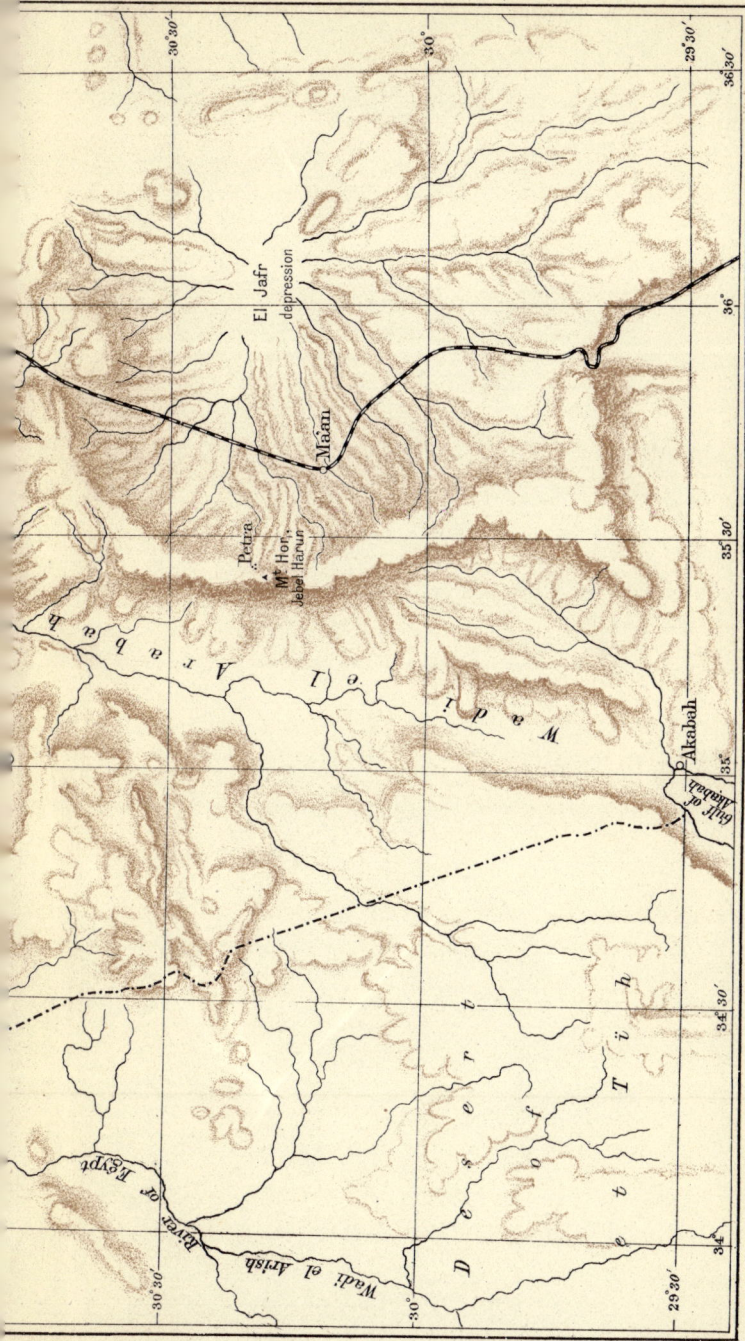

El Jafr
depression

Máan

Petra
Mt. Hor.
Jebel Harun

Arabah

El
Wady
Ghor

Akabah
Gulf of Akabah

Desert
of
Tíh

River of Egypt

Wadi el Arish

30° 30'
30°
29° 30'
36° 30'
36°
35° 30'
35°
34° 30'
34°
29° 30'
30°
30° 30'